Taj Mahal

Taj Mahal

Passion and Genius at the Heart of the Moghul Empire

DIANA AND MICHAEL PRESTON

Walker & Company
NEW YORK

07 MAY 4
B+T
25.95 (14.40)

Published by Walker Publishing Company, Inc., New York
Distributed to the trade by Holtzbrinck Publishers

ART CREDITS
Diana and Michael Preston: pages iv, 27, 43, 45, 58, 86, 121, 123, 124, 132, 154, 160, 174, 176, 178, 181, 187, 202, 246, 264, 276, 277, 279, 285; plates 4a, 4b, 5A, 5B, 7, 8A, 8B. The Bridgeman Art Library: pages 2, 4, 14, 34, 64, 101, 172, 208, 215, 227, 229, 248; plates 1, 2, 3, 6. The Freer Gallery of Art/Smithsonian Institution: pages 25, 61, 82, 95, 117, 131, 133, 197, 219. Precise Graphics: pages 161, 162. Spaceimaging.com: page 199. New York Botanical Garden: page 200. ASI: page 265. Archnet.org: page 270. Peter Mundy: pages 128–129, 144.

All papers used by Walker & Company are natural, recyclable products made from wood grown in well-managed forests. The manufacturing processes conform to the environmental regulations of the country of origin.

LIBRARY OF CONGRESS CATALOGING-IN-PUBLICATION DATA HAS BEEN APPLIED FOR.

ISBN-10: 0-8027-1511-7
ISBN-13: 978-0-8027-1511-1

Visit Walker & Company's Web site at www.walkerbooks.com

First U.S. edition 2007

1 3 5 7 9 10 8 6 4 2

Typeset by Westchester Book Group
Printed in the United States of America by Quebecor World Fairfield

1. Taj Mahal (Agra, India) — History.
2. Mogul Empire — History.

For friends and family

Contents

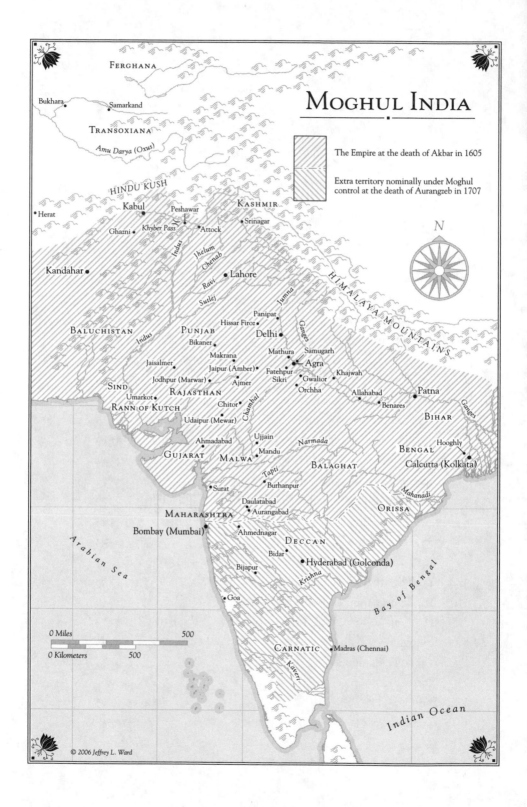

MOGHUL INDIA

The Empire at the death of Akbar in 1605

Extra territory nominally under Moghul control at the death of Aurangzeb in 1707

N

FERGHANA

Bukhara
Samarkand

TRANSOXIANA

Amu Darya (Oxus)

HINDU KUSH

KASHMIR

Herat
Kabul
Peshawar
Srinagar
Ghazni
Khyber Pass
Attock

Kandahar

Indus
Jhelum
Chenab
Ravi
Lahore
Sutlej

HIMALAYA MOUNTAINS

Panipat
BALUCHISTAN
PUNJAB
Hissar Firoz
Jumna
Delhi
Ganges
Bikaner
Indus
Makrana
Mathura
Samugarh
Jaisalmer
Jaipur (Amber)
Fatehpur
Agra
Khajwah
SIND
Jodhpur (Marwar)
Ajmer
Sikri
Gwalior
RAJASTHAN
Orchha
Allahabad
Patna
Umarkot
Chitor
Chambal
Benares
RANN OF KUTCH
BIHAR
Udaipur (Mewar)
Ganges

Ujjain
Narmada
Hooghly
Ahmadabad
BENGAL
GUJARAT
Mandu
Calcutta (Kolkata)
MALWA
BALAGHAT
Tapti
Surat
Burhanpur
Mahanadi
Daulatabad
ORISSA
MAHARASHTRA
Aurangabad
Bombay (Mumbai)
Ahmednagar
DECCAN

Arabian Sea
Bidar
Bijapur
Hyderabad (Golconda)
Krishna

Goa

Bay of Bengal

| 0 Miles | 500 |
| 0 Kilometers | 500 |

CARNATIC
Madras (Chennai)
Kaveri

Indian Ocean

© 2006 Jeffrey L. Ward

Genealogy

THE GREAT MOGHULS 1526–1707

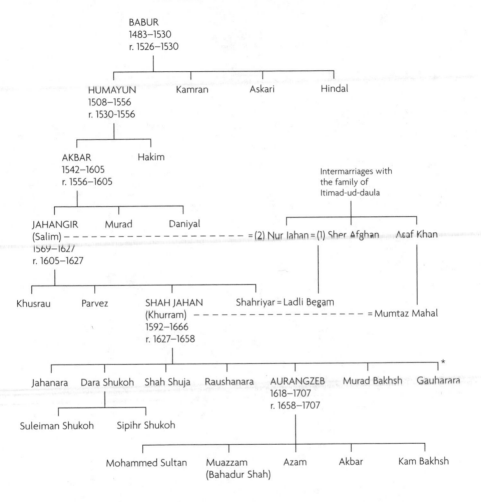

r.—reigned
=—married

* The seven of Shah Jahan and Mumtaz's children who survived into adulthood

NOTES: All the emperors had several wives
      Humayun's mother was Ma'suma
      Akbar's mother was Hamida
      Jahangir's mother was a princess of Amber unnamed by chronicler Abul Fazl
      Shah Jahan's mother was Jodh Bai

Prologue

IN A DUSTY FORTRESS ON THE HOT, AIRLESS plateau of the Deccan in central India, an army commander sat playing chess with his beautiful, bejeweled and heavily pregnant wife. The year was 1631, under the Muslim calendar 1040, and both of them were Muslims. Suddenly, as the popular version of the story goes, a severe pain gripped the woman's abdomen. Doctors were hastily summoned, but despite their efforts, the thirty-eight-year-old mother's fourteenth pregnancy was going severely wrong. Weak through loss of blood, she whispered to her distraught husband of their everlasting love and begged him not to marry again. Her final request was that he should build her a mausoleum resembling paradise on earth, just as she had seen in her dreams.

The authoritative court chroniclers recorded her death just a few minutes later after giving birth to a daughter.

> *When she brought out the last single pearl*
> *She emptied her body like an oyster.*

They related that for two years her husband, the Moghul emperor Shah Jahan, hid himself away, spurning worldly pleasures and exchanging sparkling gems and rich clothes for simple mourning garments of pure white. In the words of one of his court poets, "His eyes wept pearl drops of sadness." His hair turned white overnight. He devoted his energies to fulfilling the dream of his wife, Mumtaz Mahal, "Chosen One of the Palace," creating a tomb that was not only a representation of heaven on

Shah Jahan

earth but also a symbol of sensuality and luxury even in death. Built on a bend in the River Jumna at Shah Jahan's capital of Agra, in northern India, we know it as the Taj Mahal, the world's most famous memorial to love.

The Taj Mahal's architect is not known for certain, but this much-debated figure produced a design of flawless symmetry and exquisite elegance, a synthesis of Muslim and Hindu styles executed in rose sandstone and milk-white marble. Despite its massive size—the main dome rises more than 240 feet and throws a load of some twelve thousand tons on its supports—the Taj Mahal seems to float almost weightless above its surrounding courtyards, mirrorlike watercourses and vivid green gardens. Its mythic fragile beauty rarely fails to captivate even the most cynical.

Contemporaries immediately recognized the Taj as a marvel of the age. A seventeenth-century French traveler decided that this building "deserves much more to be numbered among the wonders of the world than the pyramids of Egypt." A Moghul scholar wrote that "the eye of the sun overflows with tears from looking at it; its shadow is like moonlight to the earth."

Later generations struggled to express the emotions the Taj's ethereal, melancholic beauty inspired in them. To the Nobel prize–winning poet Rabindranath Tagore, the Taj was "a tear drop on the face of time." To Rudyard Kipling, it was "the ivory gate through which all good dreams come; the realisation of the gleaming halls of dawn that Tennyson sings of . . . the embodiment of all things pure, all things holy, and all things unhappy." The artist and nonsense poet Edward Lear declared that "descriptions of this wonderfully lovely place are simply silly as no words can describe it at all. Henceforth let the inhabitants of the world be divided into two classes—them as has seen the Taj Mahal and them as hasn't." Eleanor Roosevelt visited the Taj Mahal just after dusk and wrote, "I held my breath unable to speak in the face of so much beauty . . . this is a beauty that enters the soul." Fittingly, another woman, the wife of an early nineteenth-century British army officer, best captured the sublime intensity of the love that inspired the building. She wrote simply to her husband, "I cannot tell you what I think for I know not how to criticise such a building, but I can tell you what I feel. I would die tomorrow to have such another over me."

By the end of the eighteenth century the British artist Thomas Daniell, who produced some of the best early paintings and plans of the Taj Mahal, could write after his visit, "The Taj Mahal has always been considered . . . a spectacle of the highest celebrity . . . visited by persons of all rank and from all parts." The Taj Mahal's celebrity has only grown over succeeding centuries. It is an international icon and, like the Statue of Liberty, the Eiffel Tower, the Leaning Tower of Pisa and the Great Wall of China, one of the world's most readily identifiable structures. Despite being built by an occupying dynasty, it is a symbol of India adopted by numerous tourist organizations, restaurant owners and manufacturers in India and worldwide. It has also become a symbol of enduring love. By the time of Princess Diana's visit in February 1992 to India

The Taj Mahal, Agra, Taken in the Garden, *by Thomas and William Daniell*

with her then husband, Prince Charles, the power of the Taj Mahal's image was such that when she visited the Taj alone and allowed herself to be photographed—a single, disconsolate and melancholy figure seated on a white marble bench before a monument to an abiding royal romance—no words were needed.

The Taj Mahal is an expression not only of supreme love but also of confident power and opulent majesty. It was the creation of an emperor whose dominions stretched westward across the Indus into present-day Afghanistan and Pakistan, eastward to Bengal and southward to the central Indian plateau of the Deccan. Shah Jahan's ancestors, the four preceding emperors, had acquired these huge—and hugely wealthy—lands by persistent opportunism. Descendants of Genghis Khan and Timur, they had been pushed out of their traditional territories on the plains of central Asia beyond the mountains of the Hindu Kush by fierce rivalries among the rulers of the local clans. In the early sixteenth century, under the leadership of Babur, the first Moghul emperor, they had begun probing down through the Khyber Pass into Hindustan—northern India. Their hold on their territorial gains had at first been precarious as local rulers had forced them back. Not until the reign of Babur's grandson—Shah Jahan's grandfather, Akbar—from 1556 to 1605, was the Moghuls' hold on India secure.

With stability and prosperity came the opportunity for the Moghuls to indulge their traditional aesthetic interests. Nostalgic for the cooler· climes they had left behind them, they had a particular love for exquisite gardens, cooled by fountains and streams and with airy pavilions in which to relax. They were the prototype for the gardens of the Taj Mahal, and several survive to this day. The emperors also became enthusiastic builders, constructing in their new lands fortresses and palaces and within their pleasure gardens their own beautiful mausolea. They brought with them a tradition of tomb building which they developed over the years into a unique fusion of Islamic and indigenous traditions. The fabulous wealth of India, piled high in the imperial Moghul treasuries, enabled them to build mausolea of extraordinary magnificence and sophistication. Shah Jahan could literally stud the Taj Mahal with jewels, inlaid into the building's white marble to form the glowing flowers of an earthly representation of the heavenly paradise where Mumtaz awaited her grieving husband.

The Taj Mahal was the Moghul Empire's ultimate artistic expression— emulated but never equaled. However, it extracted a high price from its builder, Shah Jahan, in every sense. Creating this "heaven on earth" was an almost impossible undertaking, physically and financially. A contemporary English traveler wrote, "The building goes on with excessive labour and cost . . . Gold and silver esteemed common metal and marble but an ordinary stone." The Taj's construction and the emotional impact of Mumtaz Mahal's loss depleted Shah Jahan's treasuries and distracted him from the business of government. It also fueled the tensions within a motherless imperial family, inserted the seed of Shah Jahan's own downfall and helped precipitate what was then the world's most powerful empire into religious fundamentalism and decline.

While Shah Jahan still lived, he witnessed four of his and Mumtaz Mahal's sons fight among themselves for his throne and the victor, the strictly orthodox Aurangzeb, murder two brothers and several of Shah

Jahan's grandchildren. As for Shah Jahan himself, he passed his final years a prisoner in the fort at Agra. Here he reputedly passed his days gazing across the Jumna toward the Taj Mahal, piling recriminations on his son for the divisions he was creating in the empire, and regretting what might have been had Mumtaz Mahal, the Lady of the Taj, survived.

The seventy-three years of Shah Jahan's life, from 1592 to 1666, were a pivotal period in the fortunes of the Moghuls, but also a time of rapid change in the wider world, which itself had a growing influence on the Moghul Empire.

In the Middle East, the Ottoman Turks were trying to rebuild their power after their great naval defeat by Spanish and Venetian fleets at Lepanto. Under Mehmet III, who had in 1595 murdered twenty-seven of his brothers and half-brothers to win power—a number which puts into perspective the fratricidal tally at the end of Shah Jahan's reign—and his successors, the Ottomans reconquered much of the Balkans. In 1639 they recaptured from Persia what is now Iraq and established a permanent border with the Persians. Persia would henceforth need to turn east in search of any further conquests.

Persia had been alternately ally and adversary of the Moghuls. The Persian emperors had provided support to the earlier Moghul emperors in time of crisis, but more recently, under the Safawid dynasty, they had sheltered and encouraged rebels and, as the other major regional power, disputed the Moghuls' shifting northwest borders.

Despite their nomadic origins in central Asia, the Moghuls looked toward Persia for their cultural inspiration. From Emperor Akbar onward, the Moghuls had adopted Persian as the language of their court, and members of the imperial family, as well as courtiers, were skilled in the composition of both Persian poetry and prose.

The Moghuls also looked to Persia as a reservoir of talented manpower. Many Moghul courtiers, generals and artists were Persian-born or of Persian descent. Among the former was Amanat Khan, the calligrapher from Shiraz, who was the only man Shah Jahan allowed to sign his work on the Taj Mahal. Among the latter was Mumtaz Mahal herself. Her grandfather had arrived at the Moghul court from Persia a penniless immigrant and had risen to be the chief minister of Shah Jahan's father, Jahangir.

Mumtaz and her family were, like most Persians, Shia Muslims, while the Moghuls were Sunnis. The Moghul court was considerably more tolerant of differences between and within religious faiths than were Europeans of the time. The Moghul emperors married not only members of the rival Shia sect but also Hindus. Each of their wives continued to follow her own religion. Shah Jahan himself had both a Hindu mother and paternal grandmother. By contrast, many of the political divisions in Europe had their origin in religion. In the first half of the seventeenth century, as Shah Jahan consolidated his power and married Mumtaz, much of northern Europe was exhausting itself in the Thirty Years War, as much about the conflict between Catholic and Protestant, which had fed the fires of the Inquisition, as about territory.

Shah Jahan's lifetime was a period of vigorous expansion in European trade and of a shifting balance between European powers. The outcome of the Thirty Years War would keep Germany fragmented until the rise of the Prussian Empire some two hundred years later. Catholic France, however, would soon reach the summit of its power under Louis XIV, whose centralized, autocratic court bore many resemblances to that of the Moghuls and who, like the Moghul emperors, believed in the Divine Right of Kings. The Protestant English parliament did not share such views and in 1649, after a bloody civil war, tried and executed their king, Charles I, substituting for him a Puritan republic under Oliver Cromwell and later, in 1660, replacing that with a restored monarchy restricted by a parliament from which democracy eventually grew.

The English founded their first colony in America at Jamestown in Virginia in 1607, the year of Shah Jahan's betrothal to Mumtaz Mahal. In 1664, two years before Shah Jahan's death, the English acquired from the Dutch the town of New Amsterdam and renamed it New York. The Dutch consoled themselves with their burgeoning, monopolistic spice trade in the East, where the Dutch East India Company had already established its headquarters at Batavia (modern Jakarta) in 1619.

The Spanish had long been masters of much of South and Central America, oppressing its people to exploit the mineral wealth such as the mines in the 15,381-foot silver mountain at Potosí in present-day Bolivia. However, by the time of Shah Jahan's death the Spanish were a fading power. Like their contemporaries, the Moghuls, they had failed to develop a trading system independent of regal bureaucracy and cupidity. In 1655 the English republic had captured Jamaica from Spain, and from there its privateers or pirates (the designation depending on whether you were English or Spanish) plundered Spanish wealth. More insidiously, English free traders began to cooperate with local Spanish merchants to trade outside the bounds of the Spanish customs regime. The English were also bringing their own brand of free trade to other parts of the world. In Africa they traded with local rulers for the black slaves they first took to Virginia in 1619, and in the East Indies they began to encroach on Spanish and Dutch monopolies.

When Shakespeare and his contemporaries, such as Christopher Marlowe, referred to India, it was as a synonym for exotic wealth in gems and spices. The English East India Company was chartered in 1600 and began trading for cotton, spices and gems on India's west coast, where the Portuguese had been established since 1510. In 1661, when Shah Jahan was in the third year of his imprisonment by his son in the Agra fort, the recently restored Charles II received Bombay (Mumbai), just outside the Moghul domains, as part of the dowry of his Portuguese wife, Catherine of Braganza. The English were, however, mere lowly observers at the court of the Moghuls. A miniature portrait of Shah Jahan's father, Jahangir, shows him ruling the world while an insignificant James I of England is pictured beneath in a subordinate position looking somewhat sour even if he is wearing only slightly fewer pearls and jewels on his person and clothes than Jahangir. British power would, in due course, rise in India as that of the Moghuls declined.

The English and the Portuguese were by no means the only Europeans to visit Moghul India. Others included the Dutch, the Italians and the French. Whatever their nationality, many were in search of trade. Some were Catholic priests in search of souls. Others were simply curious visitors, eager to learn more about the fabled Great Moghul and his dominions. Yet others were soldiers of fortune or pirates seeking refuge from the European authorities and prepared to share their martial skills, in particular that of gunnery, with the Moghuls for a price. Whatever their initial motivation for travel, many when they returned home wrote memoirs to satisfy increasing public demand for information about the Moghuls' lands, their lives and their magnificent jewelry, works of art and buildings.

Shah Jahan had been born just as St. Peter's in Rome was finished and died just as Christopher Wren was preparing to work on his masterpiece, the world's first Protestant cathedral, the new St. Paul's in London. In comparison with these major works of Western architecture, the walled enclosure of the Taj Mahal was big enough to enclose the whole of St. Peter's, including the later piazza designed by Bernini and constructed during Shah Jahan's last decade. And while St. Paul's rises 365 feet above the ground, 125 feet higher than the Taj Mahal, its footprint is much smaller.* In Persia, in the southern city of Isfahan, Shah Abbas had built the beautiful Shah Mosque between about 1611 and 1630. It shares many architectural features with the Taj Mahal, such as a swelling, double-skinned dome with a massive, weight-saving void between the outer and inner surfaces, as well as grand rectangular *iwans* (recessed entrance arches) dominating the main façades. However, covered in blue, soft yellow and green tiles, its patterned exuberance contrasts with the opalescent serenity of the Taj Mahal's white marble and shows how far Moghul architecture had diverged from its Persian influences, despite the continuing employment of Persian immigrants in the design and decoration of Moghul buildings.

During Shah Jahan's lifetime Europe's most prominent artists included Caravaggio, Velázquez and Rubens but also a most notable collector of Moghul drawings and paintings, Rembrandt. He made sketches based on these works and seems to have taken a particular interest in the jewelry displayed. That Rembrandt copied paintings made by Shah Jahan's painters, who had themselves been influenced by European works given by travelers to his father, Jahangir, is just one example of how artistic influences could migrate around the world. Chauvinistic European historians conscious of the Taj's greatness would soon claim that its intricate semiprecious stone inlay, and perhaps its design, were influenced or even undertaken by Europeans. Such rivalries about the Taj's origins persist. In India today some even claim the Taj Mahal as an entirely Hindu achievement rather than a Moghul synthesis of Islamic and indigenous

---

* For about 4,400 years, until the nineteenth century, the Great Pyramid of Cheops at Giza was, at more than 450 feet, the tallest building in the world.

influences. Others insist that it is a wholly Muslim creation which should be managed under sharia law.

Yet the story of the Taj and the love that created it has universal appeal. It has the cadences of Greek tragedy and the ripe emotion of grand opera. It is a tale of overwhelming passion, set against a world of imperious patriarchs, jealous sons and powerful, charismatic women dominating court politics from behind the silken screens of the harem. The fate of an empire of 100 million souls hung on the relationships within the imperial family as sons sought to depose fathers, brother killed brother, and empresses and would-be empresses plotted and schemed. Yet a veil of glittering wealth, supreme power and an exotic location cannot obscure the deeply personal nature of the emotions behind the Taj Mahal. At the heart of the Taj are questions transcending time and cultures about the nature of love, of grief and of beauty and of whether these intangible qualities can be given substantive and enduring earthly expression.

CHAPTER ONE

"A Place of Few Charms"

BABUR, THE FOUNDING FATHER OF THE Moghul Empire, came from the kingdom of Ferghana, a small state to the east of Samarkand in central Asia. His father, the king, was, in Babur's words, "short and fat . . . he wore his tunic so tight that to fasten the strings he had to draw in his belly, if he let himself go the ties often broke." He was nonetheless "brave and valiant, good-natured, talkative and affable. He was strong in the fist, however, and no one was ever hit by him who did not fall. His urge to expand his territory turned many a truce into a battle and many a friend into a foe." On 8 June 1494, this small, stout man was inspecting a dovecote on his castle walls when the parapet collapsed, precipitating him into the ravine below. Thus, wrote Babur, "in the twelfth year of my age I became ruler in the country of Ferghana."

Ferghana was only one of several principalities in what is now Uzbekistan and Afghanistan, whose rulers were in constant conflict to claim a greater share of the fragmented legacy of two preceding dynasties, those of Ghenghis Khan and of Timur. Most of the contenders could claim descent from one or the other; Babur could claim both. On his mother's side Babur was a direct descendant of the legendary Ghenghis Khan. When Ghenghis was born in 1167, the son of a local headman on the Mongolian plains, he is said to have been clutching a blood clot in his fist, the symbol of his warrior destiny. When he died in 1227, he was known as the "Oceanic Ruler." He and his horde of horsemen had plundered half of the known world from Beijing to the Danube.

Timur was Babur's great-great-great-grandfather on his father's side. Better known to Europeans as Tamburlaine from a corruption of his nickname, "Timur the Lame," he was a chieftain of the nomadic Barlas Turks and, a hundred years before Babur's birth, had once again estab-lished a vast empire stretching from the borders of China to Turkey, with its capital at the fabled golden city of Samarkand.* Like that of Ghenghis Khan before it, the empire of Timur was divided on his death among his family rather than being left to a single heir, hence its rapid fragmentation into such kingdoms as Ferghana.

Babur was much prouder of his Timurid, or what he thought of as his Turkish, descent than of his Mongol inheritance. His comment that "were the Mongols a race of angels it would still be a vile nation" encap-sulated his view of them, and he would have been much affronted that the dynasty he would initiate in India would soon become known as the "Moghuls" from a corruption of the Persian word for Mongol. (The Moghuls' fabled power and luxurious wealth were first invoked as an epi-thet for Hollywood's own movie emperors in the 1920s.)

Nevertheless, it was his Mongol grandmother who steered Babur through the early adolescent years of his rule. The first but not the last woman to guide the Moghuls from behind the purdah veil, she was, ac-cording to her grandson, "intelligent and a good planner. Most affairs were settled with her counsel." Under her tutelage and aged just four-teen, Babur took advantage of a civil war that had erupted in Samarkand following the death of two rulers in quick succession to besiege and cap-ture the city which for him embodied Timur's glory.

Inspecting his new acquisition, Babur took particular delight in the lovely gardens laid out by Timur. Despite his reputation in Europe as

---

* In 1941 a Russian anthropologist opened Timur's sarcophagus and examined his skeleton. His work confirmed that the emperor had indeed been lame—from a wound in his right leg. Reputedly founded by Alexander the Great, Samarkand sits on the Silk Road from China to Europe where it meets the Zerafshan—"Gold-Sprinkling"—River.

a savage nomad and, in Christopher Marlowe's words, "the scourge of God," he had been a cultivated man. A European ambassador described how Timur's gardens in Samarkand "were traversed by many channels of water which flowed among the fruit trees and gave a pleasant shade. In the centre of the avenues of trees were raised platforms." True to his nomadic background, Timur had lived in these gardens in large tents, some made of red cloth, others of sumptuously embroidered silk, but he had also built domed mosques and tombs, each with a perfect symmetry of plan.

However, Babur had little time to savor his new possessions. His soldiers began to drift away as Samarkand's booty ran out, while in Ferghana disaffected nobles took advantage of his absence to replace him with his younger brother. Forced to abandon Samarkand, Babur hurried back to his ancestral kingdom. His rule of Samarkand had lasted only one hundred days. "It was difficult for me," he wrote. "I could not help crying a good deal."

Babur spent the next two years struggling to regain at least some of his territory in Ferghana from his brother. He also married, in March 1500, but did not enjoy the experience. "In the early days after the wedding I was bashful, I went to her only every ten, fifteen or twenty days. Later on I lost my fondness for her altogether . . . Once every forty days my mother drove me to her with all the severity of a quartermaster." Babur confessed that his affections were engaged elsewhere in an adolescent crush on a market boy named Baburi: "I developed a strange inclination for him—rather I made myself miserable over him. Before this experience I had never felt a desire for anyone. Occasionally Baburi came to me but I was so bashful that I could not look him in the face, much less converse freely with him. There was no possibility of speaking coherently." After some three years of marriage Babur's wife left him, as he recorded, "at her elder sister's instigation."

In July 1500, less than three years after he had been forced to abandon it, Babur retook Samarkand. The city had recently been seized by a chieftain from the Uzbek tribe—nomad Mongols from the northern steppes who coveted the Timurid lands. However, Babur's second reign in Samarkand lasted less than a year. The Uzbek chieftain he had

Babur receiving tribute in Kabul

ejected besieged the city, reducing its occupants to surviving on the flesh
of asses and dogs. Babur had no choice but to sue for peace and slip
quietly away with only a few followers. With the Uzbeks also advancing
into Ferghana, this was the nadir of his fortunes. He later admitted "that
to wander from mountain to mountain, homeless and houseless had
nothing to recommend it."

However, news that Kabul, three hundred miles to the south of

Ferghana and another ancestral Timurid territory, had fallen to an outsider on the death of its previous ruler, one of Babur's uncles, brought him some cheer. Babur had as strong a claim to the throne of Kabul as anyone and determined to capture it. As he advanced, his forces grew and the incumbent ruler decamped, leaving only chaos. Babur recalled, "In the end I rode there and had four or five people shot and one or two dismembered. The riot ceased." On 14 June 1504, still only twenty-one, he took possession of Kabul. It would remain his power base and spiritual home for the rest of his life. Here in Kabul Babur for the first time had the leisure to indulge his inherited passion for books and for gardens.

In his honest and intimate memoirs based on his diary, the *Baburnama*—the first autobiography in Islamic literature—Babur described how he established his favorite garden in Kabul: "I laid [it] out on a hillside facing south. In the middle a stream flows constantly past the little hill on which are the four garden plots. In the southwest there is a reservoir round which are orange trees and a few pomegranates, the whole encircled by a meadow. This is the best part of the garden, a most beautiful sight when the oranges take colour. Truly," he congratulated himself, "that garden is admirably situated." Later, when ruling in India, Babur still found time to write to his governor in Kabul that his garden should be well watered and properly stocked with flowers.

When Babur conquered new lands, one of his first acts was to plunder the ruler's libraries to add to his own collection. Central Asian royal libraries contained only manuscripts. Although the world's oldest printed book, Wang Jie's *Diamond Sutra*, was produced in China in AD 868 by the painstaking hand engraving of wooden blocks, and printed books were becoming commonplace in Europe following Johannes Gutenberg's invention in the mid-fifteenth century of reusable type and the printing press, neither process was used in central Asia or Moghul India. While this resulted in a greater reliance on oral communication, it also produced beautiful illuminated manuscript copies of key documents such as the chronicles of kings. Babur himself wrote poetry and prose, and the breadth of his interest in the arts is summed up in the education he enforced on a young cousin: "calligraphy, reading, making verses, epistolary style, painting and illumination . . . such crafts as seal-engraving, jewellers' and goldsmiths' work."

However, Babur was keenly aware that if he did not keep his troops on the move in search of new territory and plunder, their minds might turn to revolt. With Persian backing he attacked the Uzbeks, forcing them back from some of the Timurid lands they had seized, and in 1511 he regained his beloved Samarkand from them. This was the third time he had taken the city, but again he failed to hold it, relinquishing it to the Uzbeks after just eight months. His third failure to retain the city was a watershed in Babur's thinking. Whatever dreams he might still have entertained of possessing Timur's lost capital, Babur accepted that the obstacles were too great. Instead, he would turn his aggressive attentions southward to the lands beyond the Khyber Pass—Hindustan (northern India).

THE INDIAN SUBCONTINENT had a long history and a highly developed series of civilizations dating back at least until 3000 BC. In 326 BC Alexander had crossed the River Indus, one of the major natural defensive barriers protecting northwest India, and reached the plains of the Punjab. Here he defeated the forces of an Indian ruler named Porus, which numbered two hundred war elephants in their ranks, before being forced to turn back by his homesick generals and troops. Just over fifty years later, the emperor Ashoka established a Hindu empire which stretched from Afghanistan in the west to Assam in the east and from the Himalayas to the southern Indian state of Mysore. Ashoka maintained his empire by raising revenue from taxation on everything from agriculture to prostitution. He ordered that "no wasteland should be occupied and not a tree cut down" without permission because all were potential sources of state revenue.

Within fifty years of Ashoka's death in 232 BC, his empire had disintegrated. Over the next millennium India was mainly ruled by a series of regional kingdoms, although for some 150 years from AD 320 the Gupta Empire dominated much of the north Indian plains around the River Ganges. Around AD 1000 the Turks and Afghans made their first forays into India. They brought with them their Islamic religion and traditions in art and architecture. They won major victories and by the early thirteenth century had established their rule over much of northern and central India. They created a series of kingdoms at the expense of the established Hindu rulers. Nevertheless, many Hindu kingdoms remained, particularly those of the Rajputs in northwestern India. India was rich in natural resources including iron, gold and gems, being the world's only source of diamonds until the eighteenth century. Although subject to occasional droughts and consequently famines, it produced large amounts of grain. Under the Islamic rulers, trade with Arabia and other parts of the Middle East in goods such as spices, indigo dye and textiles increased. Even if the majority of the people remained poor, the rulers, both Muslim and Hindu, grew hugely wealthy.

Control over the most important of the new Islamic kingdoms, known as the Delhi Sultanate, changed five times over the next three centuries as rival Muslim dynasties contested this strategic prize. Despite these power struggles, the sultanate grew in size and importance as successive rulers expanded its boundaries. At its greatest extent it incorporated Bengal to the east, Gujarat to the west and, to the south, Malwa and parts of the Deccan. Under their rule Delhi first became a major capital. However, although the sultanate was extensive, it was not unified. Local governors frequently took advantage of their distance from Delhi to try to carve out their own independent fiefs.

Attracted by the sultanate's wealth, Babur's own ancestors had twice interrupted the rule of succeeding dynasties of sultans of Delhi. In 1221 Ghenghis Khan had reached the barrier of the River Indus and turned back. At the age of sixty, in 1398, Timur, whose cold, determined eyes a contemporary likened "to candles without brilliance," crossed the Indus over a bridge of boats with his marauding troops. He and his men plundered and pillaged all the way to Delhi, leaving "a multitude of dead carcasses which infected the air" in their wake. Timur entered Delhi in December and put the city to the sword and flame so efficiently that "nothing stirred not even a bird for two months."

However, before the flames consumed the city, Timur assembled as many of Delhi's craftsmen—particularly stonemasons—as he could to accompany him back to Samarkand to work on his construction projects such as the splendid turquoise blue domed tomb he was building for himself. Indeed, after each of his conquests Timur selected skilled artisans to beautify his capital. Glassblowers came from Damascus and silversmiths from Turkey. An ambassador described how there was "such a multitude" of workers that Samarkand "was not large enough to hold them, and it was wonderful what a number lived under trees and in caves outside."

So laden with booty that according to one report they could move at no more than four miles a day, Timur and his army left India less than six months after entering it. However, before departing, Timur had established a new dynasty—the Sayyids—to rule in his name. This gave Babur some pretext, albeit slender, that Hindustan was Timurid territory and his by right.

BEFORE BABUR EMBARKED on his own conquest of India, both his army and his family received reinforcements. The army acquired cannons and matchlock muskets from the Ottoman Turks; Babur, another wife, Ma'-suma Sultan Begim. Although he described how "upon first laying eyes on me she felt a great inclination toward me," he did not in his writings reveal his feelings about her. But Babur greeted the birth of a son, Humayun, around nine months later, in March 1508, with unequivocal joy: "I gave a feast in celebration. More silver coins were piled up than had ever been seen before in one place. It was an excellent feast." *Humayun* means "fortunate," but by no means would all his fortune be good. Other sons from different wives followed: Kamran in 1509, Askari in 1516 and Hindal in 1519.

Beginning in 1519, Babur made four preliminary expeditions into Hindustan before he finally unleashed a full invasion in the autumn of 1525. At this time the Delhi sultanate—by then in the hands of the Lodi dynasty, whose weakening writ ran, at least in name, from the upper Punjab in the northwest to Bihar in the east—was riven by internal feuding against the ruling sultan, Ibrahim. Therefore Babur was able to descend the snowy passes of Afghanistan and Pakistan, cross the Indus, march on through the foothills of the Punjab and reach Panipat on the hot, dusty plains only fifty miles from Delhi before, in April 1526, he had to face any determined opposition.

The one hundred thousand men deployed there by Sultan Ibrahim, who took personal command, outnumbered Babur's troops by five to one. But Babur made best use of his only superiority—his Turkish cannons and matchlock muskets, both being employed in northern India for the first time. He drew his seven hundred wagons, joined by their leather harnesses, into a defensive perimeter behind which he placed his cannons and matchlock men. When, just after dawn on 20 April, the sultan's forces attacked with almost one thousand war elephants in the van, fire from muskets and bronze cannon halted their advance and threw their ranks into panic and confusion. Next Babur's mounted archers attacked the disordered mass of trumpeting elephants and yelling, bewildered and frightened men from the side and rear. Within five hours, twenty thousand of his enemy were dead, including Sultan Ibrahim. Babur was master of northern India.

Once Babur had been proclaimed ruler in Delhi by having Friday's midday sermon, the *khutba*, read in his name in the main mosque as a public statement of his sovereignty, he marched south along the banks of the River Jumna to the city of Agra, which the Lodi sultans had made their capital in 1502. Here his son Humayun presented him with a huge diamond, which Humayun had, in turn, been given by the royal family of Gwalior in gratitude for their protection after their ruler's death fighting for Ibrahim at Panipat. Babur recalled, "A gem merchant once assessed its worth as the whole world's expenditure for half a day . . . but I returned it straightaway to [Humayun]." It was the famous Koh-i-Nur, the "Mountain of Light," that would reappear several times in the Moghul story.

Babur took stock of his new realm and was not overly impressed, writing: "Hindustan is a place of few charms . . . The cities and provinces are all unpleasant. The gardens have no walls and most places are flat as boards. There is no beauty in its people, no graceful society, no poetic talent, no etiquette, nobility or manliness . . . There are no good horses, meat, grapes, melons or other fruit . . . no ice, cold water, no good food, no baths, no madrasas . . . no running water in their gardens or palaces and in their buildings no pleasing harmony or symmetry." At first Babur could only think of one satisfactory characteristic: "The one nice aspect of Hindustan is that it is a large country and has masses of gold and money." After a little more reflection, he managed another: "the unlimited numbers of craftsmen and practitioners of every trade." Like his ancestor Timur, he particularly prized the excellent stonemasons. He and his descendants would employ them to spectacular effect.

Babur soon remedied some of the faults he perceived by building a garden on the banks of the Jumna in Agra, opposite where the Taj Mahal now stands. "In charmless and inharmonious India marvellously regular and geometric gardens were laid out . . . and in every border rose and narcissus in perfect arrangement," he wrote.

Babur had treated the family of his defeated enemy, Sultan Ibrahim, well, keeping the sultan's mother, Buwa, at court. However, she did not reciprocate his kindness. Babur had retained four of Ibrahim's cooks to allow him to try Hindustani dishes. On 21 December 1526, Buwa persuaded one to sprinkle poison on Babur's food. Babur takes up the story. "There was no apparent bad taste. While seated at the meal I was near vomiting on the tablecloth . . . I got up and on my way to the toilet I almost threw up. When I got there I vomited much. I never vomited after meals, not even when drinking. I ordered the vomit given to a dog. [The dog] became pretty listless. No matter how many stones they threw at it, it refused to get up but did not die." Babur had the cook arrested. After he confessed under torture, two old women who had acted as messengers and Babur's taster were in turn arrested. "They also confessed . . . I ordered the taster to be hacked to pieces and the cook skinned alive. One of the two women I had thrown under the elephant's feet and the other shot. I had Buwa put under arrest." To cure himself, Babur drank some opium mixed in milk. "On the first day of this medicine I excreted some pitch black things like burnt bile. Thank goodness now everything is alright. I never knew how sweet a thing life was."

Although Babur cheated death on that occasion, he had less than four years to live. Part he spent in quelling uprisings against Moghul rule and repelling incursions by neighboring powers, part he spent in composing poetry and in compiling his memoir, the *Baburnama*. According to the court chronicles, Babur's death resulted from the severe illness of his son Humayun. Indifferent as he might have been to his wives,

Babur loved his children, declaring Humayun "an incomparable companion." When his son was deep in delirium, seers suggested to Babur that if he gave up one of Humayun's valued possessions he might recover. They seem to have meant the Koh-i-Nur, but Babur took it that he should offer his own life to God. He did so crying "I shall be his sacrifice . . . I can endure all his pain," and "when his prayer had been heard by God . . . Babur felt a strange effect on himself and cried out 'We have borne it away!' Immediately a strange heat of fever surged upon his majesty and there was a sudden diminution of it in [Humayun]."

Babur's health did deteriorate after the incident, but several months elapsed before his death in December 1530, which, less romantically, was more likely to have been related to the rigors of his youthful life and his overindulgence in wine, opiates and other drugs. (Babur described how in a drug-induced trance, hippylike, he enjoyed "wonderful fields of flowers.") But before he died, Babur called upon his supporters to recognize Humayun as his rightful successor and lectured Humayun, "Do nought against your brothers, even though they may deserve it." Unlike some of his descendants, Humayun would follow his father's injunction, which derived from a general Timurid principle that the lives of royal princes should be protected. Babur was buried in his new garden opposite the future site of the Taj Mahal. Later his body was returned to Kabul, as he had wished, and interred in his hillside garden overlooking the city. At his request, and in accordance with Islamic tradition that tombs should lie beneath the open canopy of the sky, no building was constructed over his marble cenotaph.

THE TWENTY-TWO-YEAR-OLD HUMAYUN was "a dignified and magnificent prince, kindhearted and generous, mild and benevolent." He was personally brave but crucially lacked the determination and decisiveness necessary to consolidate his energetic and charismatic father's four-year-old rule over Hindustan. He was easily distracted and so superstitious that he always entered a room right foot first and sent others who did not back outside to reenter properly. Astrology infatuated him. He wore different colored clothes and varied his pursuits to suit the governing planets of the days of the week. On Sunday, for example, he wore yellow and

dealt with state affairs, and on Monday green and made merry. On Tuesday he wore warlike red and acted wrathful and vengeful. His wrath
could be both whimsical and cruel. One Tuesday he claimed to fit punishments to the crime, removing the heads of those he considered "head-
strong" and chopping off the hands and feet of those he thought lacked
judgment, that is who failed to "distinguish between their feet and
hands."

His natural lethargy was multiplied manifold by what one chronicler
called his "excessive" use of opium, which he took mixed with rosewater.
As a result of such failings, Humayun lost Hindustan and was forced to
wander, a ruler without a throne, as had Babur in his youth. The agent of
his expulsion was the astute, stout and subtle Sher Shah. From humble
origins as an officer in a small Muslim state along the Ganges in Bihar, he
had over a number of years quietly established himself as the virtual ruler
of much of Bihar and Bengal.

When he eventually realized the threat that Sher Shah posed to his
rule, Humayun led a large army down to the Ganges. His approach was
leisurely and allowed Sher Shah plenty of time to prepare. After much
maneuvering, the two armies finally joined battle at the end of June 1539.
Sher Shah's forces routed Humayun's troops, and the emperor was forced
to flee ignominiously. He only succeeded in escaping across the Ganges
with the aid of one of his water bearers named Nazim, who blew up his
animal skin water bottle and gave it to Humayun as a flotation aid.*

Humayun fled first to Agra and then northwest to Lahore to meet his
half-brothers Kamran, Askari and Hindal. Their loyalty was suspect.
Mindful that Ghenghis Khan and Timur had divided their kingdoms
among their sons, rather than appointing a single heir as Babur had
done, each of the other brothers had sought a return to the old tradition
and had already been involved in rebellions or near rebellions, seeking to

---

* Much to the annoyance of his brothers and courtiers, the quixotic Humayun made
  good a promise he had given Nazim in the heat of the moment to allow him to sit
  on the imperial throne. Nazim was only allowed to occupy it briefly and only gave
  a few orders, all designed to enrich himself and his family. However, Humayun's
  action did nothing to increase his regal dignity at a crucial point in his reign, even
  if it did show him to be a man of his word.

carve out territories for themselves. Each time they had been tearfully forgiven by Humayun, who, as well as respecting his father's injunction, was sentimental and affectionate by nature. According to their sister Gulbadan, faced with a common danger, the four siblings "conferred and took counsel and asked advice but they did not settle on any single thing." Kamran secretly tried to negotiate a separate peace with Sher Shah that would secure him Kabul. Humayun, equally privately, offered Sher Shah peace on the basis that "I have left you Hindustan. Leave Lahore alone and let Sind be a boundary between you and me."

Sher Shah rejected both. When he advanced on Lahore, Humayun, his brothers and, it is said, two hundred thousand of their followers fled. Gulbadan wrote, "It was like the day of resurrection, people left their decorated palaces and their furniture just as they were." Accompanied by Hindal, Humayun fled toward Sind and spent months in fruitless efforts to persuade the local ruler to support him. However, he did succeed in another task of persuasion, but only after a month of trying. He convinced Hamida, the fourteen-year-old daughter of one of Hindal's advisers, to agree to marry him. At first both she and Hindal were vehemently opposed to the marriage, perhaps because they were mutually attracted. Eventually, Hindal marched angrily away to Kandahar, and Humayun's mother induced Hamida to accept her thirty-three-year-old son by arguing, "After all, you will marry someone. Better than a king, who is there?" Humayun "took [an] astrolabe into his own blessed hand" and himself carefully worked out the astrologically most auspicious date for their marriage: 21 August 1541.

When Hamida and Humayun left Sind in May 1542, they crossed the Rajasthani Desert back into India, where Humayun had hopes of alliance with the raja of Marwar (Jodhpur). However, these soon came to naught, and the party turned back across the blistering, shimmering desert in the hottest months of the year. Hamida was by then eight months pregnant. Even so, the disdain some of his officers now had for Humayun was such that when, one day, Hamida was left without a horse, none would lend her one. Eventually, Humayun gave her his own and clambered on a camel—an undignified and inauspicious mount for an emperor. Finally, an officer relented and handed Hamida his horse, allowing Humayun to climb down.

Soon the party reached Umarkot, a desert town whose ruler had been
killed by Humayun's enemies. It was a case of "my enemy's enemy is my
friend," and Humayun's exhausted party was welcomed and feasted.
There, on 15 October 1542, Hamida gave birth to a son: the future emperor Akbar. In later years Akbar's chief chronicler, Abul Fazl, described
the birth thus: "The unique pearl of the viceregency of God came forth
in his glory." The proud new father, the astrology-obsessed Humayun,
of course cast his son's horoscope. It was most propitious. However, Humayun's own position remained inauspicious. He once more left India,
with his brothers Askari and Kamran among the opposition hemming
him in. He decided that his only hope was to seek assistance from the
shah of Persia as his father had once done in similar straits.

Because the journey would be across harsh terrain in winter, the two
fond parents entrusted their only son, then fourteen months old, to the
care of his rebellious uncle. Askari was no Richard III, and, in line with
the best Timurid prescriptions on the treatment of princes, his wife cared
well for his nephew. However, the boy's father was by now suffering. "My
very head was frozen by the intense cold," Humayun recalled. Both food
and cooking pots were scarce, and the party were reduced to killing one of
their horses and boiling some flesh in a helmet. Nevertheless, in January
1544 they reached Persia. The shah welcomed Humayun as an honored
guest and seemed inclined to grant him considerable support, a benevo-
lence no doubt encouraged by the Moghul wanderer's production, from
beneath his robes, of a green flowered purse. From it Humayun extracted
the Koh-i-Nur and other jewels, placed them in a mother-of-pearl box and
handed them to the shah. Abul Fazl later wrote that the jewel reimbursed
all the shah's expenditure on Humayun "more than four times over."

Nevertheless, before granting assistance, the shah insisted that Humayun, a Sunni Muslim, should change his sect and become a Shia. The
Safawid dynasty had made the Shia practice of Islam the state religion of
Persia in 1501. The distinction between Shia and Sunni derived from
the first century of Islam and the rivalry over who was the prophet
Muhammad's legitimate successor and whether the office should be an
elected one or restricted, as the Shias claimed, to the descendants of the
prophet through his cousin and son-in-law, Ali. *Shia* is the word for party
and comes from the phrase "the party of Ali." *Sunni* means those who

follow the custom, sunna, of Muhammad. By the sixteenth century further differences had grown between the two sects, such as the nature of
required daily prayer.

Humayun could only reluctantly acquiesce, at least while under the
shah's sway.* So a Persian army was provided, and Humayun advanced
into Afghanistan, where in 1545 he captured Kandahar from his brother
Askari and Kabul from his brother Kamran. In Kabul he and Hamida
were reunited with Akbar, by then in the care of Babur's sister, Khandura, who, in the way of the women of the Moghul royal family had become a frequent intermediary between the warring brothers. As part of
the celebrations, the important public ceremony of the three-year-old
Akbar's circumcision took place. Humayun participated in a celebratory
wrestling contest with his nobles.

Humayun and Hamida reunited with Akbar

---

* His decision is comparable to that of Henry of Navarre, Henry IV of France, who
  in 1593 renounced his Protestantism and became a Catholic to win the French
  throne, declaring, "Paris is worth a mass."

Although the brothers were reconciled once more, they could not agree for long. Both Kamran and Askari rebelled on further occasions. Hindal died in 1551 fighting Askari's forces. Humayun eventually dispatched Askari on a pilgrimage to Mecca—a common form of Moghul exile—on which he died. After Kamran had twice recaptured Kabul from Humayun and twice lost it again, Humayan's forces captured him in 1552. Humayun's counselors, according to the chroniclers, argued for Kamran's execution: "Brotherly custom has nothing to do with ruling and reigning. If you wish to be king put aside brotherly sentiment . . . This is no brother! This is your majesty's foe."

Humayun reluctantly agreed that Kamran should be blinded, a stratagem used in Timurid kingdoms to disable rivals. Some of Humayun's men held the wildly struggling Kamran down, repeatedly lanced his eyeballs and rubbed salt and lemon juice into the wounds. Later Kamran is said to have told his weeping brother, "Whatever has happened to me has proceeded from my own misconduct." Kamran departed on a pilgrimage to Mecca, where he too died.

In 1554 news came to Humayun in Kabul of the death in Hindustan of Sher Shah's son and successor Islam Shah. (Sher Shah himself had died in the explosion of a gunpowder magazine in 1545 while on campaign.) Soon afterward came further welcome news: Three rival claimants were fighting for the throne of Hindustan. Even the normally indecisive Humayun could not ignore such a clear opportunity. Taking his young heir Akbar with him, he advanced quickly into India, twice defeated his main rivals and in July 1555 retook Delhi—some fifteen years after he had fled before Sher Shah.

Back on his throne Humayun unsurprisingly devoted himself to astrology and to literature. He established an observatory and refurbished a small octagonal sandstone pavilion in Sher Shah's palace, known as the Sher Mandal, to become his library. (His collection of manuscripts including his father's memoirs had, like his other prize possession, his jewels, accompanied him on his wanderings.) But his fate continued to belie his name of "fortunate." One evening toward sunset in late January 1556, he was sitting on the flat roof of the Sher Mandal discussing with his astronomers when Venus would rise into the night sky, since he thought this would be a propitious time for important announcements.

The Sher Mandal

After a while he decided to return to his living quarters. As he was setting foot on the Sher Mandal's narrow, steep and sharp-edged stone steps, he heard the call to prayer from the neighboring mosque and "his blessed foot caught in the skirt of his robe . . . He lost his feet and fell upon his head, his right temple receiving a serious blow so that blood issued from his right ear." He slipped in and out of consciousness, dying three days later with the words, "I hear the divine call." He was forty-seven years and ten months old, just a few days older than his father, Babur, had been when he died.

Humayun had lived less than a third of his life in India. By contrast, his son Akbar, who died like his contemporary Shakespeare on his own birthday, would live precisely sixty-three years, fifty of them in India, forty-nine of them as emperor. He would transform Moghul rule in India from a foreign occupation into a structured, integrated, stable empire.

CHAPTER TWO

Allah Akbar

THE FIRST SIX YEARS OF YOUNG AKBAR'S RULE were conducted, as Abul Fazl put it, "behind the veil," first under the tutelage of his father's leading general and then under that of his chief foster mother or wet nurse, Maham Anga, and her family. According to Abul Fazl, when Akbar was born in the Rajasthani Desert, he was first put to suckle at his fifteen-year-old mother's breast, "his honeyed lips in contact with the benign breasts, his life was sweetened by the life-giving fluid." However, and according to Timurid custom, he was then passed to a series of high-born wet nurses. Theirs was a coveted position because they acquired great influence and their sons were considered foster brothers of the royal infant. Akbar had at least ten foster mothers, rather more than usual, because at the time of his birth Humayun had little other way of rewarding loyal followers.

Power soon went to the head of Maham Anga's son, Adham Khan. In the words of Abul Fazl he became increasingly "intoxicated by youth and prosperity," and "the cap of his pride was blown away by the wind of arrogance." He withheld treasure due to the emperor from captured cities and attempted to keep for himself the choicest inhabitants of captured harems. Then, one hot May afternoon in 1562, the chronicles record that he coolly walked with his guards into the imperial palace at Agra, where a rival minister was giving public audience. As the minister, the husband of another of Akbar's wet nurses, rose to greet him, Adham gestured to one of his henchmen to knife him. Sword in hand, Adham made for the adjoining harem where Akbar was asleep, but a eunuch slammed the door shut and bolted it from the inside. Nineteen-year-old Akbar, now wide-awake, emerged from a side door, rushed toward Adham and smashed his fist into his face. (Akbar's chroniclers boasted that it looked as if he had been hit with a mace.) Akbar ordered Adham's still unconscious body to be thrown from the palace wall, which was more than thirty feet high, but the first fall did not kill him. Akbar had him hauled back up by his hair and flung down again, this time headfirst. Thus, in Abul Fazl's words, "his neck was broken and his brains destroyed. In this way the bloodthirsty profligate underwent retribution." Akbar had emerged from behind the veil with a vengeance.

Akbar was personally brave as shown by his confrontation with Adham. He was also ambitious to extend the boundaries of the empire he had inherited from his father. According to Abul Fazl, he believed "a monarch should be ever intent on conquest, otherwise his neighbours rise in arms against him. The army should be exercised in warfare lest from want of training they become self-indulgent." During his lifetime he waged many wars of conquest. Most often dressed in glinting gilded armor, he led his troops from the front. He was a good and innovative general and never defeated in battle. Adept at the surprise attack and hit-and-run raid, he once covered five hundred miles in nine days with his mounted troopers to surprise and defeat a much larger force. He contrived pontoons to float elephants and artillery more quickly to the front, had a mortar cast which reputedly needed one thousand oxen to move it and even rigged up a device to fire fourteen matchlocks simultaneously.

The first of the conquests of his reign, those of Ajmer, Gwalior and Juanpur, were made on Akbar's behalf while he was still behind the veil. Early in his personal rule Akbar defeated some of the leading rajas of the principalities of Rajasthan (Rajputana). The Rajputs, whose name means "sons of kings" and who claimed descent from the sun, moon and fire, were, and are, some of the bravest warriors in the world, with a strict code of honor equivalent to that of the Spartans and a clan spirit to

match that of the Scottish Highlands. They were in many ways the
knights of Hindu India and had held out for many years against Islamic
invaders. Legends and songs are full of their deeds. From the ninth century the Rajputs had gradually risen to power in the northwest of India,
where they formed the majority of the ruling dynasties. However, they
frequently fought among themselves, and their strong tribal rivalries
helped Akbar in an initial policy of "divide and rule."

Akbar's siege of Chitor in late 1567 and early 1568 marked a high
point of Rajput courage but also the virtual end of their independence.
The fortress at Chitor tops a rocky sandstone outcrop three quarters of a
mile long, rising sheer from the plains below. To allow his forces to approach the fort, Akbar ordered the construction of large, covered attack
corridors, *sabats*, wide enough for ten horsemen to pass through abreast
and built of stone and rubble with wood and hide roofs. Each day musketeers on Chitor's ramparts shot down hundreds of those constructing
these deadly tentacles advancing slowly, sinuously but inexorably up and
around the rocks. After months of siege Akbar saw flames and smoke rise
suddenly from different areas of the fort. An onlooker explained that the
Rajputs saw defeat as inevitable, but, before the men sallied out to die in
their battle robes of saffron yellow, their families were making *jauhar*—
"the last awful sacrifice which Rajput despair offers the gods." The fires
were those of the funeral pyres on which the Rajput women were throwing themselves.

After the Rajput warriors had died fighting and in contrast to his
usual policy of reconciliation, Akbar ordered a massacre of those remaining alive within Chitor, mostly farmers seeking shelter. Perhaps he
did so because Chitor was a long-standing symbol of Rajput power, or
perhaps he was simply showing future enemies that the greater the resistance the greater would be his retaliation. By 1570 all the major Rajput
princes but one, the rana of Mewar (Udaipur), who retreated into the
mountains, had acknowledged Moghul suzerainty.

Akbar's next target was the west coast kingdom of Gujarat. The state
was a particularly rich one, benefiting from its position as a major gateway for trade with Arabia and beyond as well as being a departure point
for many of the pilgrim ships for Mecca. As the Moghuls often did,

Akbar made a claim to legitimacy for his actions on the flimsy pretext that Gujarat had fleetingly been a part of Humayun's realm. Akbar also typically took advantage of squabbles among the ruling elite of the state, one faction among whom Akbar claimed had invited him to restore order. Later in life Akbar would disingenuously claim that his conquests "did not proceed from self-will and self-indulgence . . . we had no object except to be kind to mortals and to obliterate the oppressors." The campaign was short, and Akbar emerged victorious. He demonstrated his personal courage once more by routing one thousand of the enemy by charging them at the head of only one hundred men of his own. By the end of 1573 Gujarat was safely incorporated into the Moghul realm.

Among the more significant of Akbar's later campaigns were those to consolidate and extend Moghul rule in Bengal, the expansion of his territories in Afghanistan including the taking from the Persians of the then, as now, strategic city of Kandahar, the conquest of Sind and Baluchistan in what is now Pakistan and incursions into the Deccan to the south.

However, it was Kashmir, captured in 1586 after a short campaign, which won the heart of Akbar and his descendants. The vale of Kashmir nestles among high mountains in northern India and is only about ninety miles long and twenty-five miles wide. Watered by the River Jhelum, it is a verdant Shangri-la, its slopes cloaked in rhododendrons and juniper, spruce and cedar, while poplars and pines fringe its lakes. Akbar particularly enjoyed the blazing colors of autumn and the violet saffron fields of summer. A measure of how secure Akbar felt on his throne is that he made three separate visits to this remote, secluded area in the last few years of his reign.

By the end of his life Akbar could be well pleased that he had extended his borders to natural geographic boundaries such as the Himalayas, Hindu Kush and other high mountains in the north, the desert borders of Persia in the west and in the east the jungles bordering Arakan in present-day Burma (Myanmar) and to the south toward the tablelands of the Deccan. Akbar did not venture far into the central Asian homeland of his fathers. He did, however, once think of sending an embassy into China, because, although China was linked by major trading routes to India, "for a long time there had been no news of that country nor was it known who ruled it," but he never took the proposal further.*

EVEN WHILE FIGHTING the Rajputs early in his reign, Akbar had recognized the need to reconcile them and the other people of his overwhelmingly Hindu empire to his rule. He did this in a number of ways. Abul Fazl described the first: "His Majesty forms matrimonial alliances with princesses of Hindustan and of other countries and secures by these ties of harmony the peace of the world." In 1562, at the age of nineteen, Akbar had married the first of several Rajput princesses, the daughter of the raja of Amber (Jaipur). By the time he died, Akbar had more than three hundred wives, many of them dynastic brides, married to cement alliances both at home and abroad. The Koran permitted a man four wives but in one verse seemed to sanction implicitly a kind of second-tier marriage with an unspecified number of women. In the view of both Akbar, who was a Sunni Muslim, and of Shia clerics, this provision gave legality to Akbar's extra marriages. When the Sunni divine who was Akbar's chief adviser on religious law would not sanction the marriages, even after lengthy debates, Akbar replaced him with a more compliant Shia.

However, Akbar gave none of his daughters in marriage to other rulers, and, in fact, from his time it became customary that Moghul princesses should not marry at all, presumably to avoid the creation of further rival dynasties. Akbar also integrated senior Rajputs into his service. Soon, like the Scots in the British imperial armies, they provided a disproportionate number of his generals and of his troops, and were given special privileges such as mounting guard on imperial palaces or beating drums as they entered the royal citadel.

---

* China was already deep in a period of chauvinistic isolation in which it would remain for many centuries despite the displacement of the Ming dynasty in 1644 by the Manchus, invading from the north from beyond the Great Wall, and the appearance in the Far East of Russian fur traders who reached the Pacific in 1637, twenty-four years after the Romanovs had taken power.

Akbar banned the desecration of Hindu temples, and when, in 1563, he discovered that his officials were charging Hindu pilgrims a special tax to visit the holy site of Mathura, forty miles from Agra and believed by Hindus to be the birthplace of the god Krishna, he immediately forbade any such pilgrim taxes anywhere in his dominions. In 1564 he went further, much to the discontent of the Islamic mullahs, and abolished the *jizya*, a poll tax on "infidels," prescribed in the Koran and thus seen by them as an essential part of the sharia, or "straight path," of Islamic law. Akbar also cleared away a mass of petty, degrading and discriminatory practices, such as the bizarre right of Muslim magistrates to spit in the mouth of Hindus who were late in paying their taxes.

With the guidance of his ministers and advisers, Akbar instituted a series of administrative and land reforms to integrate his expanding empire. In doing so Akbar, who built on measures introduced by Sher Shah, himself a highly competent administrator, converted a loosely knit military aristocracy into a highly regulated imperial bureaucracy in which anyone of importance was a servant of the state. With the exception of the Rajput principalities and other subordinate states whose rulers acknowledged Moghul suzerainty and paid tribute to the imperial treasury while conducting their internal affairs autonomously, Akbar made all the land in his empire into his own imperial property and divided it into fiefs (*jagirs*). He appointed nobles to rule the fiefs on his behalf for a period. In return for taxes collected from their *jagirs* by government officials, the nobles had to maintain a stated number of troops. Whether they exercised military command or not, he had both nobles and officials graded hierarchically as commanders of a certain number of troops, from ten to ten thousand. Even the head of the royal kitchens was "a commander of 600."*

Akbar decreed that when his nobles died their property was forfeited to the crown. Because he could arbitrarily remove nobles from their fief or transfer them to another on the opposite side of the empire as well as

---

* Akbar's use of "tens" was based on zero, an Indian invention. What we know as Arabic numerals are really Indian numerals. They were simply brought to Europe via the Middle East.

Abul Fazl presenting the manuscript of his book to Akbar

control their posthumous estates, Akbar hoped to secure greater loyalty from them and to prevent them establishing rival power bases. Nevertheless, according to the chronicles, he suffered 144 rebellions—all unsuccessful—during his reign. Akbar also overhauled his empire's central administration, sharing the responsibility for the main functions—finance, army, justice and religion and the royal household—with four different ministers.

The importance of good communications, in both senses of the word, to his empire was well understood by Akbar. While the British later used English and railways to rule India, Akbar imposed Persian as the language of the court and built great trunk roads planted with shading trees.*

At regular way stations along the improved roads, travelers could rest and imperial messengers change horses or transfer messages. Relays of messengers and horses could thus carry imperial instructions up to 150 miles in twenty-four hours. To remind travelers of imperial power, as well as to reassure them about their safety, at some way stations piles of severed heads showed the fate of robbers and rebels. An English traveler described how the heads were cemented into little towers or turrets "in form like a pigeon house, not exceeding 3 or 4 yards in height." In a move designed to put an end to fraud and to increase his people's confidence in his government's conduct of business and trade, Akbar reformed the currency, replacing the old coinage with a new, square-shaped silver rupee, and introduced a new system of weights and measures.

FOR AKBAR, RELIGION was throughout his reign key to both his rule and his personal life. He had seemingly always had a mystical streak. In his late teens he had suddenly ridden alone into the desert one day, released his horse and, after meditating intensely, claimed to have heard a divine voice. Years later, while preparing under a fruit tree for a hunt in the Punjab, "a sublime joy took possession of his bodily frame, cognition of God cast its ray." He was so shaken by the experience that his mother, Hamida, rushed the considerable distance from Agra to care for her son.[†]

His inherent spirituality, combined with the political imperative to turn religion into a uniting rather than a dividing factor within his empire, led Akbar into ever-deeper contemplation of comparative religion. He built what he called the Ibadat Khana—"the House of Worship"—and

---

* Urdu, today the official language of Pakistan, is the mixture of the Persian spoken by the Moghul rulers with Hindi. It was originally spoken in the Moghuls' military camps, and the word *Urdu* means "camp."

† Some commentators have suggested that this and other trances seemingly experienced by Akbar may, in fact, have been epileptic fits.

invited theologians from all the major faiths to enter and to expound and debate their beliefs.

When disputing Islamic scholars descended to calling each other "fools and heretics," he issued a decree of infallibility on his own behalf. If Islamic experts disagreed about the interpretation of the Koran, Akbar himself would make the final decision. Even more important, the measure stated that when Akbar issued any decree on whatever subject, it could not be disputed unless demonstrably against the provisions of the Koran. Just as Henry VIII had done in England in 1534, he was making himself the clear temporal head of his faith, a decisive diminution in the power of the mullahs.

Akbar also introduced a new form of salutation of the imperial presence: prostration, with the forehead touching the ground. This was anathema to the Muslim faithful, who believed such salutation should only be made to God. The clerics objected to other more minor innovations of Akbar's, such as his decision to bathe before rather than after sexual intercourse. He also prohibited the slaughter of animals on Sunday, because the day was sacred to the sun. He discouraged the growth of beards, a facial adornment favored by the strict Muslim, as well as the consumption of garlic and onions. He thought "that to remove a piece of skin [circumcision] is not seeking after God" and therefore decreed that boys should not be circumcised until they were twelve years old, when they should be allowed to decide for themselves whether the operation should go ahead.

Akbar's questioning of the representatives of other religions in the Ibadat Khana revealed a genuine curiosity and openness of mind. From Hindu holy men he learned of the complex religious traditions that had evolved in the Indian subcontinent over several thousand years and were practiced by the majority of his subjects. They explained how Hinduism had no particular founder, prophets or creed and was based on dharma— the right way of living—rather than upon doctrine. The main gods of Hinduism were Brahma, Vishnu and Shiva, but the Hindu tradition embraced wide variations in practice and belief—from deities worshipped to festivals celebrated. Common to most Hindus, however, was a profound belief in reincarnation—a process of birth and rebirth governed by karma, the law by which the consequences of a person's actions in one life were carried through to their next existence. The holy men discussed how people's social and religious status was governed by the group—or caste—into which they were born and how they considered the cow a sacred animal whose killing was forbidden. An interested Akbar ordered Hindu epics to be translated, attended Hindu festivals and appeared with the red Hindu *tilak* mark on his forehead. He allowed his Hindu wives—as he did all his non-Muslim wives—to practice their faith within the harem. A disgusted Muslim complained that Akbar had been persuaded "to venerate fire, water, stones and trees and all natural objects, even down to cows and their dung."

There was, however, one Hindu custom that Akbar opposed vehemently: the rite of suttee, whereby Hindu women burned themselves alive on their husband's funeral pyres. Such a death was considered honorable, and many chose it in preference to a life of isolation and neglect—the alternative fate of Hindu widows who were not allowed to remarry. An English traveler wrote of women "following their dead husbands unto the fire" and how "the parents and friends of these women will most joyfully accompany them, and when the wood is fitted for this hellish sacrifice and begins to burn, all the people assembled shout and make a noise, that the screeches of this tortured creature may not be heard." Akbar tried to prohibit the practice, but in many regions it persisted.

Akbar was intrigued by the creed of the Zoroastrians, whose religion had originated in Persia in the first millenium BC and who believed in a supreme being: the Good Spirit Ahura Mazda, who was engaged in a constant but ever victorious battle against the spirit of evil. Central to their rituals was the veneration of fire as the symbol of the pure, divine source of life. In the seventh century AD Muslim invaders had driven the Zoroastrians out of Persia, and many, known as Parsees, had settled in India, where they continued to guard the "purity" of their faith. They never sought converts, and marriage to non-Parsees was forbidden. Akbar was especially interested in their reverance for the sun and, like them, prostrated himself before it.*

---

* The wise men or Magi who attended Christ's nativity are thought to have been Zoroastrian priests (*majus*).

By talking with the Jains, Akbar became convinced of the benefits of vegetarianism. The followers of this ancient and indigenous religion of the Indian subcontinent seek to liberate their souls through conquering their attachment to worldly things. The Jains follow a strict ascetic code, and one of their core beliefs is the practice of *Ahimsa*—causing no harm to living things. Akbar also found merit in the traditions of Buddhism, which had originated in India around the sixth century BC after the Buddha, a prince born in northern India (modern Nepal), found enlightenment. Like Hinduism, Buddhism focuses on the law of karma by which good and evil deeds result in punishment or reward and people progress through a series of rebirths. Only by adhering to the true path can human beings break the cycle of karma and attain the ultimate goal of nirvana—the extinguishing of earthly desires and absorption into the infinite.

From followers of Confucius, Akbar learned of the Chinese philosopher's moral teachings, especially of his war against a biased mind, arbitrary judgments, obstinacy and egotism and his emphasis on filial piety and brotherly respect. Sikhs too found Akbar "an attentive listener." Sikhism was a recent development, founded by Guru Nanak in the Punjab area of northern India. (The term *Sikh* derives from the Punjabi verb *sikhna*, "to learn.") Nanak, who had died in 1539, preached that God was neither Hindu nor Muslim but beyond narrow religious definition. What mattered was to find and follow God's path. In so doing, Hindus and Muslims would combine into a single brotherhood without distinctions of caste or rank.

From Jewish travelers to his court, Akbar learned of the tenets of Judaism. According to some sources, Jews had settled in India from as early as the sixth century BC, although the earliest firm evidence of their presence is a copper inscription dated AD 388. By the thirteenth century Jewish traders had established several small settlements on the western coast of India.* Curious, too, about the third of the great monotheistic religions that shared the Old Testament with Islam and

---

* The beautifully tiled synagogue in Cochin in the southern Indian state of Kerala, dating from 1568 and rebuilt in 1662, is still in use, though the community has now dwindled to only a handful of families.

Judaism—Christianity—in 1579 Akbar summoned Jesuits from the Portuguese colony of Goa on the southwest coast of India.

Akbar had first met Europeans—Portuguese traders—in 1572 during his conquest of Gujarat. The Gujaratis had invited them into their state with the intention of securing their aid in resisting Akbar's invasion, but when they saw the strength of Akbar's forces the Portuguese had wisely declined to become involved. The Portuguese coastal base of Goa, considerably to the south of Gujarat, had been established in 1510, only twelve years after Vasco da Gama had pioneered the passage around the Cape of Good Hope at the tip of southern Africa to India, and sixteen years before Babur first proclaimed himself emperor of Hindustan. The Portuguese had thus been in India longer than the Moghuls. They were also, at this time, the only European nation with a territorial foothold in India. Their "official" possessions included Goa and several other ports on the western coast, but other Portuguese had set up virtually independent enclaves on the eastern coast and in the Ganges delta. Their overall purpose was trade, but the Catholic Jesuit priests who followed in the merchants' wake were, just as in the New World, keenly interested in converts.

Akbar treated the Jesuits with much courtesy, and they reported that he received four volumes of the Bible "with great reverence," kissing each in turn and placing it "on his head which amongst these people signifies honour and respect." He even removed his turban when entering the priests' small chapel and was sometimes persuaded to wear a crucifix and hang one over his bed. Although the priests remained hopeful for more than two years that he would emulate Constantine and bring an empire to Christianity, he never did.

To Akbar, Christianity was one faith among many from the four quarters of the globe, each containing elements of truth. Instead of embracing any, Akbar inaugurated a new religion—known as Din Ilahi (the Divine Faith)—that would unite his people without compelling them to forego their original beliefs. His was a loosely defined faith in which the principles of reincarnation and karma were accepted, and forgiveness, toleration and kindness toward all living things were encouraged. Ten vices and ten virtues were enumerated. The sun was worshipped as the body of the divinity, and unification with God was the ultimate aim.

Because "the divine will manifests itself in the intuition of kings," Akbar himself was the only conduit between the divine and humanity, though he was never clear as to whether he was claiming any divine status for himself. He changed his coinage by inscribing on it the words *Allah Akbar* rather than, as previously, just his name. Throughout the Muslim world, then as now, the phrase means "God is *akbar*"—"God is great"—but it could also have been interpreted "Akbar is God."

Although expediency brought many of Akbar's leading nobles into his Divine Faith, he did not make it a proselytizing religion, and, consequently, it never achieved a wide following and faded away on Akbar's death. However, the very existence of the religious debates and Akbar's lifelong religious tolerance had promoted a greater sense of inclusion among his subjects, whichever of the contending religions of his empire they adhered to.

CHAPTER THREE

"Seizer of the World"

DESPITE HIS MANY WIVES, BY THE TIME Akbar was in his midtwenties he had not yet fathered a living heir and began to consult holy men. Hearing of one such, a Sufi or Muslim mystic named Shaikh Salim Chishti, dwelling in the small town of Sikri twenty-three miles west of Agra, he visited him. (Sufis preach the seeking of a more personal relationship with God through a variety of mystical paths.)* The shaikh consoled Akbar that he would have three sons. Soon afterward Akbar's principal wife, the daughter of the Rajput raja of Amber (Jaipur), became pregnant. Akbar sent her to live with the shaikh to bring good fortune upon her pregnancy. On 30 August 1569 she gave birth at Sikri to a son, named Salim by Akbar after the mystic, but to be known as Jahangir when he became emperor. Two other sons, Murad and Daniyal, born to different mothers, followed within the next three years, one born at Sikri and the other at another Chishti shrine.

To honor his adviser and to capitalize on the good fortune that had come to him from Sikri, Akbar decided to move his capital from Agra to a new city to be built there. Later he would embellish Sikri's name with

---

* The word *sufi* means "those who wear rough woolen garments" and derives from the Arabic word *suf* meaning "wool." The mystics were said to have adopted such garb, as did Christian hermits, as an indication of asceticism and poverty.

the prefix *Fatehpur* meaning "city of victory" to commemorate the success of his military campaigns in Gujarat in 1572 and 1573.

Fatehpur Sikri was not, however, the first major building project of Akbar's reign; that was the tomb of his father, Humayun. The vast garden complex was built to the southeast of Delhi and, even to the inexpert eye, is a clear forerunner of the Taj Mahal. Constructed to a symmetrical plan, the mausoleum sits on a square twenty-two-foot-high arched plinth of red sandstone in a large walled garden. The tomb is faced with sandstone inset with intricate white marble designs and is topped by a broad white marble dome sitting over an *iwan* (recessed entrance arch.) Unlike most Moghul buildings, the tomb can be connected to known architects: Sayyid Muhammad and his father, Mirak Sayyid Ghiyas. Both were of Persian descent and the tomb is mainly of Persian design, with its arched portals and octagonal burial chamber. It does, however, contain indigenous elements such as the twenty-foot-high bulbous brass finial surmounting the dome, the six-pointed star—an important Hindu cosmological symbol representing spirit and matter held in balance—on the walls over the arches and the *chattris* (domed and pillared open kiosks) on the roofs of each of the main parts of the building.

Humayun's tomb was the first building in India to combine marble and sandstone in such great quantities. Some architectural historians have even suggested that in the use of white (marble) and red (sandstone), the ecumenical, inclusive Akbar was associating the Moghuls with the two highest castes of the Hindu social structure: the white of the Brahmins and the red of the military Kshatriyas.

Akbar had gone on to rebuild the sandstone fortress of Agra—known as the Red Fort—beside the River Jumna and, indeed, to show his own strength by running around the one-and-a-half-mile battlements with a man under each arm. However, Fatehpur Sikri best illustrates his architectural vision. The city is in the form of a vast quadrilateral, fortified on three sides and protected on the fourth by a ridged hill. Although the layout of the city follows Moghul principles, the design of the buildings, many of which survive today in a remarkably good state of preservation, is almost entirely Hindu in inspiration. The city is constructed of sandstone, a rock that can be carved by a skilled mason in much the same

The tomb of Humayun

way as wood by a carpenter. The sharply etched decoration therefore much resembles the ornate woodcarvings on Hindu temples. The qualities of sandstone also allowed prefabrication. A European Jesuit priest, Father Antonio Monserrate, noted, "In order to prevent himself being deafened by the noise of the tools Akbar had everything cleverly fashioned elsewhere in accordance with the exact plan of the building and then brought to the spot, and there fitted and fastened together." Miniature paintings show Akbar taking a detailed interest in the work of the stonemasons of Fatehpur Sikri. Monserrate reported that "Akbar sometimes quarries stone himself along with the other workers. Nor does he

shrink . . . from practising, for the sake of amusement, the craft of an ordinary artisan."

While prefabrication was not universal at Fatehpur Sikri, as Monserrate suggested, it may well have been one reason why the nine-gated
walled city was completed in seven years. Within the walls were the
royal mint, bathhouses, barracks, halls, gardens, mosques, quarters for
the nobles and, of course, Akbar's own palace. His personal apartments
overlooked the shining Anup Talao, or "Peerless Pool."

The huge harem, protected by a guardhouse and by thick metal-
studded gates, resembled a fortress. The women's only contact with the
outside world was through peeping out from screened balconies set high
in the walls. Yet behind these thick walls was a luxurious pleasure palace.
Fountains played among beds of bright flowers, and the azure roof tiles
shone in the sunlight. When refreshing breezes blew, the women gath-
ered in a high pavilion—the Hawa Mahal, or "Wind Palace"—to enjoy
them. The red sandstone carvings of their apartments and of the inter-
linking courtyards had a Hindu voluptuousness. Akbar, who could access
the harem through a network of screened corridors, reputedly played
hide-and-seek with his women or a kind of chess using human pieces.

The most striking building of all is a hall whose interior is dominated
by a broad, richly carved pillar supporting a platform connected by slim,
diagonal bridges to hanging galleries at each corner. Historians argue
about its precise use, but most consider that Akbar used it as an audience
chamber. When he held council, he would sit on the circular platform,
soliciting advice from those on the balconies, who could, if necessary,
approach him along the bridges.

Ralph Fitch, an early English trader, was so impressed by Agra and
Fatehpur Sikri that he wrote, "[They] are two very great cities, either of
them much greater than London and very populous." Yet the magnificent city of Fatehpur Sikri remained fully inhabited for just fourteen
years, after which, beginning in 1586, it was gradually abandoned. The
reason has been much debated but never resolved. A poor water supply
and unsatisfactory communication links may have been contributory
factors. Unlike Agra, Fatehpur Sikri did not sit on one of the great trunk
roads connecting Akbar's empire, nor was it on the Jumna, a major waterway for goods and travelers, particularly those making the journey to

Akbar's audience chamber

and from Delhi. However, Akbar perhaps never made a formal decision
to leave Fatehpur Sikri; it just happened over time in response to his
changing priorities.

BY THE MID-1580s Akbar, then in his forties, was at the height of his
pomp and power, an impressive figure, regal and charismatic in the eyes
of all who saw him, Indians and Europeans alike. Father Monserrate described him as "of a stature and of a countenance well-fitted to his royal
dignity so that one could easily recognise even at the first glance that he
is the king. He has broad shoulders, somewhat bandy legs well-suited to
horsemanship and a light-brown complexion . . . His expression is tranquil, serene and open, full also of dignity and, when he is angry, of awful
majesty . . . It is hard to exaggerate how accessible he makes himself to
all . . . for he creates an opportunity every day for any of the common
people or of the nobles to see him and converse with him; and he en-
deavours to show himself pleasant-spoken and affable rather than severe
toward all who come . . . it is remarkable how great an effect this courtesy and affability have in attaching to him the minds of his subjects . . .
He has an acute insight and shows much wise foresight."

Another priest reiterated Monserrate's praise of Akbar: "He was
beloved of all, firm with the great, kind to those of low estate and just
to all men, high and low, neighbour or stranger, Christian, Muslim or
Hindu so that every man believed that the king was on his side. . . .
Amongst his great nobles he was so predominant that none dared lift his
head too high; but with the humbler classes he was benevolent and
debonair, willingly giving them audience and hearing their petitions. He
was pleased to accept their presents, taking them into his hands and
holding them to his breast which he never did with the rich gifts brought
by his nobles." The priest went on to point out that "often with prudent
dissimulation" Akbar pretended not to see his humbler admirers. Like
modern leaders, Akbar knew that his time to meet and greet was limited.

Akbar's son Salim did, however, point to one failing. Despite the
imperial library having grown to twenty-five thousand sumptuously
bound manuscripts, his father was "illiterate. Yet from constantly conversing with learned and clever persons, his language was so polished

that no one could discover from his conversation that he was entirely uneducated." Akbar's intelligence was also evident from his deep curiosity about the wider world which made him "well disposed towards foreigners."

In 1577 a particularly well-educated foreigner, an ambitious Persian nobleman named Mirza Ghiyas Beg, had arrived at Akbar's court. Charming as he was poor, this economic migrant had deserted his homeland to travel with his heavily pregnant wife and three young children through wild and lonely country in hopes of building his fortunes in the Moghuls' service. The journey was arduous and dangerous, despite the fact that, for greater security, they had joined a caravan. While still in Persia, thieves attacked the family and stole everything they had except two mules. Taking it in turns to ride the stumbling little beasts, the bedraggled party finally reached Kandahar, where Ghiyas Beg's wife gave birth to a daughter. They named her Mehrunissa, "the Sun of Women."

According to some chroniclers, the destitute parents abandoned the baby to die of exposure, but her tiny form was spotted by the caravan's wealthy leader, who scooped her up, sought out her mother and promised to help the family. Other tales relate how the parents could not, after all, face leaving the newborn infant. Ghiyas Beg rushed back to the tree under which they had left her to find the gurgling Mehrunissa caught in the coils of a great black serpent. At the frantic father's approach the snake unraveled itself to slink away, leaving Ghiyas Beg to reclaim his child.

Whatever the reality, Mehrunissa survived the early, uncertain hours of her life to travel on with her family into Moghul territory. Reaching Fatehpur Sikri, Ghiyas Beg, in accordance with the custom for well-connected strangers arriving at court, was presented to Akbar. The Persian adventurer made an immediate impression. He had inherited the eloquence of his father, a smooth-tongued poet who had risen to become chief minister of Isfahan. He was also helped by the fact that other members of his family had already joined the Moghul court and rendered useful service. None would, however, achieve the success of Ghiyas Beg, whose family would capture successive emperors both emotionally and intellectually. His daughter and granddaughter would become Moghul empresses, and his great-grandson would ascend the Moghul throne.

Ghiyas Beg's progress was at first modest. Akbar appointed him to a middling rank and sent him off to be the treasurer of the northern outpost of Kabul. He proved his competence and in 1596 was placed in charge of the imperial court buildings back in Agra. During the intervening years Mehrunissa had grown into a beautiful, accomplished woman who, according to one account, "in music, in dancing, in poetry, in painting had no equal among her sex. Her disposition was volatile, her wit lively and satirical, her spirit lofty and uncontrolled." The subtext is that she had sex appeal. She had been married at seventeen to a wellborn, battle-hardened Persian soldier who had distinguished himself in Akbar's campaigns and whose courage would win him the title of Sher Afghan, "Tiger Slayer."

Several accounts suggest that, either by accident or by design, Mehrunissa had already caught the susceptible eye of Prince Salim. According to one, Salim called on her father and "the ladies, according to custom, were introduced in their veils." Mehrunissa danced before the inflamed Salim, who "could hardly be restrained by the rules of decency . . . When his eyes seemed to devour her, she, as by accident, dropped her veil; and shone upon him." Some chroniclers claim that Akbar arranged her marriage to put her out of his son's grasp, others that Salim conceived his passion for her after her betrothal and that Akbar "sternly refused to commit a piece of injustice" by halting the marriage.

The many accounts were written years after these events, some while Mehrunissa was the most powerful woman in India, others after her fall from power. Some writers were anxious to present Mehrunissa and her family as scheming parvenus, while others strove to portray a noble and enduring love. The truth is as veiled as Mehrunissa herself, living the secluded life of an aristocratic girl within the women's quarters of Ghiyas Beg's house. For Salim to have made overt advances to her there or, indeed, at court, would have been hard, if not impossible. Although as the daughter of a trusted courtier, Mehrunissa would have been invited to visit the ladies of the imperial harem, passing through the ranks of watchful eunuchs and muscular female guards into the scented, silken interior to drop her veil and sing and dance, no ungelded adult male except the emperor was allowed within the precincts.

Salim already had a clutch of wives, primarily dynastic alliances to bind the diverse elements of Akbar's empire. His first marriage in 1585, at the age of fifteen, was to his cousin, Man Bai, daughter of the Hindu raja of Amber (Jaipur). In 1587 she bore his first son, Khusrau. Salim's second son, Parvez, was born to a Muslim wife in 1589. However, it was the arrival of his third son, born on 5 January 1592 in Lahore to another Hindu princess, the graceful and witty Jodh Bai of Marwar (Jodhpur), that most pleased his grandfather Akbar. He and his astrologers saw the birth as most auspicious. The child would be "a riband in the cap of royalty and more resplendent than the sun." More significant, the conjunction of the planets at the moment of his birth was the same as at the birth of Timur; the year of his birth was the millenium year 1000 of the Islamic calendar, while the month of his birth was the same as that of the prophet Muhammad. The emperor named him Khurram, meaning "Joyous." The child, who would become the emperor Shah Jahan, was from his earliest moments Akbar's most adored grandchild.

The following year, Ghiyas Beg also celebrated the birth of a child: a granddaughter born to one of his sons and named Arjumand Banu. During her lifetime the world would come to know her as Mumtaz Mahal, "Chosen One of the Palace," and Shah Jahan's greatest love. Her early death would translate her into the emblematic "Lady of the Taj."

AKBAR PLACED THE baby prince Khurram in the care of his first wife, a childless woman who was also Akbar's cousin, being a daughter of Hindal, and was a devout Muslim. The Hindu Jodh Bai was consoled with a magnificent gift of rubies and pearls.

In line with Moghul custom, Khurram began his formal education at the age of four years, four months and four days. Akbar himself escorted the bejeweled, silk-clad princeling to the imperial mosque school, where leading scholars instructed him in the arts, literature and the history of his forebears, especially the great Timur. Perhaps predictably, the court chroniclers claimed that the young prince showed a remarkable grasp of detail and a powerful memory, but more unusually they described how, even at a young age, he demonstrated a sensual side, delighting in drenching his clothes in perfume and in the touch of brilliant, smooth-cut gems. Historians have pointed out that there is no record of Khurram's circumcision, presumably a major celebration, and have suggested that, in line with his grandfather Akbar's ambivalence toward the procedure, he may never have been circumcised.

As he grew, Akbar taught him to hunt and fight. When Khurram was only six years old, Akbar took him on campaign, appointing a formidable rider, marksman and swordsman as his tutor. On the journey he took his first shot at a leopard and wounded the beast. Shortly afterward Khurram caught smallpox but survived unblemished, to his grandfather's relief. When he was nine years old, Akbar invited the boy to join his war council.

Akbar's love for his grandson contrasted with the ambivalent feelings he developed for his son Salim, who recalled somewhat wistfully in his memoirs Akbar's attentiveness to Khurram and how the emperor lauded the young prince as his own "true son." Abul Fazl was also struck that "the affectionate sovereign loved grandsons more than sons." Yet Akbar had once doted on Salim. As a child, he too had been the indulged darling of the harem, and his early signs of prowess at hunting and the martial arts had delighted Akbar. Aged just twelve he had been given command of a large detachment and gone on campaign with Akbar. Yet as Salim grew into active and able manhood, Akbar's affection waned. The aging emperor perhaps felt threatened by what he perceived as the restless, greedy ambition of his son.

There are also hints in the account of an English visitor to the Moghul court, merchant William Finch, and in later Moghul chronicles of sexual rivalry between the two. They claim that Salim fell in love with Akbar's loveliest concubine and that on discovering the affair, Akbar had her walled up alive.

Salim certainly felt insecure. Since the Moghuls' ancestors did not always observe the rules of primogeniture, though he was Akbar's eldest son, he could not assume the throne was his. Faced with such uncertainty, Salim refused to command military expeditions to remote regions in case his father died while he was too far from the seat of power to claim the crown. Akbar in turn began openly favoring his younger sons, Murad and Daniyal, both of whom had become hopeless drunkards.

Salim too enjoyed drinking. At the age of eighteen, he tasted a glass of sweet, yellow wine, which, he confessed, "I drank and liked the feeling it gave me." He started drinking every day, soon abandoning wine for spirits. By his late twenties he was swallowing "twenty phials of double-distilled spirits" a day and existing on a meager diet of bread and radishes. Racked by hangovers and with his hands shaking so badly that he could no longer hold a glass, he sought the help of court physicians. They warned that if he did not desist he would be dead in six months. Salim cut back to six cups of wine mixed with spirits and fourteen grains of opium a day. The process of drying out, however incomplete, probably did not improve his temper or make him more forgiving of his father's neglect.

In 1601 a resentful Salim rebelled. His revolt was somewhat half-hearted, and he contented himself with marching aimlessly hither and thither with a force of thirty thousand while tentatively calling himself emperor. Father and son seem to have striven to avoid an open fight. Instead, Salim turned his aggression toward Abul Fazl, who was, as well as Akbar's chronicler, one of his closest advisers. So close that, when Akbar was gored in his testicles while out hunting, Abul Fazl proudly recalled that the application of the ointment was left "to the writer of this book of fortune." Latterly, the fifty-two-year-old had also become one of Akbar's more successful generals and was away on campaign at the time of the revolt.

By 1602 Akbar had become sufficiently perturbed to recall Abul Fazl to Agra. Salim disliked and distrusted the soldier-scholar—who, as he later wrote in his memoirs, "was no friend of mine"—and plotted his assassination. As Abul Fazl hastened to his emperor's side, he was murdered by a local raja, whom Salim offered to reward "if he would stop that sedition monger and kill him." According to some accounts, Salim ordered Abul Fazl's severed head, sent to him by the raja in triumph, to be tossed into a common latrine.

Akbar learned of the murder while playing with his tame pigeons and collapsed in tearful anguish. He wanted to punish Salim but was in a difficult situation. Murad had died, quivering in the throes of delirium tremens, and Daniyal was also busily drinking himself to death. Despite his father's frantic efforts to keep alcohol from him, his followers brought wine past Akbar's spies, hidden in cows' intestines which they wound around their bodies under their clothes. Akbar realized that he and Salim must be reconciled to protect the Moghul dynasty. In line with

Moghul tradition, the imperial ladies were the go-betweens. One of Akbar's senior wives persuaded the disgruntled prince to return with her to Agra, where he was received by his grandmother Hamida, Humayun's reluctant bride of more than half a century before. The old lady induced Salim to prostrate himself at his father's feet. In a designedly theatrical scene Akbar lifted his wayward son in his arms, embraced him and placed his imperial turban on his head—a sign to onlookers that Salim was his heir. He ordered drums to be beaten loudly and joyously to announce the reconciliation.

Yet family problems and uncertainty about the succession were not over. In 1604 the death of Daniyal, after a particularly spectacular drinking bout using double-strength spirits smuggled in a rusty musket barrel, freed Salim of fraternal rivals. However, his eldest son, the mettlesome teenage Khusrau, was emerging as a challenger for the throne, being in the eyes of his supporters less volatile and more pliable than his erratic, violent father. The last year of Akbar's reign brought a very public showdown when the emperor deliberately arranged a contest between Salim's and Khusrau's most powerful war elephants. Elephant fights were a favorite royal pastime, with the great beasts goaded into action by riders clinging to their backs. However, this occasion had a special significance. Perhaps the old man was seeking a portent for the future of the empire, or perhaps, still grieving at the death of his seventy-seven-year-old mother, Hamida, the year before, he was merely trying to discomfit his own overeager son.

Akbar watched the noisy contest from a balcony with the thirteen-year-old Khurram, who was, as usual, by his side, on this occasion acting as the referee. Salim's elephant was being mangled by Khusrau's, and Khurram at once ordered a reserve elephant into the arena to draw the contestants apart. When this did not succeed, the guards fired rockets to separate the enraged, trumpeting beasts. Khusrau's elephant bolted, frightened by the flashes and bangs, leaving Salim the unexpected victor. In the highly charged atmosphere, fighting broke out among the respective supporters, and Akbar sent Khurram with orders to Salim and Khusrau to quell the fracas. Khurram's thoughts about the feuding and jealousy between the two would-be emperors and his own intervention are not recorded, but the teenager watching closely by his grandfather's side was imbibing lessons. The future Shah Jahan would one day demonstrate a ruthlessness in eliminating family rivals unmatched by any of his predecessors.

Whatever his feelings for his father and half-brothers, Khurram loved Akbar. When, a week after the elephant fight, the old man began suffering from diarrhea and internal bleeding, a distraught Khurram refused to leave his bedside, insisting, "So long as there is a breath of life in Shah Baba [Akbar], nothing can induce me to leave him." Meanwhile his father and half-brother each schemed for the throne. As it turned out, the majority of nobles, summoned by Akbar to give their views, favored the more seasoned Salim over the youthful Khusrau. Anxious that his empire should not decline into civil war, Akbar accepted their verdict. The dying man signaled Salim to put on the imperial robes and turban and gird on Humayun's sword hanging at the foot of his bed. A few hours later that same day, 15 October 1605, Akbar was dead at sixty-three. At dawn his corpse was borne on a bier to Sikandra, five miles from Agra, to the great tomb that he himself had begun, but which was not yet complete.

Akbar's vision and vitality had forged a strong, cohesive empire of 100 million ethnically and religiously diverse subjects across two thirds of the Indian subcontinent. He had almost trebled the precarious dominions bequeathed him by Humayun. Conscious that seizing territory was far easier than holding it, he had reformed and centralized his administration, welding it into an efficient machine. Akbar's power and wealth were symbolized by the vast armies he had poured into the field and the treasuries piled with glistening diamonds, rubies, emeralds and pearls for which the Moghuls had an almost fetishistic passion. He had made his court a place of sophistication and luxury, and his grand, graceful buildings were a signal to the world that the nomadic days were over. Of all Timur's descendants, Akbar had shown himself the most able and astute, the truest successor and worthy of his name, "the Great."

The inheritor of this magnificence, the thirty-six-year-old Salim, was proclaimed emperor in the Hall of Public Audience in the Agra fort nine days after Akbar's death. He took on the name Jahangir, which meant "Seizer of the World," because, he said, "the business of kings is controlling the world."

CHAPTER FOUR

"Peerless Pearls and Heart-Pleasing Stuffs"

As HIS FATHER'S REIGN BEGAN, YOUNG Prince Khurram, the future Shah Jahan, gained greater insight into power and the threat posed by ambitious, disaffected family members. There were still those who wished to see Khusrau replace his father on the throne, so Jahangir quickly placed Khusrau under nominal house arrest in the Red Fort at Agra.

In April 1606, on the spurious pretext of visiting Akbar's tomb nearby, Khusrau galloped out of the Red Fort. Pausing only to plunder sweetmeat shops for sustenance, Khusrau rode northwest to Lahore, gathering more supporters as he went, and laid siege to the city. Jahangir himself marched in pursuit of his errant son, leaving fourteen-year-old Khurram to oversee his governing council, and departing so quickly that he forgot his morning "allowance of opium."

Jahangir's army caught and routed the rebels with ease. Khusrau fled, but Jahangir resolved, "I would not rest till I had taken him." Khusrau attempted a nighttime flight across a river, but the boatmen refused to help him and his companions. When they tried to row themselves, they ran aground on a sandbar in their nervous, inexpert haste. At first light they surrendered. Khusrau was dragged "trembling and weeping" before his father, together with two leading confederates. According to Jahangir, "Khusrau was brought into my presence with his hands bound and a chain on his leg." The emperor ordered his son's two supporters to be stitched tightly into the stinking and soaking-wet skins of a freshly killed ass and ox to which the flopping heads were still attached. The men were mounted backward on donkeys. The grotesque little cavalcade was then led around Lahore in the baking sun until the man inside the ox skin suffocated since, as Jahangir noted with interest, "the skin of an ox dries quicker than the skin of an ass." The one in the ass's skin survived and was eventually rehabilitated into imperial favor.

Khusrau himself was paraded on an elephant along a route lined with a double row of pointed wooden stakes on which three hundred of his shrieking supporters had been spitted. Jahangir wrote approvingly that there was no "more excruciating punishment, for the culprits die in lingering torture." Khusrau was so traumatized by the experience that, as his father coldly recalled, "he neither ate nor drank for three days and nights, which he consumed in tears and groans, hunger and thirst." Yet such horrors merely dampened rather than extinguished his ambition. For a while Jahangir kept him in chains, but as soon as his father showed signs of relenting and had the chains struck from his legs, Khusrau began to plot again, motivated by his suspicion that Khurram, four and a half years his junior and his father's favorite, might soon be designated his heir. Jealousy reignited his already lively sense of grievance.

Khusrau incited a group of nobles to murder Jahangir on the hunting field in early autumn 1607. Ironically, it was his rival Khurram who learned of the plot and, as Jahangir wrote, "in great perturbation instantly informed me." Jahangir at once killed four of the ringleaders and pondered executing Khusrau but decided that "paternal affection did not allow me to take his life." Instead he ordered his son to be blinded. Since Khusrau later recovered some limited vision, his eyeballs were perhaps rubbed with corrosive fluids, rather than gouged, or his eyelids stitched together. Whatever the case, his existence was a miserable one, and the sight of him irked his father, who complained, somewhat unfairly under the circumstances, that whenever he was brought into his presence, his son was "always mournful and dejected in mind." A side effect of Khusrau's rivalry with his father was that his mother, Jahangir's first wife, had in despair taken "her own life out of the zeal that is an integral part of Rajput nature." Several times, wrote the emperor, "she went beserk—it must have been an hereditary trait since her father and brothers all used suddenly to appear quite mad . . . While I was away on a hunt . . . with her mind in a state of imbalance she ate a lot of opium and died soon thereafter."

In his treatment of Khusrau, Jahangir conveniently blotted from his memory his own rebellion against an aging father. His lively memoirs, written with the same freshness if not always candor as those of his great-grandfather Babur, assert piously that "a son ought always to be the stay of monarchy." The diary reveals the emperor as a man riven with contradictions—an effective ruler when not fuddled with opium or alcohol, charming, sophisticated and inquiring at some moments, bizarrely cruel at others.

Jahangir made a pageant of torture and execution, on one occasion apparently relishing the sight of men being skinned alive. Sir Thomas Roe, England's first ambassador to India, who arrived at his court in 1615 and shudderingly witnessed elephants crushing convicts beneath their feet as the emperor looked on, thought that Jahangir took "too much delight in blood." Even more revealing of Jahangir's sadistic streak is that he beat his seven-year-old son, Shahriyar, to see whether he would cry and when the little boy stayed quiet, stabbed his cheek with a bodkin. The child bled profusely but remained silent.

Jahangir could be hypocritical. A sybarite in all things, he banned alcohol from his court but could not bear to renounce it himself, excusing his weakness with the guile of an old lady addicted to the sherry bottle. He only indulged, he insisted, while overlooking the many occasions he was too drunk to stand, "to promote digestion of my food." He also salved his conscience by deciding that "on Friday evenings I would not commit the sin of drinking wine." Later in his reign, he would somewhat ambiguously urge the benefits of wine on Khurram, at the same time suggesting caution. He recorded his advice in his diary: "My boy, you are the father of children, and kings and princes drink wine. Today is a festival, and I will drink wine with you, and I give you leave to drink on feast days, on New Year's day, and at great entertainments, but always with moderation for to drink to excess and weaken the intellect is avoided by the wise; in fact, some good and benefit ought to be obtained from wine-drinking."

Deeply curious about science and nature, Jahangir conducted original research into the loveplay of cranes and the gestation period of elephants, ordering a smoking meteorite to be dug up and fashioned into swords and the dissection of lions' intestines to investigate where their courage came from. He was fascinated how the banyan, a tree sacred to Hindus, supported its weight by sending down aerial roots. Had he lived a little later in England, he would have been a natural candidate for the Royal Society, set up by Charles II in 1660 to inquire into the natural world. A workshop of court painters accompanied Jahangir on his travels to record whatever curious creature caught the emperor's fancy. When a splendid turkey, then a novelty in India, was presented to him, he ordered its portrait painted, writing smugly that "although King Babur has in his memoirs given an able description and pictured representation of several animals, it is most probable he never ordered painters to draw them from life."

The emperor also viewed the increasing numbers of European visitors to his court with interest. Some, like Sir Thomas Roe, were envoys sent by their governments to seek trading concessions. Indian indigo—a blue dye—and cotton calicoes were highly prized in Europe as, too, were Indian pearls and gemstones. In 1608 the English East India Company had established a base at Surat, but the Portuguese, watching anxiously from their settlement farther south at Goa, had attacked the company's ships. Shortly before Roe's arrival in India, however, English ships had twice beaten Portuguese vessels off the coast of India. This attracted Jahangir's attention because, lacking a significant maritime tradition, the Moghuls relied largely on European ships to carry Muslim pilgrims across the sea to Mecca. Until then the Portuguese had provided safe passage, selling their pilgrim passengers passports incongruously bearing the images of Jesus and the Virgin Mary. Roe intended to convince Jahangir that England's ships were superior to those of the Portuguese and of the Dutch, who were also seeking a toehold in India. He hoped in return to win trading rights for the East India Company's merchants, in particular the establishment of "factories" (small settlements of traders).

Among the gifts Roe and other European visitors presented to Jahangir were miniature portraits. The emperor particularly admired these and launched a new fashion at court of bejeweled miniatures to be hung around the neck or attached to the turban. A favored few were permitted the privilege of wearing tiny likenesses of the emperor himself.

Gateway to Akbar's tomb

Jahangir, like his father, was also interested in architecture. He took great satisfaction in completing a "magnificent sepulchre" for Akbar at Sikandra near Agra. Akbar had commissioned the mausoleum during his own lifetime, but, on a tour of inspection, Jahangir did not find the design sufficiently striking. "My intention," he wrote, "was that it should be so exquisite that the travellers of the world could not say they had seen one like it in any part of the inhabited earth." Instead, while he had been preoccupied with Khusrau's revolts, the architects had built it according to their own taste and had altered the original design at their discretion. Jahangir ordered the objectionable parts to be pulled down and employed new architects so that "by degrees a very large and magnificent building was raised, with a nice garden round it, entered by a lofty gate, consisting of minarets made of white stone." The four minarets of shining white marble were then an innovation but would become one of the most distinctive features of high Moghul architecture. An inlaid tracery of lilies, roses, narcissi and other flowers, delicate as lace, covering Akbar's marble cenotaph also prefigured what was to come.

Even while the tomb was under construction, the Englishman William Finch marveled at the huge monument built to contain a monarch "who sometimes thought the world too little for him." In the early 1630s another Englishman, Peter Mundy, who sketched the building, wrote that it ranked among the seven wonders of the world. However, thirty years later a French visitor to India would write that, lovely though Akbar's tomb was, he would not describe it since "all its beauties are found in still greater perfection in that of the Taj Mahal."

WITH KHUSRAU NEUTRALIZED and his empire settling into stability and tranquillity, Jahangir's affections focused increasingly on Khurram, whom he had only come to know well after Akbar's death. The young prince excelled in the martial arts and shared his interests, even exceeding his father's love of fine buildings. In 1607 the emperor visited a house Khurram, then fifteen, had had built, and judged it "truly a harmonious structure." In 1608, and overlooking the claims of his other son Parvez, just over two years older than Khurram, Jahangir awarded the sixteen-year-old youth the territory of Hissar Firoza in the Punjab and the right to pitch a crimson tent—honors traditionally awarded to the emperor's chosen heir.

Khurram was, by then, engaged to be married. In April 1607 he had become betrothed to the fourteen-year-old Arjumand Banu, granddaughter of the Persian adviser Ghiyas Beg, and Jahangir himself had placed the betrothal ring on the young woman's finger. According to romantic tradition, Khurram first saw her at the Royal Meena Bazaar during the celebrations for the Nauroz—the New Year festival introduced by Akbar to mark the sun entering Aries. The Nauroz was an eighteen-day blaze of luxury and excess. Workmen erected a huge tent, covering two acres, in the palace gardens, with awnings of maroon velvet embroidered with gold and luxurious private chambers for the royal women where they could see but not be seen. Every surface was spread "with silk and gold carpets and hangings, rich as rich velvet embroidered with gold, pearls and precious stones can make it." Here the emperor held court or visited the resplendent tents of his noblemen, pitched nearby, to be presented with "the rarest jewels and toys that they can find."

The Royal Meena Bazaar was a courtly replica of a real bazaar. This "whimsical kind of fair," as a French visitor described it, took place by night in scented gardens lit with flickering candlelight and colored lanterns swaying from the branches of trees and in the background the splashing of fountains. The wives and daughters of the nobility spread stalls with gold and silver trinkets and swaths of silk and played the part of traders, bantering and bargaining with their would-be purchasers: royal matrons and princesses and, of course, the emperor and his favored male relations. This festive, intimate occasion was one of the few times when the women were allowed to drop their silken veils and let the soft light fall on their carefully made up faces. It was a fine opportunity for any woman to show off a handsome daughter. Khurram could therefore gaze openly on Arjumand Banu, who would hold him emotionally and sexually for the rest of her life.

Court historians recorded the betrothal in their usual flowery language, praising the young woman as "that bright Venus of the sphere of chastity" and extolling her "angelic character" and "pure lineage." All accounts, official or not, agreed that Arjumand Banu was exceptionally beautiful at a court where beauty was not in short supply. However, images of the future Mumtaz Mahal, the Lady of the Taj, are tantalizingly elusive. A contemporary Moghul portrait claimed by some to depict her shows, in profile, a fine-featured young woman with delicately arched brows, a soft, tranquil expression and with a pink rose in her hand. A golden veil half conceals her long black hair, and strings of pearls interwined with rubies and emeralds are twisted around her smooth throat and narrow wrist, and her fingertips and palms are hennaed. The only other portrait, reputedly copied in the late nineteenth century from an earlier original, depicts a girl in a bejeweled diadem, with elongated dark eyes, graceful curving brows and, once again, a rose in her hand.

Yet within just a few months of the betrothal, Arjumand Banu's family suffered a dangerous reverse. On his accession in 1605, Jahangir had appointed Ghiyas Beg to be his revenue minister, awarding him the title Itimad-ud-daula, "Pillar of Government." The Persian courtier's administrative talents were well suited to the task, but a contemporary wrote of his lavish corruption, "In the taking of bribes he certainly was most uncompromising and fearless." He was at first charged with embezzlement, but far more serious accusations followed. One of Ghiyas Beg's sons was among the only four conspirators executed by Jahangir for their involvement in Khusrau's final plot to assassinate the emperor. Ghiyas Beg himself was implicated and arrested and only narrowly escaped execution. He saved his life and secured his rehabilitation by paying Jahangir an

Itimad-ud-daula (Ghiyas Beg)

enormous sum, presumably out of the proceeds of his corruption. He cautiously resumed his rise as Itimad-ud-daula, but the damage to the family had been considerable.

Itimad-ud-daula's slip from grace and the execution of his son perhaps explain why the marriage between his granddaughter and Khurram did not take place for five years—an exceptionally protracted engagement when the partners were of marriageable age. In the meantime Khurram contracted, at Jahangir's behest, a dynastic alliance. In October 1610 he wed another Persian girl—a princess descended from Shah Ismail Safavi of Persia—who bore him his first child, a daughter, in August 1611. The cloud over her family, her protracted engagement and the thought of Khurram with another woman could not have been easy for Arjumand Banu, waiting anxiously and impotently in her father's harem.

Everything changed for Arjumand Banu in 1611 with the marriage of her aunt, Itimad-ud-daula's daughter, to Jahangir. Four years earlier, the then thirty-year-old Mehrunissa had returned to the imperial court a widow. Her warrior husband, Sher Afghan, had been slain in Bengal in revenge for killing Jahangir's foster brother—an act which deeply angered Jahangir and may have contributed further to the disgrace of Ghiyas Beg's family. European accounts of the period paint a more lurid and fevered picture, claiming that Jahangir had expressly sent his foster brother to Bengal to murder Sher Afghan so that he could possess Mehrunissa and that Sher Afghan, suspecting something, had struck first. After her husband's death, the emperor summoned Mehrunissa to Agra, where she joined the household of one of Akbar's senior widows in the imperial harem. However, once there, she apparently remained "for a long time without any employment," and there is no evidence that she and Jahangir met.

Most likely Mehrunissa first attracted Jahangir during the Nauroz celebrations of 1611. According to one chronicle, "Her appearance caught the King's far-seeing eye, and so captivated him that he included her amongst the inmates of his select harem." According to another, "The stars of her good fortune commenced to shine, and to wake as from a deep sleep . . . desire began to arise." Within two months the two were married at a glittering ceremony. Jahangir's love of finery and luxury far exceeded his father's, and he delighted in jewels, wearing a different set every day of the year. Given that he had inherited 125 kilos of diamonds, pearls, rubies and emeralds alone—amounting to 625,000 karats of gems—he could indulge his tastes. To the English ambassador he appeared not so much clothed as laden with gems "and other precious vanities, so great, so glorious . . . His head, neck, breast, arms, above the elbows, at the wrists, his fingers every one, with at least two or three rings, fettered with chains . . . Rubies as great as walnuts, some greater; and pearls such as mine eyes were amazed at." The Great Moghul on his wedding day must have been a brilliant spectacle.

Jahangir gave his new bride the title Nur Mahal, "Light of the Palace," and she was to be his last official wife. In 1616 he would bestow on her a yet more exalted name: Nur Jahan, "Light of the World." In his memoirs he wrote, "I do not think anyone was fonder of me." Jahangir promoted her family again and rewarded them. Itimad-ud-daula, his previous indiscretions forgiven, received increased rank and a huge amount of money. Jahangir honored his son, Arjumand Banu's father, with the gift of one of his special, razor-sharp swords, Sarandaz, "Thrower of Heads." (In 1614 Jahangir would award him the title Asaf Khan, the name by which he would be known for the rest of his long and influential career.) However, amid all her new glory Nur had at least one critic. Jodh Bai, Khurram's quick-witted, sharp-tongued mother, was scornful of the new arrival in the imperial harem. According to one story, when Jahangir told Jodh Bai that Nur had praised his sweet breath, the acerbic Rajput princess snapped that only a woman with experience of many men could judge whether one man's breath was sweet or sour.

The following year, on 10 May 1612, a date selected by court astrologers as guaranteeing the couple's perfect happiness, Khurram and Arjumand Banu were finally wed. Court chroniclers related how, on this auspicious night, "the lights of the lamp-festival of the stars and the illuminations of torches and lanterns shone respectively on the earth and on the sky." "A night brighter than the day of youth" added "to pleasurable delight and fulfillment of desire."

As if to compensate for the long delay, the nuptials were celebrated with all the pomp and ostentation that a hugely wealthy empire could provide. Jahangir took personal charge, making arrangements for "the means of festivity and the requisites of joy and pleasure on such a scale as

*Nineteenth-century portrait said to be of Arjumand Banu, who became Mumtaz
Mahal, and said to have been copied from a seventeenth-century original*

befits the emperors of very great grandeur." He spent a day and a night at
Khurram's house, where his son presented him with lavish gifts including
"peerless jewels and heart-pleasing stuffs." Khurram's friends carried gifts
of money and precious gems to the bride's house, and he followed them
in sumptuous state, mounted on a huge elephant.*

Before the ceremony, Moghul noblewomen, concealed behind a cur-
tain, painted Khurram's hands with henna and turmeric for good luck,
and Jahangir himself "tied the marriage tiara of glittering pearls" upon
his son's head. Mullahs read verses from the Koran, for Khurram, though
three quarters Hindu through his Rajput ancestry, had been brought up
as a Sunni Muslim, while Arjumand Banu was a Shia. Next, the young

---

* The Moghuls had adopted the Hindu custom of the wedding procession. From Akbar's reign, with the marriage of Hindu brides into the imperial Moghul family,
  they had also borrowed the Hindu tradition of holding the marriage ceremony in
  the bride's house.

bride gave her formal consent, and the two families exchanged gifts—
"costly products of mines and quarries and the choicest harvest of the
Garden of Eden."

As the ceremony drew to a close, Khurram's hands were rinsed in
rosewater and he drank a goblet of water to confirm the union. The wedding feast was held at the house of the bride's father. The celebrations,
noisy with "the drum of festivity and the clarion of joy," and with glittering processions and firework displays, lasted a month.

Imperial chroniclers as a matter of course hinted at the sexual potency of the emperors whose deeds they recorded, but in Khurram's case,
they had no need to exaggerate. He would remain, throughout his life, a
deeply sensual and sensuous man. Twenty years old at the time of his
wedding to Arjumand Banu, barrel-chested and athletically built, he was
at the height of his sexual powers and a deft, experienced lover, well tu-
tored in a court where fleshly pleasures were unashamedly enjoyed.

The Moghuls had readily embraced the sensual traditions of their
new lands. India was known throughout the Islamic world for its sexual-
ity and sensuality and for its love manual, the Hindu Kamasutra, believed
to date from between the third to fifth century. Sheikh Nefzawi, who
wrote The Perfumed Garden for the bey of Tunis in the fifteenth or sixteenth century, acknowledged that "the people of India had advanced
further than we in the knowledge and investigation of coitus." He reported that, whereas in the Near East there were a meager eleven sexual
positions, the Indians had many more, including the twenty-five imaginative postures he described in The Perfumed Garden.

Wedding nights were, by tradition, carefully managed to ensure
the maximum sexual gratification. The bride and groom were bathed,
scented and oiled and laid upon a magnificent platform of a bed by
attendants who skillfully caressed their bodies to ready them for intercourse. Sexual pleasure was regarded as one of the rights, indeed necessi-
ties, of life for both men and women. After Khurram and Arjumand
Banu's first couplings the bedding was inspected to confirm that coitus
had taken place and that she had, indeed, been a virgin. Six weeks later
the woman later praised in the court chronicles as a "mine teeming with

gems of royalty" for her prodigious fertility was pregnant with their first child.

Khurram's chroniclers related that, having found his new wife "of perfect assay against the touchstone of experience; and finding also, in respect of her appearance of beauty, that she was chief and elect (mumtaz) from among the women of the time and the ladies of the universe, he [Khurram] gave her the title Mumtaz Mahal Begum, so that it may on the one hand serve as an indication of the pride and glory of that select one of the age, and on the other, that the real illustrious name of that reputed one of this world and the hereafter, befittingly may not occur on the tongues of the common people." The award of such a title was a tradition of the Moghuls "when they wish to distinguish with greater honor from among those who grace the royal bedchamber of fortune."

THE IMPERIAL CAPITAL Agra, where the young couple began their long-delayed married life, was a thriving city of 750,000 inhabitants. English visitors thought it "populous beyond measure."* The houses of ordinary people were of brick and tiles, if they could afford it, or of clay or mud if not. Floors were beaten earth, varnished over with cow dung mixed with water. Roofs were often just simple thatched awnings to protect against the hot sun and were vulnerable to fire; the hot, searing winds of summer, for which Agra was notorious, whirled sparks from cooking fires high into the air, causing the tinder-dry roofs to ignite. Sometimes women chose to burn to death in their houses rather than break purdah and run outside to reveal themselves to strangers.

The Moghul capital drew visitors from across the empire and far beyond. Afghan, Uzbek, Turkish, Persian and European merchants and soldiers of fortune alike found shelter in the ninety caravanserais spread throughout the city. Weary travelers sloughed off the dirt and dust of their journeys in one of eight hundred *hammams* (bathhouses).

---

* London, with a population of about three hundred thousand, was then Europe's third largest city after Paris and Constantinople.

Then, as now, the streets of Agra swarmed with hawkers energetically striving for a living. An English clerk described how "every evening is like a fair, where they resort, make their bargains, take and choose the whores sitting and lying on their cots." He saw little slave girls being trained as dancers, their virginity offered "at first at dear rates, after prostituted for a small matter." The streets were so crowded that people pressed themselves against the walls as chariots drawn by white, gilded-horned oxen trundled past, carrying nobles to court. More dangerous were the great elephants, tramping by with their burdens of swaying howdahs from which veiled women peeped into the world. Some of the wealthy prefered to loll in palanquins, a kind of bed with satin or brocade draperies, borne on the shoulders of slaves whose bare feet beat out a dusty tatoo as they ran.

The rituals of the court modulated the lives of all when the emperor was in residence behind the massive sandstone battlements of the Red Fort. The day began in the bleached dawn light when the beat of the great *dundhubi* (drum) announced the arrival of the emperor at the *jharokha-i-darshan* (the balcony of appearance), built high in the outside wall of every palace and fort. By making an appearance, the emperor showed his people that he still lived and that the empire was safe. Akbar had introduced this ceremony, which had its origins in the courts of the Hindu rulers. It was so vital, Jahangir wrote, that nothing, not even "great pain and sorrow," would deflect him from appearing. Jahangir did, however, confess that he returned to bed for a couple of hours afterward.

Those bold enough could seek direct redress for their ills from Jahangir. Anxious to be considered a just ruler who could "win the hearts of all the people and re-arrange the withered world," early in his reign he devised what he called a chain of justice. This was an eighty-foot-long rope festooned with sixty golden bells, and its task was to "remove the rust of oppression from the hearts of his people." Englishman William Hawkins wrote of the long rope stretched between a stone pillar on the riverbank and the battlements of the Agra fort: "This rope is hanged full of bells, plated with gold, so that the rope being shaken the bells are heard by the king, who sendeth to know the cause and doth his justice accordingly."

Those judged to have pulled on the chain for insufficient reason risked punishment, thus it took courage to seek an audience with the emperor. Imperial etiquette was complex and demanding. Profound silence was the rule, and no one, not even royal princes, could move from their allotted position in the chamber of audience without approval. Punishments were often carried out immediately in front of the emperor. Hawkins described how "Right before the king standeth one of his sheriffs, together with his master hangman, who is accompanied with forty hangmen wearing on their heads a certain quilted cap, different from all others, with a hatchet on their shoulders; and others with all sorts of whips being there, ready to do what the King commands."

Other bells rang in Agra, like those of the churches built by the Jesuits in Akbar's reign, whose sonorous clang mingled with the muezzin's call to prayer. Jahangir was, on the whole, tolerant of different religions, writing in his memoirs of his wish, like Akbar, to "follow the rule of universal peace with regard to religion." Pietro della Valle, an Italian visitor to his court, wrote that he "makes no difference in his dominions between the one sort and the other and both in his court and armies, and even amongst men of the highest degree, they are [all] of equal account and consideration." Cows ambled at will through Agra's streets since, out of regard for his Hindu subjects, Jahangir forbade their killing on pain of death. His tolerance was, however, more erratic, than Akbar's.*

As far as his own religion was concerned, Jahangir observed the tenets of Islam but enjoyed listening to debates between Jesuits and mullahs. Sir Thomas Roe observed shrewdly that his religion was "his own invention" and even suggested that Jahangir was really an atheist. In 1610 he allowed the Jesuits to baptize three sons of his dead brother Daniyal, summoning the amazed and delighted priests to the palace at midnight so he could hand the boys over to them. The conversion of his nephews

---

* Jahangir executed the Sikh guru Arjun Singh, who thus became one of Sikhdom's most holy martyrs, though that was for his part in Khusrau's rebellion rather than on religious grounds. In fact, all the guru had done was to bless the prince and mark his brow with saffron to bring him good fortune.

did not, however, last. The Jesuits wrote with disgust that the princes "rejected the light and returned to their vomit."

ALONG THE RIVER Jumna were the elegant, luxurious mansions of the courtiers with their flower-filled, tree-shaded gardens and cooling fountains. Because river frontage was so sought after, the city was, according to one European visitor, "much longer than it is broad," curving like a half-moon with the course of the river. Among the great palaces was Khurram's, where Mumtaz settled into her own apartments within the traditional enclosed courtyard hidden from public view—"the harem"—in conformity with the prescriptions of the Koran. The word harem derives from the Arabic harim, meaning something sacred or forbidden. Accounts are silent on the fate of the Persian princess Khurram had wed two years earlier. He would later take at least one other wife for political reasons, but as the court historians later wrote under his direct supervision, "his whole delight was centered in this illustrious lady [Mumtaz], to such an extent that he did not feel towards the others one-thousandth part of the affection that he did for her." For her part, Mumtaz had the happiness of a relationship that mirrored close marital bonds within her own Persian family. Her grandparents, Itimad-ud-daula and his wife, loved each other devotedly, and her aunt Nur Mahal, the former Mehrunissa, was already developing a powerful bond with her new husband, Jahangir.

Nur was consolidating her central position within the huge imperial harem—a place whose seeming "lascivious sensuality, and wanton and reckless festivity" fascinated Western visitors to the Moghul court, at this time all male of course. They speculated enthusiastically about what went on within this world of women and wrote titillating accounts of how the sentinels would allow nothing of a phallic shape, not even a cucumber or a radish, to reach these female sanctums. The eccentric English pedestrian Thomas Coryat, who arrived on foot at the Moghul court in 1615, went further: "Whatsover is brought in of virile shape" was "cut and jagged for fear of converting the same to some unnatural abuse." In fact, the women of the harem had no need of such crude devices. Artificial phalluses of gold, silver, copper, iron, ivory, horn and wood, with a number of small protuberances for extra sensation, were available in India.

The imperial harem was, of course, a sexual playground. Jahangir had at least three hundred sexual partners, girding himself for love by swallowing aphrodisiac potions. Female harem officials kept a careful record of his lovemaking, from its frequency to the name of his partner. If Moghul miniatures are accurate, they were sometimes even present during the emperor's couplings, albeit with eyes decorously averted from the writhing couple.

But the harem was many other things besides. It was home to large numbers of imperial family members—mothers, aunts, sisters, cousins and widows—together with superannuated concubines, put aside as their sexual attraction waned. The harem also functioned as a nursery for the imperial children, who, as Khurram had been, were on occasion brought up by senior matrons of the imperial family, rather than by their own mothers.

Akbar had paid great attention both to the aesthetics and to the governance of his vast harem of five thousand women, and his rules were faithfully observed by his successors. Traditionally, the mother of the reigning emperor ruled the harem, followed by the emperor's chief and secondary wives. Beneath them, the harem was administered by various departments overseen by "chaste women" well salaried for their work. One of the most important was the harem accountant—a "clever and zealous writer"—who controlled day-to-day expenditures and calculated each year's budget. When a woman wished to make a purchase, she applied to a "cash keeper," who submitted the request to the accountant for her approval. If the ordinary systems of household management failed, the female astrologers of the harem were consulted. When a valuable pearl disappeared from a harem apartment, an astrologer prophesied correctly, or so the story goes, that it would be found within three days by a pale-skinned woman who would place it in the emperor's hand. At the bottom of the huge hierarchy of female officials, attendants and servants were the female scavengers employed to clean the underground tunnels into which the latrines emptied.

The seraglio in the Red Fort at Agra was spacious, airy and light with terraces, gardens, avenues of trees and swimming pools. Rooms and halls were richly furnished, with highly colored and patterned silk carpets in summer and woolen ones in winter, layered on top of soft matttreses. No indoor floor was ever left bare. Swaths of silk in glowing colors and sensuous velvets were draped gracefully around windows and doors.

Products from the imperial perfumery established by Akbar scented the air. Incense distilled from ambergris, rosewater, aloewood and sandalwood wafted seductively from bejeweled censers. Fragrant soaps and unguents helped the women cool and and freshen their skin. There was also attar of roses invented by Mumtaz's grandmother, Asmat Begum. Jahangir called it the discovery of his reign and praised its potency: "When she was making rose-water, a scum formed on the surface of the dishes into which the hot rose-water was poured from the jugs. She collected this scum little by little . . . It is of such strength in perfume that if one drop be rubbed on the palm of the hand it scents a whole assembly and it appears as if many red rose-buds had bloomed at once. There is no other scent of equal excellence to it. It restores hearts that have gone, and brings back withered souls."

Wives and concubines maintained their own households in interconnecting suites and apartments. A secret network of underground corridors and staircases provided not only ventilation but a means of checking on the activities of the women. The emperor could move swiftly and silently through the complex, appearing now here, now there, giving him the appearance of supernatural powers. A network of female spies, set up in Akbar's time, also kept him informed. Discipline within the harem was strict and ruthless. A former concubine of Jahangir's caught dallying with a eunuch was placed in a pit with her feet tied to a stake and earth rammed up to her armpits and left exposed to the sun without food or water. She died thirty-six hours later. The eunuch was "condemned to the elephant," victim of the fact that castration does not always destroy sexual desire.*

---

* Castration could be total removal of penis and testicles, meaning that a quill was needed for urination, or, more simply and hygenically, the removal of the testicles alone. The wife of a eunuch of the latter type told the Victorian traveler Richard Burton that her husband could even be aroused to a kind of ejaculation, presumably a prostatic fluid, after a protracted period of erotic stimulation.

There was no safer place for an emperor than the imperial harem, where he ate and slept as both master and guest. In many ways it was a return to the security of childhood, perhaps even of the womb. His drinking water was entrusted to a special servant, who kept it sealed, and all his food was tasted before it touched his lips. The same guards who prevented ardent young lovers from stealing into the harem were also a good line of defense against any would-be assassin. The inside of the harem was protected by tall, powerfully built women skilled with bow and arrow; Uzbek, Turkish and Abyssinian women were especially prized. Their reputation for ruthlessness reflected the terrible punishment they would suffer for neglecting their duties. They reported to the khwajasara, the senior official of the harem, and the most trusted of these amazons guarded the apartments of the emperor himself.

All gates were closed at sunset except the main gate, where torches burned through the night. Eunuchs guarded the immediate approach to the harem. The Englishman Peter Mundy described how "great men . . . employ them in matters of greatest trust, of which the chiefest is to guard their women, their treasure." Some, as was often the case in China, had themselves chosen emasculation as a means of advancement. Others had been gelded by force, sometimes on their parents' instructions. A senior imperial eunuch of the period later refused to see the parents who had denied him "the greatest pleasures attainable in this world."

Beyond the eunuchs, on duty twenty-four hours a day, was a detachment of Rajputs backed up by further detachments of guards and imperial troops. Entering the imperial harem was thus no easy matter. When the wife of a nobleman wished to pay a visit, she had to apply to the harem officials and await a reply. Those granted admission were, if unknown to the guards, rigorously searched by the eunuchs, "with no respect being paid either to the position or rank of the person." The Venetian traveler Niccolao Manucci complained that "the tongue and the hands of these baboons act together, being most licentious in examining everything, both goods and women, coming into the palace; they are foul in speech, and fond of silly stories." The examinations were ostensibly to ensure that no male disguised as a woman slipped inside. Several European doctors, who were allowed to enter the harem to tend women too sick to be brought to the outside gate, wrote of their experiences. François Bernier described how his head was first covered with a Kashmir shawl, "hanging like a large scarf down to my feet, and an eunuch led me by the hand, as if I had been a blind man."

Many accounts suggest that surgeons were asked to procure abortions. Jealous wives, anxious that concubines and slave girls should not usurp them in their husband's affections, paid doctors well for such services. One account relates how a princess "in one month had caused miscarriages to eight women of [her husband's] harem, as she would not permit any children but her own to survive."

Troupes of dancing girls, mimics and acrobats entertained the ladies of the harem, who chewed fragrant betel, told stories, played games and admired their reflections in tiny, pearl-ringed mirrors mounted on thumb rings. But they did not pass all their time in narcissistic idleness. Wealthy, well-educated, well-connected women of the imperial harem like Nur conducted successful businesses, using their male relations or specially appointed officials as intermediaries. They traded internally but also with the outside world, chartering ships, hiring captains and exporting Indian goods to Arabia and beyond. They financed their commercial activities from allowances and gifts, but also from estates settled on them and the award of perks like customs dues. They prudently reinvested their profits in further ventures, building up immense fortunes, but also spent lavishly on parties, feasts and festivals and the extravagant gift giving so integral to court life. They endowed charitable institutions and commissioned new buildings. A Dutch traveler wrote of Nur that "she erects very expensive buildings in all directions—*serais*, or halting places for travellers and merchants, and pleasure-gardens and palaces such as no one has ever made before." The women resented competition in commerce almost as much as in love. William Hawkins found himself in disgrace with Jahangir's mother for cornering the market in indigo and thus preventing her from acquiring a cargo of the valuable dye.

On 30 March 1613, Mumtaz gave birth to a baby girl. This "early fruit of the garden of auspiciousness" was named Princess Hur al-Nisa. However, Mumtaz's life of courtly comfort, playing with her new daughter, was about to end. Jahangir was once again focusing on the military campaigns which Khusrau's revolts had forced him to suspend and, in 1614, called on Khurram. His mission was to subdue the rana of Mewar (Udaipur), the greatest of Rajasthan's rulers, who, from a mountain stronghold, had continued to defy the Moghuls.

Though pregnant once more, Mumtaz accompanied Khurram on the campaign, and this was to become the pattern of their marriage. He steadfastly ignored his ancestor Babur's advice never to take women on military campaigns. One of his chroniclers observed that "he never allowed that light of the imperial chamber to be separated from him whether at home or abroad." Throughout hardships, misfortune and, on occasion, real danger, she would remain at his side, and twelve of their fourteen children would be conceived and born in their wanderings.

CHAPTER FIVE

The Warrior Prince

JAHANGIR INTENDED THE CONQUEST OF Mewar to be a precursor to extending Moghul control over the troublesome sultans of the Deccan, the rugged plateau to the south, and then to regaining the hereditary kingdom of his ancestors far to the north in central Asia, in particular that holy of holies, Timur's lost capital of Samarkand. Jahangir moved the imperial court to Ajmer, three hundred miles west of Agra and closer to Mewar and his son's operations.

Khurram opened his campaign by advancing into the hills of Rajasthan and setting up a string of military checkpoints. So thorough and ruthless was the future Shah Jahan's scorching of the countryside that even his own army was sometimes left without food, and in the face of such vigorous attrition, the rana of Mewar sought terms. Khurram took care not to humiliate this proudest of enemies. He did not ask the rana to yield any lands or to make obeisance in person to Jahangir. His only requirement was that the rana should send his son to wait on the emperor. The rana's young son Karan Singh arrived at court, where Jahangir lavished gifts on him and was amused by the lack of sophistication of a boy who "was of a wild nature and had lived among the hills"—a description that not so long before would accurately have described the Moghuls.

The twenty-two-year-old Khurram had proved his talents as both soldier and diplomat and had succeeded where his father had not. Akbar

had twice ordered Jahangir to move against Mewar, and twice he had ob-
fuscated. On his arrival at court, the triumphant Khurram presented his
father with a brilliant ruby worth sixty thousand rupees. Jahangir decided to wear it on his arm but felt it needed "two rare and lustrous
matched pearls" to set it off. A courtier, taking the hint, found a single
splendid pearl, but then Khurram recalled that, in the days of his boyhood with Akbar, he had seen "a pearl of this size and shape on an old
headband." Courtiers tracked down the venerable turban ornament and,
wrote Jahangir, "upon examination it was found to contain a pearl of exactly the right size and shape . . . the jewellers were astonished." Khurram's prodigious memory was clearly as sharp as claimed in his boyhood,
but this incident also reveals the passion that would make him one of the
Moghul Empire's greatest authorities on gems.

KHURRAM'S YOUNG FAMILY was growing. During the Mewar campaign
Mumtaz had presented him with another daughter, Jahanara, born on 2
April 1614 and, the following year, bore his first son, Dara Shukoh, on
30 March 1615. The whole court celebrated. An Italian traveler observed that "when a princess is born in the mahal the women rejoice
and go to great expense as a mark of their joy" but "if a prince is born
then all the court takes part in the rejoicings, which last several days . . .
Instruments are played and music resounds."

Yet once again the couple had little time to enjoy a tranquil family
life. The following year, in 1616, Jahangir ordered Khurram south to the
Deccan to replace his older brother as commander of the imperial forces.
"Since the leadership and command of the Deccan campaign had not
gone as well as I had wished under my son Sultan Parvez," he reasoned,
"it occurred to me to summon him and then make Baba Khurram, who
was clearly competent, the vanguard of the imperial forces and go myself
in his wake."

The Moghuls viewed the independent Muslim sultanates of the
Deccan—Ahmednagar, Bijapur and Golconda—on the southern edge of
their empire as a threat. Sometimes these kingdoms waged war on each
other, but there was always the risk of them joining forces against their
northern neighbor. It was therefore important for Moghul security that

they acknowledge Moghul suzerainty—something they were of course reluctant to do. The Deccani kingdoms were and would continue to be a crucible of resistance to the Moghuls. This time the enemy was a former Abyssinian slave, Malik Ambar, who had achieved high office under the sultans of Ahmednagar, some of whose lands Akbar had annexed. Malik Ambar had been waging a clever and effective guerrilla war to regain the lost territories and had found an ally in the wealthy sultan of Bijapur.

The appointment came at a traumatic time for Mumtaz and her husband. In the early summer of 1616 their eldest daughter, three-year-old Hur al-Nisa, died of smallpox. Mumtaz's emotions are not recorded but can be imagined, especially as she was at the time more than eight months pregnant with their fourth child. Khurram was "very much grieved," and Jahangir, too, was distraught at the loss of his grandchild, writing, "Although I was greatly desirous of writing it down, my hand and heart have failed me. Whenever I took my pen, my state became bewildered and I helplessly ordered Itimad-ud-daula to write it." Itimad-ud-daula, the baby's great-grandfather, duly took up the sad tale, describing in the flowery language of the court how "the bird of her soul flew from her elemental cage and passed into the gardens of Paradise." The weeping Jahangir remained secluded for two days and ordered that Wednesday, the day of the child's death, should henceforth be known as "the lost day." On the third day Jahangir went to Khurram's house but "could not control himself."

Less than three weeks later, however, the family's sorrow was mitigated. Jahangir described how "there came from the womb of the daughter of Asaf Khan (wife of Khurram) a precious pearl into the world of being. With joy and gladness at this great boon the drums beat loudly, and the door of pleasure and enjoyment was opened in the face of the people." Mumtaz had given birth to her second son, Shah Shuja.

While Mumtaz recovered, she got ready to accompany Khurram as he again prepared for war. His base would be the city of Burhanpur on the Tapti River, noted for its bright chintzes and opium, and which had long been the Moghuls' command center for their operations against the recalcitrant Deccani kingdoms that lay farther south across a barren landscape of eroded tablelands. On 31 October 1616, the day fixed by the astrologers for his departure to Burhanpur, Khurram paraded the pick of his troops for his father's inspection. Some six hundred richly caparisoned elephants and ten thousand cavalrymen, aglitter in cloth of gold and with white egrets' feathers fluttering in their turbans, saluted their emperor. Jahangir kissed his son, who was dressed "in a coat of cloth of silver, embroidered with great pearls and shining in diamonds like a firmament" and presented him with gifts, including what Jahangir himself called a "wind-footed" horse with a jeweled saddle.

The English ambassador Sir Thomas Roe captured Khurram's rising star. "It is true," he wrote, "all men awe him more than the king [emperor], now that he is to receive the army" and "all men [are] fawning on this idol." Roe himself was not an admirer of the young prince, whom he characterized as "ravenous and tyrannical" and with such a pride "as may teach Lucifer." Khurram had complained to him about the loutish behavior of English merchants, "their drinking and quarreling in the streets, and drawing swords in the custom house." The prince had also consistently frustrated Roe's attempts to win trading concessions—the primary reason for which King James and the English East India Company had dispatched him to the Moghul court—and Khurram's men had seized gifts Roe had brought from England to help ingratiate himself with Jahangir. In fact, the only presents that pleased the emperor from what, to the Moghuls, must have seemed a remote and retarded island, which no one from Hindustan had yet been recorded as having visited, were an English coach and some paintings. For the Nauroz, or New Year festival, of 1616, Jahangir had the alcove behind his throne festooned with images of the English royal family.

Jahangir followed Khurram's armies toward the Deccan, as he had promised, moving his court south from Ajmer to the hill fortress of Mandu high on an escarpment some one hundred miles northwest of Burhanpur. Roe accompanied him. The ambassador's waspish dispatches to England sometimes bemoaned Moghul vulgarity. He likened their love of display to that of a lady who in her determination "to show all . . . set on a cupboard her embroidered slippers with her [silver] plate." This time, though, the pageantry unequivocally impressed him. Before he left, Jahangir, glittering with jewels and fanned with feathers by two eunuchs, appeared on the palace balcony to give and receive presents. Roe described how "what he bestowed he let down by a silk string . . . what was given him, a venerable fat deformed old matron, wrinkled and hung with gimbels [rings] like an image [idol], pulled up at a hole with another."

Roe thought he caught a glimpse of Nur Jahan, with another of Jahangir's wives, watching these operations: "At one side in a window were his two principal wives, whose curiosity made them break little holes in a grate of reeds that hung before it to gaze on me. I saw first their fingers, and after laying their faces close now one eye, now another; sometime I could discern the full proportion. They were indifferently white, black hair smoothed up; but if I had had no other light, their diamonds and pearls had sufficed to show them. When I looked up they retired, and were so merry that I supposed they laughed at me."

Roe described how, when the moment of departure came, Jahangir "descended the stairs with such an acclamation of 'Padshah salamat,' 'health to the king' as would have out cried cannons." An attendant buckled on his sword "set all over with great diamonds and rubies." On one side of his turban hung an unset ruby "as big as a walnut," while on the other dangled "a diamond as great" and, in the middle, an enormous, heart-shaped emerald. Jahangir's tunic of cloth of gold was tied with a sash "wreathed about with a chain of great pearls, rubies and diamonds." The ambassador was gratified to see Jahangir rattle off in a luxurious replica of the English coach he had commissioned, lined with Persian velvet. Nur Jahan followed in the original conveyance, "newly covered and trimmed rich." Jahangir had had it sumptuously refurbished because the original upholstery had mildewed on the long, damp, salty sea voyage from England.

Roe also admired the superb organization that enabled the emperor to move with an entourage equivalent to a small town. His chaplain thought it was like an "ambulans respublica," a mobile state. Over one hundred thousand bullocks lumbered along, pulling creaking wooden carts laden with provisions. When Jahangir made camp, it covered an area of twenty miles in circumference. Roe measured Jahangir's own accommodation, erected at its heart, and found it nearly three hundred yards in diameter. To Roe it was "one of the wonders of my little experience," though he was disconcerted by the arrival of a camel swaying under a putrescent burden of three hundred rebels' heads, a thoughtful gift to Jahangir from the governor of Kandahar.

As Jahangir made his leisurely progress south in Khurram's wake, Nur demonstrated her skill as a huntswoman. Jahangir recorded proudly, "She shot two tigers with one shot each and knocked over two others with four shots . . . Until now such shooting was never seen, that from the top of an elephant and inside of a howdah, six shots should be made and not one miss."

Khurram also gave his father cause for pride. In another short and cleverly managed campaign, the prince quelled Malik Ambar and the sultan of Bijapur, at least for the present. Roe's chaplain caught the drama of battles between armies which "in these eastern wars oftentimes consist of incredible multitudes . . . The music they have when they go to battle is from kettle-drums and long wind instruments. The armies on both sides usually begin with most furious onsets." Khurram forced his adversaries to retreat from the Moghul lands they had invaded and extracted huge amounts of treasure and their promise that henceforth they would remain, in Jahangir's words, "quiet and loyal."

When reports of Khurram's victory reached Jahangir, he, in his own words, "ordered the drums of rejoicing beaten" that "the troublemakers who had dared to rebel had admitted their inability and powerlessness." In October 1617 Khurram returned "in wondrous triumph," as Roe reported. Roe himself was prevented from waiting on the prince, "having the emralds [hemorrhoids, or piles] still bleeding," a condition which had already lasted "a scouring twenty weeks." Jahangir's memoirs make clear his delight with Khurram: "After he had paid me his respects, I called him in the window where I was sitting, and with the impulse of excessive paternal affection and love, I immediately rose up and took him in my arms. The more he expressed his reverence and respect for me, the more my tenderness increased towards him." The emperor showered his son's head with trays of jewels and golden coins and announced that from then on he would be known as Shah Jahan, or "Lord of the World." Jahangir also ordered, "Henceforth a chair should be placed for him in the court next to my throne, an honour . . . never before known in my family" and appointed him governor of the wealthy province of Gujarat.

Nur held a victory feast costing a staggering three hundred thousand rupees at which she presented bejeweled robes, horses and elephants to

Shah Jahan and dresses of honor to Mumtaz and the other women of his household.* A painting depicts the banquet spread on lavish carpets in a pavilioned garden. Nur is offering a dish to Jahangir, kneeling beside her, a halo around his head. This nimbus, intended to convey sanctity, was an artistic innovation of Jahangir's, borrowed from Jesuit art.† Shah Jahan kneels by his father's side, and a group of bejeweled women in diaphanous clothes look on admiringly. One of them is, perhaps, Mumtaz, sharing this high point in her husband's fortunes. Barely a month before the victory feast Mumtaz had delivered their fifth child, another daughter, named Raushanara.

In his father's eyes Shah Jahan personified everything a Moghul prince should be. "My consideration for this son is so unbounded," wrote Jahangir, "that I would do anything to please him, and in fact, he is an excellent son, and one adorned with every grace, and in his early youth has accomplished to my satisfaction everything that he has set his hand to."

There was, however, something else that Jahangir required of his son—to take another wife—which he did on the very day of his daughter Raushanara's birth. The bride was the granddaughter of Jahangir's Khan Khanan, his leading general, whom Jahangir wished to reward. The marriage was, according to Shah Jahan's court historians, entirely "due to political expediency," and the girl was "content with this illustrious connection in name only." He nevertheless fathered a son, Sultan Afroz, by her. However, the child did not rank either in status or emotionally with the children of Mumtaz. Of the little boy's birth, Shah Jahan's chronicler wrote simply that "as the child was not born in an auspicious hour, His Majesty did not keep him with himself." A later incident recorded by Jahangir also reveals his insignificance to the imperial family. In 1620 Mumtaz's second son, Shah Shuja, a sickly child prone to

---

* Price comparisons are notoriously difficult to make, but the fact that, according to Abul Fazl, a sheep could be bought for only one or two rupees and an ordinary silk garment for between one and five rupees gives some idea of the extravagance.

† Originally Asian in origin, the concept of the halo reached Europe by way of Byzantium, by which time it had died out in Persia and India.

Nur Jahan serving a feast to Jahangir and Shah Jahan (Khurram)

ailments, fell ill "with an eruption so violent that water would not go down his throat," and court astrologers told the distraught parents that his death was in the stars. However, another astrologer disagreed, prophesying that "some other child would die" instead. Jahangir recorded with joy that the man had been correct—Shah Shuja indeed recovered. It was unlucky little Sultan Afroz who died, passing out of history with the briefest of mentions.

In 1618 the emperor gave further signals that he regarded Shah Jahan as his heir. He decided that the diary he had kept for the first twelve years of his reign should be bound into a single volume and copies made for favored friends or, as he conceitedly wrote, to be "sent to other countries to be used by rulers as a manual for ruling." However, he presented the first copy to twenty-six-year-old Shah Jahan, "whom," he wrote, "I consider to be in all respects the first of my sons." When, a few months later, Shah Jahan's mother, Jodh Bai, died, he again publicly showed his love and concern for his son. Although removed from his mother at birth, Shah Jahan had become devoted to her. Indeed, throughout his life the women of his close family would unleash his deepest feelings. So excessive was his grief that Jahangir went to the house of his beloved son. After "having condoled with him in every way," and finding him still inconsolable, Jahangir "took him with me to the palace" to try and assuage his sorrow.

Jahangir remained deeply attached to Shah Jahan and Mumtaz's children, sharing in the day-to-day crises that naturally arose with such a burgeoning brood. He described another illness of Shah Shuja: "Prince Shuja, my son Shah Jahan's darling son . . . of whom I am inordinately fond, contracted a childhood illness called infantile epilepsy. He was unconscious for a long time. No matter what treatments and remedies those with experience tried they did no good." Mumtaz, pregnant again, must have been poignantly reminded of the loss of her eldest daughter to smallpox two years earlier. In despair, Jahangir made a solemn vow not to harm "any living thing with my own hand" if only the child lived. Soon after, the little boy recovered, and Jahangir, true to his word, gave up hunting.

On the night of 3 November 1618, Mumtaz gave birth to her third son. She was accompanying Jahangir, Shah Jahan and the rest of the imperial court on its return to Agra when she went into labor in a small village high in the mountains dividing the Deccan from Hindustan to the north. Several days later, when the court reached Ujjain, capital of the province of Malwa, the birth was celebrated with due ceremony. During a party in Shah Jahan's quarters, Jahangir reported, "[he] brought that auspicious child before me, and, presenting as offerings trays of jewels and jewelled ornaments and fifty elephants . . . asked me for a name for him." He chose Aurangzeb.

Barely three months later, Mumtaz was pregnant once more. During the first seven years of their marriage, Mumtaz had as many children, and seven more were to follow. Even contemporaries marveled at such devotion and fecundity.

IN MARCH 1620 Jahangir, Nur, Shah Jahan and Mumtaz arrived among the bluebells and pale pink almond blossoms of the vale of Kashmir. The journey from Agra had taken more than five months, and the latter stages had been hazardous, "full of hills and passes, ravines and ascents," as Jahangir described, and through drizzling rain that sometimes turned to snow. On one particularly dreadful day, traveling along narrow mountain tracks, horses and elephants laden with the paraphernalia of the imperial household and weakened by the march "fell in every direction and were not able to rise again." Twenty-five elephants died. The experience had been taxing for everyone but must have been especially so for the pregnant Mumtaz, who during the journey, in December 1619, had given birth to another son, Ummid Bakhsh. However, the robustness of Moghul women surprised foreigners. According to one, "They [seemed to] suffer much less than other mortals in child-birth: for not infrequently they bear a child at the end of a day's journey and on the next day ride forward carrying the infant in their arms."

In Kashmir she could recuperate, although the rural idyll was punctured briefly when little Shah Shuja, while playing in the palace, tumbled through an open portal and down over a high wall. Luckily, a rug and the body of a man sitting beneath the wall broke his fall: The prince's head landed on the rug, while his feet hit the man's back, otherwise he would have been killed. The commander of the palace guard "immediately ran and picked the prince up, clasped him to his breast, and started up the stairs." In his confused state all the prince could do was repeat, "Where are you taking me?"

The imperial family passed lazy days floating in shikara boats on the "crystal brilliance" of the Dal Lake and plucking scarlet lotuses. They watched local farmers tend their crops of melons and cucumbers planted on floating islands which they poled about the lake and admired the soft mauve haze of the fields where the saffron-producing crocuses grew. Jahangir, ever the naturalist, described how "every parterre, every field, was, as far as the eye could reach covered with flowers . . . the flower has five petals of a violet colour, and three stigmas producing saffron are found within it, and that is the purest saffron."

Kashmir's beauty moved him to passionate, lyrical verse.

> *The garden nymphs [flowers] were brilliant,*
> *Their cheeks shone like lamps;*
> *There were fragrant buds on their stems*
> *Like dark amulets on the arms of the beloved.*
> *The wakeful, ode-rehearsing nightingale*
> *Whetted the desires of wine-drinkers;*
> *At each fountain the duck dipped his beak*
> *Like golden scissors cutting silk.*

Jahangir had begun laying out gardens in Kashmir soon after his accession and sought Shah Jahan's help with a new project: building pleasure grounds in the lower reaches of what today are the famous Shalimar Gardens on the shores of the Dal Lake.* The prince designed a wide, central waterway to channel the melted snows of the mountains down a series of cascades, then on through avenues of poplar and sycamore trees and out into the lake. His imaginative ideas made the gardens, as Jahangir admiringly wrote, one of the most idyllic and scenic in Kashmir.

---

* The gardens' evocative name dates from a ruler of the sixth century AD, who built a house there which he called Shalimar, meaning "the Abode of Love."

The vale of Kashmir

These were, however, the last days of unalloyed harmony between the
emperor and his favorite son. The tight family circle that had cocooned
Shah Jahan and Mumtaz was starting to unravel. In the early years of his
marriage to her niece, Nur had protected and promoted Shah Jahan's interests. The two of them, with Mumtaz's father, Asaf Khan, and her
grandfather, Itimad-ud-daula, had formed a powerful quartet.

As Shah Jahan had grown in his father's favor, so had Nur's hold
over Jahangir. An underlying factor was Jahangir's weakness for alcohol
and opium, which had progressively nourished his natural indolence
and hedonism. Contemporary accounts suggest that Jahangir was often
comatose through drink and drugs. Roe, a favorite drinking companion
of the emperor, described how evening council meetings with the imperial ministers were often "prevented by a drowziness which posses-
seth His Majesty from the fumes of Bacchus." Sometimes he would
simply stretch out and go to sleep. After a couple of hours his attendants would respectfully nudge him awake and bring food, which,

because he was too unsteady to feed himself, was "thrust into his mouth by others."*

Nur was lovingly indulgent to Jahangir and fussed over his health. One account describes how she undressed him, "chafing and fondling him as if he were a little child." At the same time, his weakness and befuddlement had given Nur scope to exercise her remarkable talents. Her absorption of power had begun early in her marriage. When Sir Thomas Roe first arrived at court in 1615, her influence was already such that she could order his credentials be sent to her in the harem so that she personally could check them. Roe quickly and correctly deduced Nur's influence on the emperor, reporting back to England, that she "governs him and winds him up at her pleasure." "Easy in his temper and naturally voluptuous," Jahangir became increasingly content to relinquish the tiresome, tedious business of government to his energetic, capable and ambitious wife.

Nur began exercising power directly—independently approving imperial orders and having them issued under Jahangir's name with the addition of her own name, "Nur Jahan, the Queen Begam," beside the imperial signature. She took control of the frequent appointments, promotions and demotions that were the heartbeat of Moghul administration. A contemporary complained that "her former and present supporters have been well-rewarded . . . most of the men who are near the king owe their promotion to her . . . many misunderstandings result, for the King's orders or grants of appointments etc, are not certainties, being of no value until they have been approved by the Queen." Nur also had coins struck in her name and was distinguished from Jahangir's other

---

* Jahangir was not alone in his drug addiction. Peter Mundy, who would arrive in India just a few years later, noted the "many fields of poppies of which they make opium called here *afim* by this country's people, much used for many purposes. The seed thereof they put on their bread . . . of the husks they make a kind of beverage called *post*, steeping them in water a while. And squeezing and straining out the liquor, they drink it, which doth inebriate. In the like manner they use a certain [plant] called *bhang* [marijuana] working the same effect, so that most commonly they will call a drunken fellow either *afimi* [opium eater], *posti* [opium drunkard] or *bhangi* [drug taker]."

wives by the title shahi (empress). The only right she never acquired was that of having the *khutba* read in her name as a statement of sovereignty before midday Friday prayers in the mosque.

While Nur attended to the administrative aspects of government on behalf of her husband, Shah Jahan had conducted Jahangir's military campaigns. Their interests had, for a while, run in tandem, but Shah Jahan had become wary of Nur's growing domination and suspicious of her ambitions. In 1617 they had sparred over the awarding of trading concessions to the English—the first time there was open disagreement between them. However, a far more serious issue for them both was what would happen when Jahangir died. Around this time Nur had begun seeking a more malleable candidate for the imperial throne than the clever, increasingly independent Shah Jahan; a man through whom she could rule as she governed through Jahangir. The best way of achieving this objective was through yet another alliance between her family and the imperial house.

Some accounts suggest that Nur had originally considered trying to marry her only child, Ladli—her daughter by her first husband, Sher Afghan—to Shah Jahan. However, this seems implausible. Her niece Mumtaz was so obviously and absolutely his beloved principal wife and had borne him a clutch of children, including male heirs. Instead, Nur's first thought seems to have been to marry Ladli to Shah Jahan's half-brother, Prince Khusrau. The partially sighted prince would, she reasoned, be more tractable than Shah Jahan. Yet although the marriage would have freed Khusrau from the prison where he was currently confined, he declined. According to the many and various accounts, this decision was made out of love for the wife who had insisted on sharing his imprisonment with him and had "utterly refused any other comfort than to be the companion of her husband's miseries." Not even her selfless pleadings to Khusrau to marry Ladli and thus to secure his freedom had moved him to accept Nur's offer.

The negotiations had, however, alerted Shah Jahan and Mumtaz to Nur's strategy. Rifts began to open within Itimad-ud-daula's hitherto united family. The ambitions of Nur Jahan, as consort of the current ruler and aspiring mother-in-law of any pliant prince who might succeed him, and those of Mumtaz Mahal, already wife of the most powerful claimant to the throne and devoted mother of his copious children, came into direct conflict. Mumtaz's unequivocal loyalty was to her husband, not to her aunt, whose hand would soon be guiding Jahangir's increasingly antagonistic moves against Shah Jahan. The situation also left Mumtaz's father, Asaf Khan, in an ever more sensitive position. Though a loyal supporter of his empress sister and her mouthpiece in the council, he had his daughter's future and his own to consider. The aging Itimad-ud-daula himself needed all his considerable skills to steer between the interests of daughter and granddaughter, while retaining Jahangir's confidence as his chief minister.

These underlying tensions were brought into sharper relief while the imperial family was still in Kashmir. The fifty-one-year-old Jahangir was "seized with a catching and shortness of breath . . . in the air-passages on my left side near the heart, an oppression and catching was felt. It gradually increased and became fixed." A "course of warm medicine" brought a little relief, but, believing that "the moisture of the atmosphere" might be to blame, Jahangir prepared to leave Kashmir for the hot, dry plains. Such evidence of her husband's physical frailty induced Nur to act quickly. If she could not secure Khusrau as a son-in-law, there was another possibility. In December 1620, with the court now at Lahore, Nur persuaded Jahangir to betroth his youngest son, the indolent, pleasure-loving Shahriyar, to her daughter. He was, she believed, unlikely to challenge her authority. According to contemporary accounts, though "the most beautiful of all the princes," he was also showing signs of a "feeble mind and imbecile character." He must have seemed ideal.

The betrothal, with its implied threat to his position as Jahangir's heir, could not have come at a worse time for Shah Jahan. That autumn news had reached the imperial court that, once again, as Jahangir wrote, "evil-disposed men in the Deccan [had] raised the standard of rebellion." The sultans of Bijapur and Ahmednagar, and their ally the sultan of Golconda, had torn up the terms of their settlement with the Moghuls and, with a force of sixty thousand, were besieging imperial troops in Burhanpur and other cities. Once again Jahangir called on Shah Jahan to go to war. He was the obvious, indeed the only, choice. Even had he been perfectly sighted, Khusrau was too disaffected to be trusted, Parvez was too incompetent as a military strategist and had inherited the family vice of alcoholism, while the adolescent Shahriyar was too young and inexperienced to take the field.

Shah Jahan had no wish to be more than one thousand miles from court at a time when Nur was scheming against him. Furthermore, if Jahangir should die while he was away on campaign, he would be ill placed to make his bid for the throne. He decided that, although he had no option but to obey his father's orders, he would make one demand: that Jahangir should give him custody of his half-brother Khusrau, who would go with him on campaign. He could at least keep one potential rival for the throne under surveillance and out of the hands of other factions.

Jahangir agreed, and Shah Jahan and Mumtaz, pregnant for the eighth time, traveled south once more to the Deccan accompanied by a force including one thousand Turkish mercenaries with the latest muskets, fifty thousand artillerymen, a sea of gray elephants and the miserable Khusrau and his loyal wife. Shah Jahan would never again see the father who had so exultantly rained golden coins over his head. Within months he would become, as Jahangir wrote angrily in his diary, "a Wretch," no longer trusted or loved, and fearful for his family's safety.

The ensuing family drama would have all the elements of a Jacobean revenge tragedy in which the principal players, picked out by a prescient Sir Thomas Roe, would be "a noble prince, an excellent wife, a faithful councillor, a crafty stepmother, an ambitious son, a cunning favourite."

CHAPTER SIX

Emperor in Waiting

ONCE AGAIN SHAH JAHAN DEALT SWIFTLY with his father's enemies in the Deccan, defeating them in a six-month campaign and this time inflicting harsher penalties including the ceding of some border territories to the Moghuls. These were, as Jahangir wrote, still days of "gladness and victory." While Shah Jahan consolidated his position in the south, the emperor attended royal entertainments organized by Nur and her brother, Mumtaz's father, Asaf Khan, in Agra at which they placed "many delicate gems and wonders" before him. Jahangir was sufficiently recovered from the painful breathing problems that had afflicted him in Kashmir to take a gleeful pleasure in such things. He was also well enough to resume his study of the curiosities of nature, writing of the exceedingly strange appearance of a zebra and of the arrival at court of a hermaphrodite eunuch from Bengal.

Far away in the monsoon heat of the Deccan, in June 1621, Mumtaz gave birth to her eighth child, a daughter named Sorayya Bano. This should have been a happy time for the family, but news from the distant imperial court was making Shah Jahan increasingly uneasy. He learned that, shortly before the birth of his new daughter, Shahriyar and Ladli had been married in Agra. A resplendent "feast of joy" had been held in Itimad-ud-daula's house during which Jahangir, under Nur's approving eye, had heaped honors on his youngest son. Even more disturbingly, messengers arrived with the news that Jahangir was again ill—a serious asthma attack had left him gasping for breath. As the malady increased, he dosed himself with goat's and camel's milk and, when that failed, turned in despair to alcohol, admitting frankly, "As I found relief in drinking, contrary to my habit, I resorted to it in the daytime, and by degrees I carried it to excess." Unsurprisingly, as the weather grew hotter, his condition worsened. An anxious Nur took charge and "exerted herself to reduce the quantity of my potations and to provide me with suitable and soothing preparations . . . She gradually reduced the quantity of wine I took, and guarded me against unsuitable food and improper things."

The usually inebriated Parvez had rushed to his only slightly less drunken father's bedside to be commended as a "kind and dutiful son," but Shah Jahan and Mumtaz, so many miles away in the Deccan, could do little but wait anxiously, and further family drama soon followed. First, Nur's mother, Mumtaz's grandmother, the inventor of fragrant attar of roses, became ill and died. Then, three months later, as Jahangir and the grieving Nur were progressing northward to the cooler climes that the emperor hoped would improve his health, Itimad-ud-daula, his "Pillar of Government," also fell sick. The old man had been devastated by the loss of his wife. Jahangir wrote how "he cared no longer for himself, but melted away from day to day." Moved by Nur's agitation, which "I could not bear," Jahangir kept vigil with her while his elderly courtier slipped in and out of consciousness at "the hour of his death agony." In January 1622, forty-four years after shepherding his family on their dangerous journey from Persia, Itimad-ud-daula died.

Jahangir regretted the loss of such "a wise and perfect Vizier, and a learned and affectionate companion." Nur mourned not only a beloved father but also her mentor. She would find consolation in planning a white marble tomb to commemorate him in Agra but, for the moment, was inconsolable. Mumtaz's reaction to the death of her grandparents is not recorded, but she, too, must have been saddened as well as apprehensive about how Nur would act without the restraining influence of the head of the family. Itimad-ud-daula had been the only person capable of moderating Nur's ambitions and of balancing the overall interests of his family. Without him Mumtaz would have known that her future and that of her husband and children were less secure.

A week after the passing of Itimad-ud-daula, news broke of yet
another—this time very unexpected—death. A simple entry in the convalescent Jahangir's diary reads: "A letter from Khurram [Shah Jahan] informed me that Khusrau had died of colic." He had apparently expired in
the fortress of Burhanpur, where Shah Jahan had incarcerated him. Although the signatures of Shah Jahan's chief nobles were affixed to the
letter confirming the truth of its contents, the timing of Khusrau's demise, just when Jahangir's own survival had seemed doubtful, was striking, indeed sinister. Virtually every foreign visitor at the Moghul court
concluded that Shah Jahan had murdered his thirty-six-year-old half-
brother to eliminate a rival in the forthcoming fight for the throne.

Such claims persisted. A luridly detailed account, written a few years
later by the Augustinian friar Sebastien Manrique, is typical. He described how Shah Jahan, "the author and engineer of this barbarous
plan," ordered a slave to murder Khusrau while he himself went off "on
the pretext of hunting" to give himself an alibi: "So this man, in the
dead of night, went with some companions to the Prince's chamber. He
knocked on the door in such a way as to deceive the Prince, calling out
that he was bringing letters from the father and some clothes which
are used on such occasions by the Mogol Emperors as an intimation
that they will show clemency and forgive crimes. On hearing this joyful
news the wretched Prince opened the door, wholly unsuspicious of the
evil tidings they were really bringing, of his sudden death. For no sooner
had the executioners entered than they threw themselves upon him,
gagged him, and putting a rope round his neck throttled him. When he
was dead they placed the corpse on his bed, and leaving it there went
away, fastening the door carefully and firmly on the outside as if they had
done nothing." A few hours later, according to another European account, Khusrau's faithful wife came to his room: "Her husband seemed to
be sleeping in his bed. Seeing that he did not move, she touched his face
with her hand, and found that he was cold and dead. She ran out and began to scream."

One of Shah Jahan's own chroniclers wrote blandly that "Khusrau got
delivery from the prison of existence and instead became confined in the
prison of non-existence." A Moghul historian, writing later in Shah Jahan's lifetime, also believed Shah Jahan to be responsible, though he

claimed more boldly that Khusrau's death had been necessary for the empire's security.

Whatever the actual circumstances, Khusrau was undoubtedly murdered, very probably by his brother. Shah Jahan had on several previous occasions attempted to gain custody of Khusrau, but Jahangir had resisted. He had only agreed this time either because, as alleged in some accounts, he was drunk when Shah Jahan petitioned him or, as seems more likely, he needed Shah Jahan to subdue the Deccan and wished to please him. Nur probably also played a part in securing Jahangir's consent. As her focus shifted away from Khusrau to Shahriyar, it must have seemed a neat device for removing both Shah Jahan and Khusrau from court and their father.

Shah Jahan certainly had the motive for killing Khusrau. Despite his blighted sight, he was still the eldest son and commanded a following. Furthermore, his abilities far exceeded those of the drunken Parvez and the somewhat dim-witted Shahriyar. His death was, at the very least, convenient for Shah Jahan. It was also consistent with his later ruthless elimination of other family rivals. However, by ordering his murder, Shah Jahan had committed an act that would haunt his reign and establish a bloody precedent among his children. As an unsympathetic early commentator put it, he was "laying the foundation of his throne in a brother's blood."

Jahangir himself, slowly recuperating, seems at first to have accepted Shah Jahan's explanation of Khusrau's sudden end. However, accounts suggest that a letter from a Moghul nobleman, who had been in Burhanpur at the time and believed the death to have been planned, changed his view. The emperor wrote angrily to the nobles in Burhanpur "enquiring why they had failed to write to him the truth, whether his son had died a natural death, or been murdered by some one." He ordered his son's corpse to be exhumed and sent to Allahabad for reburial in the garden housing Khusrau's mother's tomb. He also ordered Khusrau's widow and little son to the imperial court, then at Lahore, for safekeeping.

However, Jahangir was soon facing another crisis, which left little room for reflections on fratricide. Reports reached him that Shah Abbas, the emperor of a renascent Persia, was advancing on Kandahar, a Moghul border post three hundred miles southwest of Kabul and

Jahangir Embracing Shah Abbas *by Abul Hasan*

defended by only a scant garrison. The city had been a source of grievance between the two empires ever since a humble Humayun had presented it to the shah in 1545 in return for help in regaining his throne.
Since then it had been batted back and forth four times. Ownership was
a point of principle rather than an issue of real significance. Though
Kandahar had once been a wealthy entrepôt on the trade route to India,
its importance had, by this time, waned as traders and pilgrims had taken
to the sea instead. Nevertheless, Jahangir was anxious to retain the city
for strategic reasons, particularly since he feared its capture might
presage a Persian invasion of his empire. He mobilized an enormous
force, including "artillery, mortars, elephants, treasure, arms and equipment," and in March 1622 ordered Shah Jahan and his armies from the
Deccan to join it.

The summons came at a poignant and difficult time for Shah Jahan
and Mumtaz. Only a few weeks earlier, their son Ummid Bakhsh, born
on the mountainous route to "Paradise-like Kashmir" two years before,
had "shifted to the eternal world," as the chroniclers euphemistically reported the little boy's death. He was the second child that they had lost.
Nevertheless, Shah Jahan set out at the head of his forces, with the
grieving and once again pregnant Mumtaz as ever following loyally behind with the women of the household, in curtained howdahs, bullock
carts or panniers hanging against the bony ribcages of camels. He advanced as far as the hill fortress of Mandu, some one hundred miles
northwest of Burhanpur, but then paused. The excuse he gave his father
was that he wanted to wait until the monsoon rains had passed. Jahangir
himself had once written that "in the rainy season there is no place with
the fine air and pleasantness of this fort" with its airy buildings surrounded by large lakes. One of Mandu's former Muslim rulers had also
built a white marble tomb there, probably the first in India, for himself in
1440. However, Shah Jahan also chose this moment to make a series of
demands of Jahangir. He asked to be given sole command of the Kandahar campaign and to be appointed governor of the strategic province of
the Punjab, which would be to his rear as he marched northwest to Kandahar. Most important to him of all, perhaps, he asked for the huge
Rajput fortress of Ranthambhor in Rajasthan, seized by Akbar fifty years
earlier, as a safe refuge for Mumtaz and their children.

Shah Jahan's conditions reflected his belief that his stock at court was falling. No new honors—either literal or metaphoric—had been heaped on him to mark his victories. Neither had he been recalled to his father's side. Furthermore, the long march to Kandahar would isolate him from the power base he had been consolidating in the Deccan and leave him vulnerable. At the same time, he would surely have noticed that Nur's position had been yet further enhanced. Jahangir had awarded her all of her father's money and lands, ignoring the custom whereby such assets reverted to the crown to be apportioned at the emperor's pleasure among all the deceased's family. Even more significant, Jahangir had ordered her drums to be beaten immediately after his own in court ceremonials. It must have seemed to Shah Jahan that Nur was profiting from his extended absence to tighten her already forceful grip on government. Later, when Shah Jahan was emperor, his official chronicler blamed his fall from grace on those at court "whose coin of sincerity was impure and who had been suffering from the torture of jealousy for a long time" and who estranged Jahangir from his son, thereby inflaming "the fire of intrigue and disturbance which kept burning in Hind for the next four or five years." Although he did not say so, the writer clearly meant Nur and her faction.

Jahangir's response to Shah Jahan's requests, no doubt encouraged by Nur, was unsympathetic. "His report was read, I did not like the style of its purport nor the request he made, and, on the contrary, the traces of disloyalty were apparent," he wrote. Jahangir was further angered by news that Shah Jahan had seized lands belonging to Shahriyar and Nur and that his men and Shahriyar's were brawling openly so that "many were killed on both sides." Deciding that Shah Jahan's mind was perverted, the emperor wrote, "[I] warned him not to come to me, but to send all the troops which had been required from him for the campaign against Kandahar. If he acted contrary to my commands, he would afterwards have to repent."

In his irritable and agitated mood, Jahangir revoked the vow he had made five years earlier, when Shah Jahan's son Shah Shuja had fallen so ill, to give up hunting if he recovered, writing, "[As] I was greatly distressed at [Shah Jahan's] unkind behaviour, I took again to sporting with a gun." A more serious signal of his displeasure was that, in August 1622, he decided to hand command of the Kandahar expedition to, as he put it, his "fortunate son" Shahriyar. A delighted Nur gave her husband a pair of "priceless" Turkish pearls that very day. Jahangir also transferred the traditional fief of the heir apparent, Hissar Firoza, which he had bestowed on Shah Jahan fourteen years earlier, to his youngest son. There could have been no clearer statement of intent.

Suspecting correctly that he had gone too far, Shah Jahan apologized to his father and was shocked to find that it was too late. Jahangir wrote, "I took no notice of him, and showed him no favour." Just as years earlier he had hardened his heart against Khusrau, he now turned his face from the most talented, and once the most beloved, of his sons. Ironically, at the same age as Shah Jahan—thirty years old—he had staged his own coup against his father, Akbar. Perhaps this fact did not escape him.

In late 1622 Mumtaz gave birth to a son, but the child died before he could be named. Sorrow at the loss, and a growing fear of what would become of his family if he did not act decisively, perhaps contributed to Shah Jahan's next move: open rebellion. It was a dangerous stratagem which he would not have embraced without careful thought, but Shah Jahan knew his father's powers were waning and that many others, like himself, resented Nur's influence over the emperor and might be induced to declare in his favor. He also knew he could rely on the personal loyalty of the emirs and officers in the Deccan and in Gujarat, of which he was governor. He knew them well and had cultivated their favor with promotions and gifts. Therefore, in January 1623 Shah Jahan, with Mumtaz, their children and an army of supporters, set out northward from Mandu to Agra. Rebellions need funds, and he was intent on seizing the imperial treasure which informants told him was about to be dispatched from the Agra fort to Lahore to finance the Kandahar campaign. According to some accounts, Mumtaz's father, Asaf Khan, had secretly tipped him off about the shipment.

Asaf Khan must certainly have been watching events with growing concern. He had inherited none of his father's riches; everything had gone to his sister Nur. More significant, Nur's blatant maneuverings to supplant his son-in-law with hers in Jahangir's affections meant that her daughter, Ladli, and not his beloved Mumtaz, would become empress. Asaf Khan was too skilled and cautious a courtier to make an open move just yet, but providing a little covert assistance to the prince he privately wished to be the next emperor must have seemed only prudent.

Reports that Shah Jahan had heard that the treasure had been sent for and was marching on Agra further enraged Jahangir, who declared that his rebellious son "had taken a decided step in the road to perdition." "Fire had fallen into his mind," he raged, and he had "let fall from his hand the reins of self-control." Jahangir turned southward to confront him, relegating "the momentous affair of Kandahar," which had in any case fallen to Shah Abbas the previous June, 1622, to a literary tussle. In a letter oozing ritual courtesies, Jahangir hailed the shah as "the splendid nurseling of the parterres of prophecy and saintship" but peppered his text with subtle insults implying he was being greedy and grasping. Why, Jahangir inquired of Shah Abbas, did he want such a "petty village" as Kandahar? Surely, it was beneath his dignity.

"What shall I say of my own sufferings?" Jahangir complained in his diary as he set out to deal with the wayward Shah Jahan. "In pain and weakness, in a warm atmosphere that is extremely unsuited to my health, I must still ride and be active, and in this state must proceed against such an undutiful son." He ordered that henceforth Shah Jahan should be called Bi-daulat—"the Wretch"—and railed against his son's ingratitude: "From the kindness and favours bestowed upon him, I can say that up till the present time no king has conferred such on his son."

Jahangir was not in time to forestall Shah Jahan's attack on Agra. His son plundered the city but failed to capture either the fort or the treasure waiting to be shipped to the Kandahar campaign. Jahangir's ministers had prudently decided not to risk sending the latter from the fort. Instead they had concentrated on strengthening the fort's red sandstone towers and thick gates to help them withstand attack. Disappointed though not downcast at his lack of success, Shah Jahan wheeled his forces northward toward Delhi to engage the imperial troops advancing under Jahangir. To many still wavering on the sidelines of the rebellion, it seemed as if the young, vigorous Shah Jahan would prevail over the forces of his aging father.

On 29 March 1623 the two forces, numbering over fifty thousand men in total, clashed on an arid plain encircled by low, barren hills dotted with rocks and scrubby lantana bushes. Neither the ailing Jahangir nor Shah Jahan took part themselves. Contrary to expectations, Shah Jahan's forces were routed and many of his commanders killed despite the fact that during the battle the leader of Jahangir's advance guard changed sides, bringing ten thousand soldiers with him. Ironically, Asaf Khan was in command of part of the imperial forces, but he was not among those whom Jahangir rewarded for their bravery that day. Doubts about Asaf Khan's true allegiances may already have been troubling the emperor.

Shah Jahan and Mumtaz fled southwest through Rajasthan, finding a temporary refuge with the new rana of Mewar (Udaipur), Karan Singh, the wild hill boy whose arrival at court nine years earlier, after Shah Jahan's defeat of his father, had so amused Jahangir. The young rana, who had become close to Shah Jahan at court, lodged his guests for four months in an exquisite domed marble pavilion—the Gul Mahal—which he had recently built on an island in the shimmering lake at Udaipur. From there, Shah Jahan, Mumtaz and their six young children could gaze out on the surrounding hills and find respite as the summer heat grew fiercer.

For form's sake, in May 1623 Jahangir entrusted the campaign against Shah Jahan to his second son, Parvez, but its true commander was his most trusted general and childhood friend, Mahabat Khan, who had also been Shah Jahan's tutor and came from another of the Persian families that had prospered at the Moghul court. Jahangir's orders were succinctly brutal. Mahabat Khan was to pursue Shah Jahan and capture him alive or, if that proved difficult, to kill him.

However, Shah Jahan's and Mumtaz's most determined and dangerous opponent was Nur. Though bereft of her father's advice and increasingly unsure of her brother Asaf Khan's allegiance, she had Jahangir's total trust and devotion. Her power over him, given that she was in her late forties in a society where, as an English visitor observed, "the King and his great men maintain their women, but little affect them after thirty years of their age," was remarkable and as much a tribute to her strong, attractive and intelligent personality as to any enduring beauty. In fact, she became a grandmother that September with the birth of a daughter to the handsome if foolish Shahriyar and her own daughter, Ladli. The arrival of her grandchild no doubt strengthened her resolve to rule.

One of many paintings said to be of Nur Jahan

Jahangir's increasing frailty made it easier for Nur to assume new powers. He was grateful to her for assuming his burdens at a time when he found himself no longer even able to keep his own diary. He confessed, "As in consequence of the weakness that came over me two years ago and still continues, heart and brain do not accord. I cannot make notes of events and occurrences." Instead he asked a courtier, Mutamid Khan—who "knows my temperament and understands my words"—to henceforth keep a record of events and submit them to him for verification. The death of Jahangir's charismatic Hindu mother in the summer of 1623 must have also reinforced Nur's authority over her increasingly dependent husband.

Shah Jahan and Mumtaz soon learned the depth of Nur's enmity toward them as they moved south from Mewar toward the Deccan. With many supporters deserting to the imperial armies, the prince's forces were dangerously reduced, and he decided he had to secure a suitable retreat for Mumtaz and the children. He chose the great hill fortress of Asir, which was close to Burhanpur and under the control of a chieftain married to a cousin of Mumtaz, whom he hoped would help them. However, this cousin was also a niece of Nur's, and upon learning of Shah Jahan's plan, Nur moved to frustrate it. She herself wrote to the chieftain, warning him, "Beware, a thousand times beware, not to allow Bi-daulat [Shah Jahan] and his men to come near the fort, but strengthen the towers and gates, and do your duty, and do not act in such a manner that the stain of a curse and ingratitude for favours should fall."

Nevertheless, Shah Jahan forced the chieftain by threats to open the gates of his fortress, but with the imperial forces marching swiftly in pursuit, he and his family could not linger long within the protection of its walls. Leaving a trusted Rajput in command of the fort, Shah Jahan took them the twelve miles south to Burhanpur, from where he made tentative overtures of peace to Mahabat Khan. When these failed, he and his family trekked yet farther south across the Tapti and other dangerously swift-flowing rivers fed by the drenching monsoon rains. He tried to form alliances with the local sultans of the Deccan, but they rebuffed him. The only help Shah Jahan received came from the ruler of Golconda, who was eager to encourage any disorder in the Moghul domains and allowed his former enemy and his entourage to pass through his kingdom northeast into Orissa, a journey through mountains and marshland during which, according to Jahangir's memoirs, the bedraggled force "had to endure great hardships" such that many more of Shah Jahan's supporters slipped away.

However, Shah Jahan's luck turned when the governor of Orissa, a cousin of Nur's and of Mumtaz's, was so struck with terror at his arrival that he fled, leaving everything behind him. Shah Jahan seized the governor's rich treasure, rebuilt his armies and advanced with fresh recruits, artillery, horses and war elephants into Bengal and Bihar, capturing several important cities and forcing their nobles to swear allegiance to him. In the spring of 1624 he killed Nur's uncle, the governor of Bengal, in a fierce fight on the banks of the Ganges. The governor had not only been brother to Nur's mother, but was also Mumtaz's great-uncle. At times, Mumtaz's flight across India must have seemed to her like a grotesque game of chess in which many of the main pieces eliminated or elevated were her close relations.

Yet Mahabat Khan was soon nipping at Shah Jahan's heels again and pushed him back into Orissa. From there the prince and his family could do little but retrace their tortuous path back to Golconda. Once more in the Deccan, Shah Jahan found an unlikely ally. Malik Ambar of Ahmednagar, the former Abyssinian slave he had twice defeated on Jahangir's behalf, was anxious to join forces with Shah Jahan "on the basis of common enmity to the Imperial government." This seasoned guerrilla fighter was glad of the opportunity to exploit Shah Jahan's rebellion to his own advantage. Together they mounted a number of attacks, harassing the imperial forces.

However, in 1625, as a chronicler related, Shah Jahan "was seized with illness" and realized he could no longer go on. For three years Mahabat Khan had chased him and his family thousands of miles back and forth in a game of cat and mouse through the deserts of Rajasthan, southward to the Deccan, east to Orissa and Bengal, back once more toward Agra, then southward again to the Deccan. Shah Jahan had tried to avoid pitched battles with his father's forces, but when he had been forced to fight, he had invariably been the loser. During one battle an arrow severely wounded Shah Jahan's horse, and he only escaped capture when an officer gave him his horse on which to flee. Only the ability of Shah Jahan and his followers to travel light and fast, at least by Moghul standards, had prevented the more cumbersome pursuing forces from capturing him.

Throughout all this, Mumtaz, the hitherto pampered product of the harem, had remained steadfastly by his side, sharing the hardships just as she had once shared the glory of going on campaign when Shah Jahan was still a favored son. Often, as Jahangir noted with satisfaction, they had been "in a wretched state," forced to flee in disorder "through the heavy rain, and the mud and mire" so that "if any baggage was left behind

no enquiries were made and Shah Jahan and his children and depend-
ents thought themselves lucky to save their lives." Such an existence
could not continue.

Under the circumstances, Shah Jahan decided that he had no option
but to throw himself and his loved ones on his father's mercy. His family
included a new son, Murad Bakhsh, born in September 1624 in the
citadel of Rohtas near the Hindu holy city of Benares on the banks of
the Ganges. Ill and depressed, Shah Jahan wrote to his father in late
1625, expressing his sorrow and repentance and begging pardon for all
faults past and present, and waited apprehensively for a reply.

Jahangir's response was conciliatory, unlike his brutal reaction to
Khusrau's rebellion nearly twenty years before. Perhaps Nur had decided
that Shah Jahan and his father were so estranged that a true reconciliation
would never be possible and Shah Jahan no longer posed a serious threat.
She may also have been wary of antagonizing her brother, Asaf Khan.
Perhaps the latter lobbied Jahangir on behalf of Shah Jahan. Perhaps the
emperor simply welcomed the chance to make peace with his son and to
halt a campaign that had stretched his supply lines across thousands of
miles. He replied in his own hand that not only would he grant his son
"full forgiveness," but he would also appoint him governor of the remote
province of Balaghat in central India. There was, however, a sting. Shah
Jahan was required to surrender the fortresses of Rohtas and Asir still occupied by his officers, and also had to send ten-year-old Dara Shukoh
and seven-year-old Aurangzeb to the imperial court as hostages in all but
name. To soften the blow, Jahangir sent his jewel-loving son a diamond-
studded mace.

Parting with the boys under such circumstances must have been
deeply traumatic for Shah Jahan and Mumtaz. Of the ten children born
to them by this time, three had already died. A chronicle related how,
"notwithstanding the love he had for his sons," Shah Jahan, who was
still afflicted by his bodily ailments, had no option but to send them to
his father, together with "offerings of jewels, chased guns and elephants."
Despite the death of Khusrau in his custody, Shah Jahan and Mumtaz
were placing their faith in the old Timurid custom that the lives of
princes of the blood were sacred.

CHAPTER SEVEN

Chosen One of the Palace

SHAH JAHAN AND MUMTAZ WERE EFFECTIVELY in exile. Their three-year rebellion had achieved little except to exhaust them physically and emotionally, rob them of two of their sons and demonstrate their irreconcilable differences with Nur. Their only hope was that others resentful of the empress's increasingly arrogant and autocratic behavior might act.

One such was Mahabat Khan. His defeat of Shah Jahan had made him one of Jahangir's most influential nobles. It had also brought him into prolonged contact with the thirty-six-year-old Prince Parvez as together they had hounded Shah Jahan and his family across the empire. As Jahangir's oldest surviving son, Parvez had a legitimate claim to the throne. His alcoholism was a weakness, but, Mahabat Khan must have reasoned, would also make him easier to control should he become emperor.

Mahabat Khan's growing influence over Parvez was, however, being watched with alarm by both Nur and her brother Asaf Khan, neither of whom had any interest in seeing Parvez prosper. Their first step was to detach Mahabat Khan from the impressionable prince by persuading Jahangir to appoint Mahabat Khan governor of Bengal in the distant east. At the same time, Nur and her brother accused him of misappropriating treasure and elephants during the campaign against Shah Jahan. Deducing that there was a conspiracy against him, Mahabat Khan decided to appear before his emperor and defend himself.

In March 1626, at the head of more than four thousand Rajputs, Mahabat Khan approached the dusty imperial encampment on the east shore of the deep, swift-flowing Jhelum River, a tributary of the Indus flowing down from the mountains of Kashmir, where Jahangir had paused on his way northwest to Kabul. Learning of his approach, Jahangir sent orders that he was to halt and send ahead only his elephants and a few attendants. The still respectful Mahabat Khan duly dispatched an advance party that included the young man who had recently married his daughter. When Mahabat Khan's son-in-law arrived at the imperial encampment, soldiers seized him, flogged him and put him in chains on the excuse that he had wed without the emperor's consent. To add insult to physical injury, Jahangir ordered Mahabat Khan's wedding gifts to the couple to be confiscated and sent to the imperial treasury.

When Mahabat Khan learned what had happened, it confirmed his fears that Nur and her brother were bent on destroying him. His only course, he decided, was to gain direct access to Jahangir and plead his case in person. The noble recently entrusted by Jahangir with writing his diary, and who was an eyewitness, recorded how Mahabat Khan swept into the camp at the head of his men to discover that the majority of the imperial court, including the bulk of the army under Asaf Khan and "the baggage, the treasury, the arms, etc, even to the very domestics," were already busily crossing a boat bridge over the river, so they would be ready for the next day's journey. Jahangir, Nur, Shahriyar and their immediate household, who were to follow in the morning, were still in their tents—unprotected and vulnerable.

This was an almost unimaginable circumstance and a sign of how little the emperor had regarded Mahabat Khan as a threat. Without considering the consequences, Mahabat Khan staged a coup. He ordered two thousand Rajputs to guard the boat bridge and, if necessary, to burn it, to prevent the imperial army hastening back to their master's defense. Next he led a body of one hundred dust-streaked foot soldiers armed with spears and shields to the royal tents, where the few soldiers on guard were just completing their morning prayers. Jahangir's diarist recorded an astonishing scene. Mahabat Khan strode about, searching for the emperor until, spying a group of eunuchs by the entrance to the imperial bathroom tent and suspecting wrongly that Jahangir was within, he ordered his attendants to rip down the boards around it.

Hearing the commotion, Jahangir emerged from elsewhere in his quarters into a crowd of armed Rajputs. According to Jahangir's diarist, Mahabat Khan tried to justify his actions, telling the incredulous emperor, "[Since] I have assured myself that escape from the malice and implacable hatred of Asaf Khan is impossible, and that I shall be put to death in shame and ignominy, I have therefore boldly and presumptuously thrown myself upon Your Majesty's protection. If I deserve death or punishment, give the order that I may suffer it in your presence." What he actually said was probably neither so humble nor so eloquent and left no doubt that Jahangir was his prisoner. Jahangir seemingly contemplated swiping his head from his shoulders—twice his hand reached for his sword "to cleanse the world from the filthy existence of that foul dog," as a chronicler hostile to Mahabat Khan later wrote. But he restrained himself, probably because Mahabat Khan had so many soldiers with him and he feared the consequences. Instead, Jahangir acquiesced when his former friend proposed, "It is time to go out riding and hunting; let the necessary orders be given as usual, so that your slave may go out in attendance upon you, and it may appear that this bold step has been taken by Your Majesty's order." However, Jahangir refused to mount Mahabat Khan's horse, calling imperiously for his own royal stallion.

After riding "a distance of two arrow shots," Mahabat Khan asked Jahangir to climb instead into a howdah on an imperial elephant, to make it easier for people to see the emperor and convince them nothing was amiss. However, during the swap Rajput warriors killed two of Jahangir's attendants, believing they were attempting to rescue their master. In an increasingly tense atmosphere, the kidnapped emperor was hurried away to Mahabat Khan's camp.

In his nervousness and panic, Mahabat Khan had neglected to capture Nur, who was still in the imperial camp. When she realized what had happened, she lost no time in hurrying to the river, which, the chronicles relate, Mahabat Khan's Rajputs chivalrously but ill advisedly allowed her to cross. Nur rushed to the tents of her brother, who had crossed before Mahabat Khan's arrival, and, regardless of the rules of purdah, summoned the chief nobles and officers and berated them and her brother: "It was through your negligence that things have gone so far and the unimaginable has happened. You have been disgraced before God and the people." Stinging from her tirade, they decided to recross the Jhelum the next day and rescue their emperor.

The operation was a fiasco. Mahabat Khan's men had by then burned the boat bridge, and the ford chosen for the crossing by the imperial forces was, according to Jahangir's diarist, "the worst possible," full of deep holes. As the imperial troops plunged in, many men and beasts simply tumbled over. Futhermore, as they began struggling toward the opposite bank, they saw more than seven hundred of Mahabat Khan's Rajputs drawn up "in firm array" with their armored war elephants, ready to repel them. Many of the imperial troops were hacked or shot down as they tried to come ashore, while others, seeing their fate, veered away in a panic. Some battled the deep water and swift currents until they came to other crossing places undefended by the Rajputs. A courageous few of these, gasping and soaked, made their way toward the tent where Jahangir, together with Shahriyar, who had also been captured by Mahabat Khan, was being held, but most were cut down. Others fled, including Asaf Khan, who hurried to the safety of a stout fortress built by Akbar.

The Rajputs had killed some two thousand imperial troops, and another two thousand had drowned, their bodies mingling with the carcasses of horses, camels and elephants in the chilling, blood-flecked waters. The Rajputs had, as usual, proved fearsome opponents. According to a European mercenary who fought both with them and against them, "They all eat opium, and on the day of battle they swallow a double dose. They also give some to their horses to enable them to endure fatigue . . . Many of them wear gold armlets, so that, if killed, those finding the body may see to its cremation."

Nur had participated in the attack across the river, riding high in a howdah, her granddaughter in her arms and the child's nurse beside her. She had been caught in a storm of Rajput arrows and spears which lacerated her elephant's tough hide. When the baby, or according to one account the nurse, was hit in the arm, Nur pulled out the arrow "with her own hand, and threw it out, bloodying her clothes in the process" and emptied three quiverfuls of arrows into the Rajputs in return. Her elephant driver urged the stricken animal away from the ford and into deeper waters where it could swim, and eventually Nur and her party gained a section of the far bank free of Rajputs. Having witnessed the bloody chaos of the crossing and learning that her brother had fled, Nur accepted the impossibility of rescuing her husband and surrendered to Mahabat Khan, insisting on joining Jahangir in captivity. Within days Asaf Khan, removed from his mountain hideaway and kept for a while in chains, also joined the royal prisoners.

With the entire royal household firmly in the grip of his Rajput forces, but under the pretense of being still a loyal subject, Mahabat Khan set out for Kabul, about two hundred miles away to the northwest, in line with Jahangir's original intention. To the ordinary onlooker all appeared normal as, in May 1626, the royal entourage passed into the ancient mud-walled city beyond the Khyber Pass. Jahangir, on a gorgeously caparisoned elephant, scattered gold and silver coin as usual to the admiring and deferential crowds.

Over the following uneasy months in Kabul the strange charade continued. Mahabat Khan had seized Jahangir on impulse with no defined plans and seemingly no thoughts of taking the throne for himself. He probably heartily regretted his hasty action but was unable to see a way out of it. Meanwhile, under Nur's careful tutelage Jahangir contributed to the pretense of calm and continuity, graciously acceding in public to Mahabat Khan's requests. Privately, he reassured Mahabat Khan that he intended him no ill and blamed his previous suspicions on Nur. According to Jahangir's diarist, the emperor even warned the general, "The begum intends to attack you. Beware." Mahabat Khan was reassured by such confidences. He even seems to have convinced himself that Jahangir was happy to be released from the yoke of a wife who had assumed far too much power.

Nur was quietly and patiently awaiting the chance to wrest control back from Mahabat Khan. She had her own imperial cavalry, which Mahabat Khan had allowed her to keep, no doubt to preserve outward appearances and prevent a confrontation. As Jahangir's diarist noted, Nur courted them, ensuring that she kept "her battle-tried warriors appeased and in a good frame of mind," presumably discouraging desertions through bribes. Through her eunuchs she also secretly bought the services of large numbers of mercenary foot soldiers and cavalry. Her chance came when, in August 1626, to avoid the approaching chill of autumn, the royal entourage journeyed southeast again on a five-hundred-mile progress down from Kabul through the stark Khyber Pass back toward the welcoming warmth of Lahore. By November they were nearing the Jhelum River, where Mahabat Khan had staged his oppor-tunistic coup. On Nur's advice, Jahangir told his general that he wished to review the empress's cavalry and asked him to march ahead with his own forces "lest an argument ensue and battle break out" between Nur's Muslim soldiers and Mahabat Khan's Hindu Rajputs.

As Nur had hoped, the increasingly nervous and uncertain Mahabat Khan recognized a chance to extricate himself from what had become an impasse. According to Jahangir's diarist, without demur he "did as he was told" and set out with his men. As his distance from the imperial forces grew, an orderly advance became an undignified scramble and then a heedless flight. As a precaution, Mahabat Khan had taken hostages with him, including Asaf Khan and his son. Such was his fear of Nur's power, however, that when she ordered Mahabat Khan to release them, he did so as soon as he judged he had placed enough distance between himself and the vengeful empress.

MORE THAN ONE thousand miles away to the south, Shah Jahan and Mumtaz, pregnant once more, had anxiously been following the strange events of that summer as news and rumor, difficult to distinguish be-tween and in any event many days old, filtered through to them. Their chief worry must have been the possible dangers for their young hostage sons, who had reached their grandfather's camp in the aftermath of Ma-habat Khan's coup. Yet at the same time Mahabat Khan's seizure of Ja-hangir offered Shah Jahan fresh possibilities for advancing his own interests. On first learning of Mahabat Khan's action, Shah Jahan gath-ered one thousand horsemen and, in June 1626, announced that he was marching out to Jahangir's aid. However, as he and Mumtaz made the long and arduous journey northward, desertions reduced their forces and they found themselves "in great distress and poverty," as Jahangir's diarist noted. Shah Jahan made a detour to besiege Tatta, a port in Sind in northwestern India, to give himself a base, but his attack faltered after its governor, who was loyal to his half-brother Shahriyar, blocked his advance. Furthermore, the debilitating sickness that had ended his own revolt still troubled him. At one point he was so weak he could only travel in a litter. The result was that before Shah Jahan could reach the imperial camp, Mahabat Khan had fled and Nur and Jahangir were once more in control.

Alarmed by Shah Jahan's advance from the south and suspecting that his motives were more than mere solicitude for his father, Nur ordered him back. According to one contemporary account, she wrote informing him that "his march had alarmed Mahabat Khan, whose forces had been driven away and dispersed, and that the prince had better return to the Deccan and await a change of fortune." Shah Jahan contemplated fleeing to Persia but, receiving little encouragement from Shah Abbas, retreated obediently southward with Mumtaz. Nevertheless, Nur still doubted his intentions. She decided to neutralize her two enemies by setting them against each other, ordering Mahabat Khan to block Shah Jahan's path should he try to advance again. However, Mahabat Khan was astute enough to know that Nur would never forgive his seizure of the emperor and would ultimately seek his destruction. His interests, he decided, would be far better served by joining forces with his erstwhile pupil and onetime opponent.

Another factor in Mahabat Khan's thinking, no doubt, was that in October 1626 Shah Jahan's thirty-eight-year-old half-brother Parvez had died. So lost to alcoholism that "little by little he developed an aversion to food," as Jahangir's diarist recorded sadly, he had been suffering fits during which "the physicians had resorted to burning brands and placed five of them on his forehead and temples." Despite, or perhaps because of, such ministrations, he had finally succumbed at Burhanpur—the fortress where Khusrau had been murdered. A few contemporaries speculated whether Shah Jahan might have had a hand in his brother's death, but, far more likely, the hereditary family weakness for alcohol was to blame.

Whatever the case, with Parvez's demise, the contest for the imperial throne on Jahangir's death would be between Jahangir's two surviving sons: Shah Jahan and his younger half-brother, Nur's son-in-law, Shahriyar. It was also clear that that struggle was not far off, for the wheezing, asthmatic Jahangir was growing ever weaker. A sojourn in "the peerless perennial garden of Kashmir" failed to improve his health, and Jahangir returned wearily toward the heat of the plains, having lost even his appetite for the opium on which he had fed for forty years. He seems to have sensed his impending end. His diarist wrote of the "aroma of hopelessness" he exuded. The sight of one of his huntsmen plunging over a high cliff while pursuing an antelope seemed to Jahangir an inauspicious omen, "as though he had thus seen the angel of death." Three days later, on 28 October 1627, as the first pale shafts of morning light penetrated his tent in the mountains above the plains, the fifty-eight-year-old "Seizer of the World" drew his last, labored breaths. He had not named a successor.

A dazed, grief-stricken Nur attempted to convene a council of nobles, but few came, a clear if brutal signal that her power had expired with her husband. Asaf Khan acted swiftly to outmaneuver his sister. On the excuse that "the young princes were not safe with Nur Mahal," but in reality to gain control of them, he removed his grandsons Aurangzeb and Dara Shukoh. After some debate, he entrusted them to a nobleman married to another of his and Nur's sisters who "fluttered around them like a butterfly" in her eagerness to please. He placed Nur under guard in her tent, ordering that no one should have access to her, and ignored her repeated summonses to go to her.

However, Asaf Khan was in a delicate position. His daughter Mumtaz and Shah Jahan were far away. Although he had immediately and secretly dispatched a trusted Hindu messenger bearing his signet ring to inform them of Jahangir's death and urge them to hurry northward, he knew the man would take up to twenty days to reach them. In the meantime, Asaf Khan needed to ensure that Shahriyar, then in Lahore, was not proclaimed emperor. Shahriyar had gone to the city in hopes that the climate of the Punjab would alleviate the symptoms of a disease—possibly leprosy—that had attacked him while in Kashmir and "robbed him of his honour"—a contemporary euphemism for the fact that his beard, mustache, eyebrows and eyelashes and all the rest of his hair had fallen out. Such loss of bodily hair was considered shameful.

Within just hours of Jahangir's death, Asaf Khan found a cunning solution. He convinced his fellow nobles that, with both Shah Jahan and

Shahriyar absent from court, the only way to prevent a vacuum was to offer the throne to Dawar Bakhsh, one of Khusrau's young sons whom Nur had recently ordered to be kept in chains "as a precaution." By this move, Asaf Khan ensured that when Shahriyar challenged for the throne—as he surely must—he would be forced into the mode of rebel and usurper. This would prevent him from mobilizing the imperial armies against Shah Jahan. As for Dawar Bakhsh, he was, as Jahangir's diarist wrote after his master's death, to be "a mere sacrificial lamb." His slaughter would only be deferred until the arrival of Shah Jahan. A European observer predicted that "there is very little hope or chance" for him.

Dawar Bakhsh was an intelligent youth who shared Jahangir's obsession with nature's eccentricities. Several years earlier he had presented his grandfather with, as Jahangir's diarist described, "a tiger, which had an extraordinary affection for a goat, which lived in the same cage with it. They used even to couple and consort together, as if they were animals of the same kind." Dawar Bakhsh was initially suspicious, especially given his father's fate, that he was being induced to accept "a phantom rulership." However, he was eventually won over by the silken-tongued Asaf Khan and the solemn oaths of his confederates. The boy allowed them to proclaim him emperor before setting out, a virtual prisoner, on horseback and surrounded by Asaf Khan and the leading nobles to confront Shahriyar at Lahore. Nur followed a day later, with the body of her dead husband. Asaf Khan had issued strict orders that she was to accompany the cortege every slow step of the journey to the corpse's final resting place.

In Lahore, Shahriyar had indeed been quick to act, spurred by a terse message from Nur—the last she was able to send before being confined—and by the urgings of his wife, Nur's daughter, Ladli. He too claimed the throne, using 7 million rupees purloined from the imperial treasury in the city to buy support and raise an army. However, Asaf Khan's army swiftly defeated his inexperienced forces when they clashed some eight miles from Lahore. A Turkish slave rushed from the battlefield to Shahriyar, hovering indecisively just outside the city, with news of the defeat. The prince took refuge within the Lahore fortress, which soon fell to the attacking forces. A eunuch dragged the hairless, trembling Shahriyar from the sanctuary of the harem. Asaf Khan had him thrown into prison and, two days later, blinded. Dawar Bakhsh, meanwhile, mounted the throne within the citadel but would not occupy it for long.

THE MESSENGER SENT by Asaf Khan reached Shah Jahan at Junnar in the northern Deccan on 18 November. Learning of his arrival, Shah Jahan came hurrying out of the harem, where he had been with Mumtaz. The messenger flung himself to the ground before Shah Jahan, kissed it and handed over Asaf Khan's ring as proof of the story he proceeded to relate. Shah Jahan passed four days in mourning his father, as decency and decorum demanded, but did not demonstrate the deep grief which had so afflicted him as a boy when Akbar died or when, eight years earlier, he had lost his beloved mother. Affection between father and son had withered long before, the victim of ambition on one side and suspicion on the other.

Shah Jahan soon made plans for the march northward. On a day deemed auspicious by his astrologers, he and Mumtaz, who at this momentous time was again pregnant, set out to claim the throne, escorted by Mahabat Khan. As they journeyed on, Shah Jahan received a letter from Asaf Khan "filled with the good news of victory and triumph" over Shahriyar and begging that "his glorious retinue would proceed on wings of haste to rescue the world from chaos"—in other words, warning him to be quick.

Shah Jahan decided to leave as little as possible to chance with respect to the young puppet emperor. Nearing Agra, he dispatched a handwritten message to Asaf Khan in Lahore "to the effect that it would be well if Dawar Bakhsh, the son, and [Shahriyar] the useless brother of Khusrau, and the [two] sons of Prince Daniyal [Jahangir's long-dead brother], were all sent out of the world." His father-in-law obliged, ordering the murder of all four, and, for good measure, of Dawar Bakhsh's younger brother, just two days after receiving Shah Jahan's note. They were probably strangled.*

---

* Some sources state that Dawar Bakhsh in fact escaped to Persia. Jean-Baptiste Tavernier, the French jeweler, later claimed to have encountered him there.

This ruthless removal of one half-brother, two nephews and two cousins eliminated any close Timurid rivals for the imperial throne. A chronicler sympathetic to Shah Jahan excused his actions on the grounds that it was a question of kill or be killed: "Self-preservation, that first principle of the human mind, converted frequently the humane prince into a cruel tyrant, and thus necessity prompted men to actions which their souls perhaps abhorred." The dilemma was neatly encapsulated in the Moghul proverb *Taktya Takhta?* (throne or coffin?). However, this violation of the Timurid code of protection for princes, and the earlier murder of Khusrau, were deeds that would rebound on Shah Jahan.

For the moment, though, Shah Jahan's future and that of his large family seemed assured. Their journey turned into a triumphal progress as governors and local chieftains of the provinces through which they passed hurried to make obeisance and present gifts. The English clerk Peter Mundy, who was in India at the time, the French jeweler Tavernier, who first arrived in 1638, and the Venetian traveler Niccolao Manucci, who reached there in 1656, all wrote highly colored accounts of supposed dramas along the way, which hybridized into a number of far-fetched tales. According to one, the king of Bijapur attempted to prevent Shah Jahan from leaving the Deccan to claim the throne, but Shah Jahan surreptitiously swallowed goat's blood, which he spewed up in front of the king in a colorful simulation of death. Mumtaz then asked leave "to carry her husband's body to be buried in his own country." Her request was granted, and "in a coffin covered with black" the very much alive Shah Jahan was smuggled northward "with all the trappings of woe, and followed by all his people weeping and lamenting as they went." As the supposed funeral cortege approached Agra, Asaf Khan met the party and ordered the coffin to be struck open, whereupon "the fictitious defunct," Shah Jahan, "raised himself and appeared before the eyes of all the army."

Whatever the case, on 24 January 1628, a date deemed favorable by his astrologers, Shah Jahan and his family passed into Agra in a magnificent procession of swaying elephants, "scattering mountains of coins left and right" to the mob whose cheers were half drowned by the booming of the imperial kettledrums. As Asaf Khan had promised, "the high and low of this ageless city of Agra gave him a reception the like of which had not been extended to any ruler before." As the *khutba* had already been read in Shah Jahan's name in Lahore, all that remained was for him to mount the throne in the Halls of Public and Private Audience within the fort. The chosen date was 14 February 1628, the seventy-second anniversary of Akbar's succession to the throne and the 145th anniversary of Babur's birth. Among the lofty titles to which Shah Jahan laid claim were "King of the World," "Meteor of the Faith" and "Second Lord of the Auspicious Conjunctions"—a direct appropriation of the title once proudly used by Timur. Shah Jahan took equal pride that he was the tenth ruler in direct descent from the great Timur.

In a ceremony that literally glittered, jewels sent by Mumtaz and other women of the harem were poured over the new emperor's head. Shah Jahan dispensed silken robes of honor, jeweled swords, flags, drums, and piles of silver, gold and gems to his nobles and received their gifts in return. He appointed his father-in-law, Asaf Khan, who was bringing the young princes from Lahore and was therefore not present, his chief minister—the role Asaf Khan's father, Itimad-ud-daula, had fulfilled for Jahangir—and made Mahabat Khan governor of Ajmer and commander in chief of the imperial armies. Then, retiring into the silk-hung harem, Shah Jahan rewarded the thirty-five-year-old Mumtaz, "that Queen of the Age" who had stood by him through so much. He gave her two hundred thousand gold pieces, six hundred thousand rupees and an annual allowance of 1 million rupees.

A few days later, in early March, Mumtaz was reunited with the young sons from whom she had been parted for more than two years when her father, Asaf Khan, and her mother returned Dara Shukoh and Aurangzeb safely to her. Shah Jahan's official chronicler described in restrained language what must have been a highly emotional occasion: "Her majesty the Queen greatly rejoiced to hear the news of the arrival of the august princes and her respected parents. With royal permission, she rode out to greet her noble parents in the company of Her Highness princess Jahanara Begam and other royal children; and from the other side, the Princes rode onward to meet the litter of Her majesty the Queen. They met at a place . . . where tents had been pitched for the occasion and all were overjoyed to see one another again after the long separation." The next day, escorted by the elite of the nobility, the relieved,

Shah Jahan greeting Dara Shukoh

happy empress and her children proceeded into the imperial capital, where, on the *jharokha* balcony of the Red Fort, the imperial princes showed themselves to the cheering crowds. An exquisite painting in the only illustrated manuscript of the *Padshahnama*, an official chronicle of Shah Jahan's reign, shows the bejeweled emperor in purple robes greeting his sons, who are equally lavishly attired in coats of orange, gold and jade green with ropes of pearls around their necks. The chronicle records that Shah Jahan "much rejoiced at the sight of his children, who had all been born to him by his favourite wife."

These should have been days of harmony and happiness. Mumtaz could introduce the returned princes to the new brother they had never seen: the fifteen-month-old Sultan Lutf Allah, born during her uncertain exile with Shah Jahan. Of the eleven offspring born since her marriage sixteen years earlier, eight were alive and apparently thriving at this time. Yet within just three months of Shah Jahan's accession to the throne, this would change. In late April 1628, shortly before Mumtaz was due to give birth, their seven-year-old daughter Sorayya Bano died of smallpox. Then, on 9 May 1628, a court chronicler reported that "an auspicious star appeared in the sky"—Mumtaz had borne Shah Jahan another son, his eighth, Sultan Daulat Afza. Yet if joy at this event helped mitigate previous sorrows, it was short-lived. Five days later, "while everyone was enjoying the gifts of this world" and Shah Jahan was distributing largesse to everyone from high-ranking nobles to "the turbaned religious scholars, deserving persons and musicians and dancers" and lavishing gifts on his beloved Mumtaz, little Sultan Lutf Allah, "owing to the perverseness of obstinate heaven," departed suddenly "to the asylum of the world beyond."

Though people were accustomed to relatively high rates of child mortality at this time, the death of an infant in the imperial family was always deeply mourned, and the death of two children within such a short time at the outset of the reign must have seemed a bad omen. European observers were also uneasy about what the new reign would bring, but on different grounds. One wrote, "As to the nature of the present ruler, it is impossible as yet to express an opinion, though it is easy to foretell that a reign inaugurated by so many crimes will prove to be ill-starred, and that a throne buttressed by the shedding of so much innocent blood will prove to be insecure."

CHAPTER EIGHT

The Peacock Throne

DESPITE THE DIFFICULTIES OF HIS LATTER years, Jahangir had not been unsuccessful. Although he had not significantly increased the Moghul territories and had, indeed, lost Kandahar to the Persians, he had curbed the ambitions of the ever-restive rulers in the Deccan, eliminated pockets of resistance in Rajasthan and left a relatively stable empire. His greatest problems had been the rebellions of his own sons—the recklessly impatient Khusrau at the beginning of his reign and Bi-daulat (the Wretch) Shah Jahan—toward its end.

By contrast, in 1628, as Shah Jahan took control, with Mumtaz beside him, he was, at thirty-six, in his prime and had no fear of internecine struggles. He was also a very different character from his father. Though both were sensualists, deeply receptive to beauty and appreciative of luxury, Shah Jahan was the more vigorous and self-disciplined. Unlike Jahangir, he had proved himself early on the battlefield and also unlike him he was not an excessive drinker. His historian recorded that despite his father's urgings he had drunk only sparingly as a young man "during festivals and on cloudy days" and in 1620 had renounced wine entirely.

A portrait from the first year of his reign—one of a stream of paintings the image-conscious Shah Jahan commissioned to celebrate his achievements—shows the new emperor in profile against a rich green background. His black, neatly trimmed mustache and beard accentuate a strong, finely modeled face. His large pearl earring, and the ropes of pearls interlaced with gems around his neck and wrist and binding his orange turban, accentuate rather than diminish his masculinity. Shah Jahan looks, as he no doubt intended, the picture of virility and control, his right hand gripping the hilt of his sword while, with his left, he holds the royal seal on which are etched the names of his ancestors going back to Timur.

For the next eighteen months Shah Jahan, Mumtaz and their children would live a peaceful existence in the Red Fort at Agra. The sumptuous quarters of the imperial harem must have been welcome to Mumtaz. After her peripatetic life as Shah Jahan's faithful "companion during travels," she could now be his "source of solace at home." With more than one hundred female attendants and a personal staff of eunuchs she could take her ease in the richly furnished apartments once dominated by her aunt Nur.

Shah Jahan not only loved architecture but was conscious that undertaking building projects was one way in which he could forge for his new reign a new image to distinguish him from his predecessors and inspire awe at his majesty. He was therefore already considering how to remodel the Agra fort to make it yet more impressive in its public apartments and luxurious in its private ones. In particular he decided to replace some of Akbar's robust sandstone structures with airy "sky-touching" pavilions of pure white marble and spacious courtyards where rosewater fountains would play.

In Shah Jahan's private apartments overlooking the Jumna, sunlight was filtered through thin, flower-etched marble panels that reduced its harshness to a soft radiance. The Moghuls lived much of their lives in subdued light. When the summer sun grew too bright, their attendants excluded it with silken hangings. To enhance the cooling effect of breezes, they covered the arched windows with *tattis*, screens filled with the roots of scented kass grass, down which they trickled water, creating fragrant drafts of air. In winter they hung velvets and brocades around the royal chambers to keep out the sometimes chilling winds.

Anticipating future visits to "paradise-like" Kashmir with Mumtaz, Shah Jahan also sent orders for extending the Shalimar Gardens. In particular, he ordered the governor of Kashmir to oversee the building of a domed, open-sided black marble pavilion to counterpoint the existing white marble one. Set among vines, apple, almond and peach trees and

Shah Jahan and Mumtaz's apartments in the Red Fort at Agra

circular pools of water, the new area of garden was to be named the Faiz Bakhsh, the "Bestower of Bounties." Mumtaz herself began to lay out a terraced pleasure garden of her own on the banks of the Jumna—the only architectural project known to have been undertaken by her and probably the only one for which she ever had time and opportunity.*

Her children had their own adjacent quarters in the harem and were frequently with her. She was especially attached to her eldest daughter, Jahanara, who, in the words of a chronicler, was "sensible, lively and generous, elegant in her person" and who closely resembled Mumtaz. Mumtaz's father and mother lived nearby in an opulent mansion along the Jumna, and Asaf Khan was daily in attendance on Shah Jahan at court in his position of chief minister. According to a court chronicler, soon after his accession Shah Jahan had begun addressing Asaf Khan affectionately as "Uncle," making him the envy of all.

---

* Mumtaz's riverside garden, today known as the Zahara Bagh, lies to the south of the Ram Bagh, a garden once cultivated by her aunt Nur.

Another symbol of Shah Jahan's esteem for his father-in-law were the visits he paid him when, with Mumtaz and his children, he went in state to his house. Asaf Khan observed the ritual niceties, "spreading a carpet under his Majesty's feet and scattering money over his head" and "presenting excellent gifts like gems, jewelled ornaments, fabrics, Qibchaqi horses and mountain-like elephants with gold and silver trappings." The imperial family used to remain there for several days of music, dancing and elaborate feasting.

Nur was not, of course, a part of this tight-knit family circle. Passion and ambition spent, she had accepted her defeat with characteristic common sense and retired into obscurity in Lahore with the daughter, Ladli, whom she had failed to make empress in place of Mumtaz. She lived on the pension of two hundred thousand rupees a year granted her by Shah Jahan. In her distant seclusion she no doubt took comfort in the recollection of the small but exquisite mausoleum she had begun building for her father, Itimad-ud-daula, and her mother six years earlier on the eastern banks of the Jumna and which was completed in the year of her fall.

The mausoleum was set within a traditional walled garden, amid channels of cool, flowing water and framed by rows of dark trees. She had created an ethereal structure clad in gleaming white marble, low and square in shape under a canopied dome and with octagonal minaret-like towers at each corner, their tapering pinnacles surmounted with lotus petals. Walls and floors were intricately inlaid, some with geometric patterns, others with the graceful, naturalistic shapes of flowers utilizing for the first time in India polished semiprecious stones—cornelian, lapis lazuli, jasper, onyx and topaz—as inlay. This tomb, and another tomb complex built in Delhi at around the same time known as the Chausath Khamba, were the first Moghul buildings to be entirely covered in the white marble that was to become a feature of Shah Jahan's buildings. Until this time white marble had, by convention, been reserved for the tombs of Islamic holy men as symbolizing paradise.* The overall effect was of some superbly bejeweled ornament rather than a quite small building.

---

* An exception is the fifteenth-century white marble tomb of Hoshang Shah, the Muslim ruler of the fortress city of Mandu.

Itimad-ud-daula's tomb in Agra

Nur next devoted herself to the creation of a mausoleum for her husband, who had wished, like Babur, to be buried beneath the open sky. She chose a site in the vast Dilkusha Garden outside Lahore, which she had built and enjoyed with Jahangir in happier days. The design was simple: a cenotaph placed on a platform, itself resting on a giant rectangular podium with minarets at each corner. There was again inlay work, but more restrained than in Itimad-ud-daula's tomb.* Nur also began building her own tomb nearby, modeled on her husband's. In the surrounding gardens she planted fragrant roses and sweet-smelling jasmine.

SHAH JAHAN, MEANWHILE, continued to foster the aura of unprecedented splendor that would characterize his reign. Like his grandfather Akbar, he

---

* Shah Jahan may also have had a hand in the construction of his father's tomb.

Jahangir's tomb in Lahore

ordered the key events of his reign to be chronicled in detail, and he selected the writers with care, changing them at intervals and approving
their work only after regular detailed personal scrutiny.* Though writing
in the flattering, flowery language of the time, they convey the undoubted
magnificence of his court. So do the accounts of bedazzled European visitors. The English ambassador Sir Thomas Roe had thought the court of
Jahangir at times a little vulgar, but in comparison with what followed it

---

* The most important official chroniclers of Shah Jahan's reign were Mirza Amina
  Qazwini, who wrote the fullest account of Shah Jahan's princehood; Abdul Hamid
  Lahori, who wrote a detailed account of the first twenty-six years of Shah Jahan's
  reign, the *Padshahnama*; Muhammed Waris, Lahori's pupil, who extended Lahori's
  account up to and including the thirtieth year of Shah Jahan's reign and Inayat
  Khan, keeper of Shah Jahan's library, whose work effectively summarized that of
  his predecessors. Muhammed Salih Kambo, although not an official court historian, was a member of the court records department and wrote a detailed account
  of Shah Jahan's reign using the official histories as a base and adding his own recollections while taking the reign through to its close.

was positively muted. According to one early chronicler, "The pompous shows of the favourite Sultana [Nur], in the late reign, vanished in the superior grandeur of those exhibited by Shah Jahan."

One of Shah Jahan's first acts was to commission the famous Takht-i-Taus, or "Peacock Throne," to display the most splendid gems in the imperial collection. A true connoisseur, he selected the stones himself from the seven treasure houses spread across his empire. The treasury at Agra alone held 750 pounds of pearls, 275 pounds of emeralds and corals, and topazes and other semiprecious gems beyond count. The Venetian traveler Niccolao Manucci, who saw two of these repositories, was impressed both by their scale and construction. They were, he wrote, "square cisterns seventy feet long and thirty feet high, with two handsome marble pillars in the middle" and sealed off from the great halls above them by trap doors.

The eight-foot-long, six-foot-wide, twelve-foot-high throne would take seven years and 1,150 kilos of gold to complete. According to Shah Jahan's court historian, Lahori, "The outside of the canopy was to be of enamel work with occasional gems, the inside was to be thickly set with rubies, garnets and other jewels and it was to be supported by twelve emerald columns. On the top of each pillar there were to be two peacocks thick set with gems, and between each two peacocks a tree set with rubies and diamonds, emeralds and pearls. The ascent was to consist of three steps set with jewels of fine water."

The design may have borrowed from the legend of King Solomon's throne. This relates how four golden palms, aglitter with green emeralds and dark red topaz, stood around Solomon's throne—two topped with golden eagles and two with golden peacocks. According to an Islamic tradition, the peacock was once guardian of the gateway to paradise. The bird consumed the devil but then carried the devil into paradise in its stomach, there to escape and set his snare for Adam and Eve.*

---

* The emerald, the oldest known true gemstone, is especially prized by Muslims, who consider green the color of Islam. Furthermore, the emerald has long been venerated in India for its religious and astrological significance. It was first found in Egypt almost five thousand years ago, and the Romans plundered Cleopatra's mines for it. By Shah Jahan's time emeralds also came from South America.

When the French jeweler Jean-Baptiste Tavernier saw the throne in 1665, he recorded just one peacock, "with elevated tail made of blue sapphires and other coloured stones, the body of gold inlaid with precious stones, having a large ruby in front of the breast, whence hangs a pear-shaped pearl of 50 carats or thereabouts." Other accounts of the actual throne also suggest slight variations to the design described by Lahori, but what is clear is that the throne contained the most important collection of gemstones ever assembled in one artifact. Casting a professional eye over it, Tavernier counted 108 large rubies, none less than 100 karats, and some 116 emeralds, all between 30 and 60 karats.

Festivals also provided opportunities to awe onlookers with Moghul might and wealth. At the first Nauroz festival of Shah Jahan's reign, celebrated in March 1628, a court historian recorded how "three thousand skilful tentmen with the traction of a thousand kinds of mechanical science" pitched a great tent of state within the Red Fort at Agra. Court tents were no longer the practical, simple yurtlike structures of Babur's day, but sophisticated, complex constructions dripping with awnings and canopies. Chroniclers eulogized Shah Jahan's giant marquee as "the great tent of the heavens" or "the mass of clouds." It was made of gold-brocaded velvet supported by columns of silver and gold. Beneath this "silver trellis tents with coverings of velvet brocaded and embroidered with gold, and many-coloured carpets and ornamental rugs were spread: thrones and golden seats were set out, and parasols, jewelled with pearls falling in drops, were erected." Doors and walls were decked with cloth of gold from Gujarat, European curtains, brocades from Turkey and China, and cloth of gold from Iraq.

As the centerpiece, Shah Jahan had to be as impressive as his surroundings. He no longer wore the relatively simple pearl-tipped heron's plume of his ancestors in his turban, but an elaborately jeweled spray designed to show off his choicest gems. As a young prince, the jeweled aigrettes brought by European visitors as gifts to his father's court had caught his eye and served as a model. The style of the turban itself also changed during his reign. The gossamer-light material weighing only some four ounces was still wound around the head in the same way, but a band of the same fabric or in a contrasting color was used to hold the turban more tightly upon the head. Like Jahangir, Shah Jahan wore lavishly embroidered, full-skirted coats of silk or brocade and, in cold weather, soft Kashmiri shawls draped elegantly over one shoulder and quilted overcoats lined with costly furs like sable. In hot weather he wore tunics of fine muslin or satin. However, with the eye for the romantic of an English cavalier, he adopted the fashion of fastening his clothes with wide ribbons a foot long, leaving some untied to flutter with negligent grace.

The most spectacular festival after the Nauroz was the ceremonial weighing of the emperor on his birthday. The ceremony, rooted originally in a Hindu tradition, had been adopted by Humayun. Akbar made it more sophisticated, introducing two weighings: a public ceremony on the solar birthday and a private ceremony on the lunar birthday, usually conducted within the harem. (The solar and lunar birthdays coincided only on the day the emperor was born and separated thereafter by eleven days a year.) On the first lunar birthday of his reign, 27 November 1628, Shah Jahan was weighed against a variety of materials including gold. Akbar and Jahangir had only had themselves weighed against gold on their solar birthday, but, reflecting his determined desire to surpass his predecessors in splendor, Shah Jahan included gold in both ceremonies.

The Augustinian friar Sebastien Manrique, witness to one of Shah Jahan's later weighing ceremonies, described how in the center of "a richly decorated private chamber adorned with all the most precious and valued products of the world . . . there hung, securely fastened by thick chains of gold, a pair of scales made of the same metal, their circular edges being set with many rich stones. The Imperial Majesty came forth dressed in a white satin robe covered with most precious stones of many colours which, while they pleased one by their many colours on the one hand, on the other astonished one by their size . . . On reaching the balance . . . the Emperor squatted in one pan, and at once officials commenced to fill the other pan with bags full of silver, coined into rupees, until the weights were equalized . . . This weighing over, they removed the silver . . . They then made a second weighing with other bags full of gold and precious stones. After adjusting this they made a third weighment with different kinds of cotton cloth, woven with gold, silver, and silk. They also added . . . certain precious spices and various drugs. The fourth and last weighment was made against eatables, such as wheaten cakes, flour, sugar, ghee, and the common kinds of cotton cloth."

Fighting of Elephants, *by Peter Mundy*

Officials carefully calculated the monetary value of the first three weighings, and the money was distributed as alms to the poor, together with
the commonplace goods of the last weighing. However, as the friar
noted, the emperor was more than compensated for his generosity by
the enormous quantities of gifts he received from all the grandees of the
court, writing sourly of his "insatiable avarice."

Festivals often concluded with an elephant fight. The elephants were
named for their attributes, like Good Mover, Mountain Destroyer, Ever
Bold. An earth rampart, four feet high and six feet wide and intended
initially to keep the elephants apart and define their respective "territory," was thrown up on the plains near the River Jumna. The emperor
and women of the court looked down from their respective apartments
within the Agra fort, screened of course in the case of the ladies, as two
great elephants faced each other from opposite sides of the earth wall,
"each having a couple of riders [so] that the place of the man who sits on
the shoulders, for the purpose of guiding the elephant with a large iron
hook, may immediately be [taken] if he should be thrown down" as a European visitor noted. "The riders animate the elephants either by soothing words, or by chiding them as cowards, and urge them on with their
heels, until the poor creatures approach the wall and are brought to the
attack. The shock is tremendous, and it appears surprising that they ever
survive the dreadful wounds and blows inflicted with their tusks, their
heads, and their trunks." The fights were also highly hazardous for the
riders, who on the day of the combat took "formal leave of their wives
and children as if condemned to death."

Unsurprisingly at a court where so much depended on outward show,
Moghul etiquette was complex and formal. Indeed, it bore many similar-
ities to that of the French court, at that time probably the most sophisticated and regulated in Europe. Knocking on a superior's door was
considered equally vulgar at both the French and Moghul courts. In
France courtiers were expected to scratch on the door with the little finger of their left hand; in Agra they dropped to their knees and respectfully rapped three times with the back of the hand. At both courts the
respective status of individual courtiers was precisely calculated. In
France the height of the chair in which a noble was permitted to sit in
the royal presence signaled the level of his prestige; at Shah Jahan's

Shah Jahan with an audience of mullahs

court to be allowed to sit at all in the emperor's presence was a coveted honor awarded only to the very few, reflecting the idea that the emperor was master and everyone else the slave. Not even the royal princes could sit unless so honored by their father.

Both Shah Jahan and Louis XIV, who came to the French throne in 1643, spent much of their long reigns on public display. Louis's day was governed by a series of public ceremonies from the *lever* when he arose, relieved himself and was dressed in public, the *debotter* when he changed after hunting, the public procession to the chapel to pray, the receiving of petitions and of foreign ambassadors and the *coucher* when he was disrobed and put to bed in front of his subjects. Shah Jahan's day began two hours before dawn, "while the stars are still visible in the night sky," when he

A stone grille behind which women viewed court proceedings

awoke in the scented air of the imperial harem in the Agra fort, washed and prayed for the first of five times. As the sun rose, he appeared to his people on the *jharokha-i-darshan*, the "balcony of viewing," jutting out over the sandy banks of the River Jumna below. As one of Shah Jahan's court historians carefully reminded his readers, "The object of the institution of this mode of audience, which originated with the late Emperor Akbar, was to enable His majesty's subjects to witness the simultaneous appearance of the sky-adorning sun and the world-conquering Emperor, and thereby receive without any obstacle or hindrance the blessing of both these luminaries." The emperor's daily appearance—known as the *darshan* from a Sanskrit word meaning "the viewing of a saint or idol"—also allowed "the harassed and oppressed of the population" to "freely represent their wants and desires." While the masses assembled beyond the fort walls stared up at their emperor, Shah Jahan watched "furious wild man-killing elephants" paraded for his amusement on the riverbank below, or soldiers drilling or sometimes the antics of jugglers and acrobats.

Shah Jahan's brass royal seal

Next, Shah Jahan proceeded to the richly carpeted, balustraded Hall of Public Audience, where his nobles and officials awaited him, eyes downcast, absolutely still and silent "like a wall." Every man's proximity to the throne was carefully calculated according to his rank. Just before eight o'clock, a cacophony of trumpets and drums signaled the aproach of the "Lord of the World" as Shah Jahan stepped through a door from the harem into the throne alcove at the back of the hall. Mumtaz watched and listened through stone grilles cut into the alcove wall as her husband dealt with petitions, received reports, inspected choice gifts and examined horses and elephants from the imperial stables, punishing their keepers if the animals looked malnourished. Any man approaching Shah Jahan was required to make a series of low bows, brushing the ground with the back of the right hand and placing the right palm against the forehead. On reaching the emperor, the man was required to bend yet lower, pressing his right hand to the ground and kissing its back. Under Jahangir he would have been expected to put his forehead to the ground, but Shah Jahan had abolished this action, which had originated with Akbar, as a concession to the Islamic clerics who considered that it too closely simulated prostration in prayer and was therefore blasphemous.

After about two hours, the emperor retired to the Hall of Private Audience with his senior advisers to discuss important matters of state, receive foreign ambassadors and, on Wednesdays, to dispense justice to "broken-hearted oppressed persons," as his court chroniclers called the supplicants. Shah Jahan, who was a skilled calligrapher, wrote out some of his orders himself. Others were recorded by "eloquent secretaries" and then checked and corrected by the emperor, after which they were "sent to the sacred seraglio to be ornamented with the exalted royal seal, which is in the keeping of Her Majesty the Queen, Mumtaz al-Zamani." This enabled Mumtaz to review important documents before they were issued. Shah Jahan also gave her the right to issue her own orders and make appointments. In a surviving document of October 1628, she directed government officials to restore a man to a position that had been usurped by another. At the same time she ordered the reinstated man "to adhere to the prescribed rules and regulations of His Majesty; to treat the peasants and inhabitants in such a manner that they should be satisfied and grateful to him . . . and to ensure that not a single rupee of government revenue should be lost or wasted." Mumtaz's round, elegant seal was inscribed with a Persian verse:

> By the grace of God in this world Mumtaz Mahal has
> become
> Companion of Shah Jahan the shadow of God.

Mumtaz was undoubtedly influential; all accounts agree that Shah Jahan sought her advice on key matters. However, she operated very differently from the imperious Nur. Her softer, more discreet approach was a factor of her personality and of the nature of her relationship with the man she had known and loved since both were in their teens. It may also have reflected her awareness that Jahangir had been ridiculed by both his courtiers and foreigners for his obvious and public subjection to Nur's strident authority. Before his rebellion Mahabat Khan had, according to an anonymous chronicler, complained that no king in history had ever been "so subject to the will of his wife" and, he could have added, so little subject to the views of his nobles. The same chronicler commented that "Nur Jahan Begum had wrought so much upon his mind that if 200 men like Mahabat Khan had advised him simultaneously to the same effect, their words would have made no permanent impression upon him."

Nur had, of course, married Jahangir as a mature, worldly wise widow.

While there seems little doubt that she genuinely loved him, it is also clear that she had an equal affection for power. She had indulged, mothered and protected him, but above all she had controlled him, influencing his decisions and, latterly, making them for him. Mumtaz did not control Shah Jahan. She was, in every sense, his partner. The physical, emotional and intellectual bonds that had sustained them through exile and flight sustained them now as emperor and empress. Unlike Nur, Mumtaz remained strictly behind the veil, and her main desire was for her husband's contentment. A court poet rejoiced that

> No dust from her behaviour ever settled
> On the mirror of the Emperor's mind.

> She was always seeking to please the King;
> She knew full well the King of Kings' temperament.

> Despite her power as the consort of the king
> She always displayed conformity and obedience to him.

The third, most secret layer of government was the private meetings of the privy council in the Royal Tower, to which, after completing business in the Hall of Private Audience and sending any documents into the harem for Mumtaz to see, Shah Jahan summoned only "the fortunate princes and a few trusted confidants," including, of course, his father-in-law, Asaf Khan.

Shah Jahan could, however, discuss all the day's official business with Mumtaz when, at around noon, he repaired to the security of the harem to eat with the empress and other ladies of the household, including his daughters Jahanara and eleven-year-old Raushanara. After washing, they ate cross-legged on the sumptuously carpeted floor, which was protected at mealtimes by pieces of hide covered with white cloths.

The food was an elaborate and exquisite fusion. The Moghuls had brought with them to India a cuisine already containing influences from Persia, the Middle East and central Asia. From Persia and Afghanistan came the use of dried fruits such as apricots and sultanas as well as almonds and other nuts. From the Middle East and the nomadic tradition

they brought with them the spit roasting of lamb, either whole or as ke-
babs. (*Kebab* is an Urdu word.) From central Asia derived a greater use of
root vegetables, such as turnips and carrots, all mixed together with pep-
pers, mutton and buttered rice in pulaos designed to give energy to resist
the winter's cold. The Moghuls relished the sweet-and-sour contrasts today associated with the Far East. They frequently added sugar and lemon
syrups to their dishes, and salt often counterpointed sweet tastes.

The Moghuls quickly assimilated the many native flavors and influences of India, particularly those of the Hindu vegetarian tradition.
These included the use of yogurts and of many different seeds and grains.
A favorite dish of Shah Jahan's was rice and lentils mixed with butter
and spices—a sophisticated version of an Indian peasant dish known as
*khichari.** Other borrowings from Indian cuisine included the mouth-
puckering, mouth-watering taste of tamarind, so unlike any other flavor,
and the use of turmeric, both as coloring and flavoring. New conquests
brought new additions to the Moghul menu. The absorption of Kashmir
intensified the use of green vegetables such as spinach and kohlrabi, as
well as adding more waterfowl, such as ducks, to the diet.

The Moghuls also enjoyed the varieties of fruit they found in India,
prizing tastes, textures and scents very different from their traditional fare
of the apples and pears of central Asia and the pomegranates, oranges, figs
and dates of Persia and the Middle East. Even Babur said that "when the
mango is good it is really good," although he did complain that good ones
were scarce. His successors enjoyed the banana, the custard apple and, as
the records show, even the jackfruit, which Babur had dismissed as "unbelievably ugly and bad tasting—it looks exactly like sheep's intestines
turned inside out like stuffed tripe [and] has a cloyingly sweet taste." Jahangir wrote how his father, Akbar, planted another New World import,
the pineapple, "found in the Franks' ports. It is extremely good smelling
and tasting. Several thousand are produced every year . . . in Agra."

By Shah Jahan and Mumtaz's time, ingredients from the New World,
like the potato—now an Indian staple—were beginning to be brought

---

* *Khichari* was the origin of the popular Anglo-Indian dish kedgeree, which, with its
  ingredients of hard-boiled eggs and smoked fish, departed significantly from the
  original.

into India by traders from the Americas.* Cinnamon, cloves, pepper, cardamom, coriander and anise seeds and fresh ginger were the main spices, but chili—another New World import—would soon join them. Recipes were complex and subtle. An Englishman even marveled at the skill with which rice was boiled "so artfully that every grain lies singly without being added together with spices intermixt and a boiled fowl in the middle." Sophisticated recipes survive showing how chickens were boned and stuffed whole with other meats, eggs, coriander and ginger Dumpukht—meat or chicken smothered in almonds and then braised in butter and yogurt—was another favorite. The Indian *dum* means "breath," and the Moghul cooks used to allow dishes to rest, or "take breath," just before serving, as called for by modern chefs. Some recipes required dishes to be smoked by a hot charcoal being placed in the middle of a casserole full of food which was then sealed for about a quarter of an hour to allow the smoky flavor to permeate.

The royal kitchens were an independent department. Here cooks kept food in such a state of preparedness that one hundred dishes could be ready within an hour of the emperor giving the command. For feasts, gold and silver leaf was used to garnish the food, as well as fruit and herbs. The food was served in dishes made of gold and silver and sometimes of a kind of jade said to be an antidote to poison.

Buwa, the mother of the slain sultan of Delhi, had tried to kill Babur through introducing poison into the new Indian dishes he was tasting, and poison remained a constant concern. Awnings screened the cooks when they were at work to inhibit prying eyes. Cooks had to tuck up their sleeves and hems before removing the food from pans or ovens to make sure they could introduce no extraneous matter. The cooks who had produced the individual dishes tasted the emperor's meals followed by their supervisors and finally by the head of the kitchens.†

---

* A recent DNA study found that all the world's cultivated potatoes derive from a single species native to southern Peru.

† Karim's Restaurant in the teeming streets of Old Delhi is run by descendants of chefs of the Moghul court who claim that "cooking royal food is our hereditary profession."

Before the food was taken to the harem, each dish was individually wrapped in cloths and the head of the kitchen wrote a description of the contents, which he affixed to the cloth together with his seal so that no dish could be swapped. Then the cooks and other servants carried the bowls to the harem. Mace bearers and guards went before and behind them to keep malcontents away. The kitchen head accompanied the procession and remained at the gate under the eyes of the guards until the meal was completed. Once in the harem, the eunuchs and women servants again tasted the food before arranging the dishes in front of Shah Jahan and Mumtaz Mahal.

As was the custom in the Islamic world and in India, the food was eaten with the fingers of the right hand (never the left). Servants stood by to fetch more food or to brush off flies, impossible to avoid at some times of the year, with horsehair whisks. Once dinner was over, a fine flour made of pulses was used to clear grease from the fingers, which were then washed, and the mouth rinsed.

The kitchen department took much trouble in procuring the best ingredients available. A list of comparative prices produced by Abul Fazl, about thirty years before Shah Jahan came to the throne, shows that a duck, which often had to be brought from Kashmir, could cost up to half the price of a whole sheep, while a first-quality melon transported down the Khyber Pass from Kabul cost much more than either.

There was a separate department for drinking water and ice. Like mineral water connoisseurs today, each of the emperors had a different taste in water. Akbar had preferred Ganges water, and runners carried supplies to him daily wherever he was, in jars sealed to prevent tampering. Jahangir was less fussy but sensibly preferred flowing or spring water to that stored in a tank for any length of time. Shah Jahan drank only what he called "the molten snow" of the Jumna. In the summer all three liked their water and sherbets to be cooled. Boats, carts and runners brought ice from the northwestern mountains, and saltpeter was also sometimes used as a cooling agent. The imperial family drank from cups of green or white jade or pale, rose-hued agate.

———————

AFTER THE MIDDAY repast, Shah Jahan rested, but, his historian rather self-righteously claimed, did not indulge in sex at this stage of the working day. "Even in the sacred seraglio, His Majesty—unlike other negligent Kings—refrains from indulging in carnal lusts and sensual pleasures, and instead devotes himself to granting requests of the poor." Mumtaz relied on her gifted Persian friend Satti al-Nisa Khanan to bring to her attention cases of impoverished girls in need of dowries, ornaments and clothes, or of destitute widows and orphans in want of pensions or grants of land, so that she could place them before her husband, who would in turn order their needs to be met. Satti had, according to court historians, become Mumtaz's confidante "owing to her confidence, eloquent tongue, excellent service and noble etiquette." Well versed in the Koran, she instructed Mumtaz's daughter Jahanara in the writing of Persian verses and prose, a talent Mumtaz also shared.

The emperor devoted the rest of the afternoon and early evening to outstanding business, appearing again in the audience chambers and at prayers in the fort mosque. At about eight o'clock he returned to the harem for the evening meal and the night's entertainment: "beautiful songs or stirring melodies," sometimes a game of chess with Mumtaz, played with pieces of ivory, sandalwood, silver or gold, or a bout of love-making. By this hour of the evening, the imperial household was lit by the soft glow of hundreds of thousands of lamps, torches and candles. A court officer maintained the household's source of fire, a sacred flame flickering in an *agingir* (firepot). It was renewed once a year, at noon, on the day when the sun moved into the nineteenth degree of Aries in a ritual introduced by Akbar, because of his adoration of fire and light. Attendants exposed a brilliant white stone to the hot rays. Then they placed a piece of fine cotton near the hot stone until it burst into flame.

Every day at sunset, imperial servants lit twelve camphor-scented candles and carried them, in candlesticks of silver and gold, before the emperor. A court singer raised his voice in praise of God and prayed for the continuance of the auspicious reign. The whole palace was then lit up. Some candlesticks were huge. Akbar had devised a candelabra in which five candlesticks, each in the shape of an animal, stood on a base over three feet tall. White wax candles, nine feet high and more, burned in it, and attendants scaled ladders to snuff them out.

Palace lighting varied with the phases of the moon. On the first three nights of every lunar month, when the period of moonlight was briefest, eight wicks were placed in giant brass, bronze or copper *diyas*, shallow saucers filled with mustard oil. Servants positioned the saucers in niches in the walls along corridors and passages. From the fourth to the tenth day of the lunar month, they progressively reduced the number of wicks by one a night, so that by the tenth night, when the moonbeams shone brightest, only one wick burned. So it continued until the sixteenth night, when they gradually increased the number again.

The soft lighting enhanced the sensuous feel of the harem, where the weary new emperor rested after his long day. Even after sixteen years of marriage and twelve children, Mumtaz clearly still held a unique sexual attraction for Shah Jahan. She was by now in her late thirties, an age at which most wives and concubines were considered too old for sex, but as with her aunt Nur, her beauty must have endured. She could also rely on a formidable battery of cosmetics to beautify and purify her body for the imperial bed, including concoctions of flowers, seeds and oils to give added luster to black hair, black powdered antimony sulfide—kohl—to rim her eyes and pastes of burned conch shells and banana juice to remove unwanted hair.*

Mumtaz also had available the most seductive of clothes—thin silks in rainbow hues from pale apricot to lilac to ruby red and diaphanous, gossamer-thin muslins which, because of their fine texture, were given names like "running water," "woven air" and "evening dew." They were made up into tight-fitting *salvars* (pajamas)—which fastened with bunches of pearls—tight *cholis* (bodices) half concealing the breasts and a V-necked *pesvaj* (a long transparent coat open to the ankles from its fastening at the breast).

Though the clothes of Moghul women were still heavily Turkish in style, they had adopted Hindu ways of dressing their hair. Instead of simply wearing it loose and parted, they had begun twisting it "into a flat

---

* Moghul beauty aids were more appealing than contemporaneous European ones, where women mixed cat dung with urine to remove unwanted hair and fashioned false eyebrows from mouse skins.

pad at the back from which a few curls rolled on." Mumtaz draped her head with golden veils or wore turbans of bright silk with waving ostrich plumes. As the favorite wife of an emperor who was passionate about gems, she must also have possessed the most fabulous and elaborate of jewels. Some slight hint of what she must have worn comes from a European doctor allowed to treat a woman of the imperial harem. He complained that he was unable to locate his patient's pulse because of the "very rich bracelets or bands of pearls which usually go round nine or twelve times."

The sexual gratification of the emperor was paramount, and there were techniques Mumtaz could use to make her vagina, the *madan-mandir* (temple of love), slackened through constant pregnancies, contract to enhance his pleasure. She could delicately apply such fragrant pastes as camphor mixed with honey, lotus flowers crushed in milk, or pounded pomegranate skins to the vagina walls. However, the need for women to experience sexual pleasure was also understood, and a range of aphrodisiac concoctions existed to help women achieve orgasm. Some, like powdered ginger and black pepper, mixed with the honey of a large bee, were applied inside the vagina. Other aphrodisiac concoctions were smeared on the lover's penis two hours before intercourse; by stimulating and enlarging the organ, they were said to heighten the woman's sensation. There were also methods of delaying male ejaculation, some involving swallowing opium, and aphrodisiacs claimed to be so effective that they gave a man the sexual energy of a stallion. A set of stimulants collectively named the Making of the Horse was particularly popular.

Whatever techniques he and Mumtaz may have used, after making love Shah Jahan liked to be lulled to sleep by dulcet-toned women concealed behind a screen who read aloud from his favorite works, which included Babur's memoirs or accounts of Timur's conquests. However, his own call to battle came quicker than he might have hoped or wanted. As one European visitor remarked of the Moghul Empire, "[The ruler] who without reluctancy submitted to the Moghul's power, while his camp was near, immediately disclaims it when he knows the camp is at a distance, which commotions bring on the Moghul endless trouble and expense."

This time the source of trouble was once more the wealthy, disaffected sultans of the Deccan. Despite the successive Moghul campaigns against them, the rulers of Bijapur, Ahmednagar and Golconda remained ever alert for an opportunity to defy their nominal overlords. The catalyst this time was the defection from the Moghul court of Khan Jahan Lodi, a nobleman who had once been a great favorite of Jahangir. Khan Jahan had guarded Agra against Shah Jahan during the latter's rebellion against his father, and Jahangir had subsequently appointed him governor of the Deccan. This proud, independent-minded man was descended from the Afghan Lodi sultans, one of the dynasties that had ruled in Delhi until unseated by Babur. When Shah Jahan became emperor, Khan Jahan had conspicuously failed to come to Agra to make his obeisance, pleading ill health. Shah Jahan had subsequently ordered him to court, and reluctantly he had obeyed. After his arrival, a still suspicious Shah Jahan asked him to disband his followers and confiscated some of his lands.

This was too much for Khan Jahan, who, on an October night in 1629, fled Agra at the head of two thousand Afghans back toward the Deccan. Shah Jahan at once dispatched imperial troops in pursuit. They quickly caught up with Khan Jahan and confronted his forces on the banks of the Chambal River, some forty miles from Agra. After a furious and bloody struggle during which two of Khan Jahan's sons, two of his brothers and many of his followers were killed, he escaped across the swollen river and made his way to the kingdom of Ahmednagar, whose ruler welcomed him as an ally and put him in charge of his forces.

In late 1629 Shah Jahan prepared to march south with his armies. His plan was not only to crush Ahmednagar for harboring and encouraging his enemy but also to pursue a full-blown subjugation of Bijapur and Golconda. Mumtaz, well advanced into her thirteenth pregnancy, was, as usual, to accompany her husband. She would never again see Agra or her newly sown, terraced gardens just sprouting into life on the banks of the Jumna.

CHAPTER NINE

"Build for Me a Mausoleum"

A MOGHUL ARMY ON THE MOVE WAS, in the words of the English clerk Peter Mundy, "a most majestical, warlike and delightsome sight," as it was no doubt intended to be. First to appear was the artillery, the cannons pulled on wooden gun carriages. Some cannons, like the one on which Shah Jahan bestowed the name World Conqueror, had barrels as long as seventeen feet. The enormous baggage train followed with its mass of pack elephants, "like a fleet of ships" in a sea of dust, its ranks of spitting camels and patient mules and its thousands of ox-drawn carts. Laborers with spades and pick axes on their shoulders marched with the baggage train, ready to clear obstacles from the path.

Next came the leading columns of marching infantry and "thousands of horsemen going breadthwise, each in their ordained position, their rippling silken standards blazoned with the devices of their commanders." Elephants of state, gorgeous in velvet and cloth of gold and clanking with gold and silver plates, chains and bells, plodded in their wake. Especially favored beasts bore the royal ensign of a tiger against the rising sun. Then came the emperor, the royal princes and their bodyguards, followed closely by mounted musicians playing long-stemmed pipes, trumpets and kettledrums and then the mounted rearguard "whose lances, being very long, broad and clean, glittered most brightly against the sun." Tens of thousands of attendants and camp followers straggled behind.

The Moghul court on the move, by Peter Mundy

The awesome pageantry was born of much practice. Moghul emperors spent at least a third of their reigns on the move, going from camp to camp either on campaign or on tours of inspection of an empire which, according to Abul Fazl, took a year to traverse. The appurtenances of imperial government accompanied the emperor, from his throne and the imperial records and accounts—so massive that they required numerous wagons to carry them—to sacks of gold coin, silken robes of honor and bejeweled swords to be presented as gifts. As a Moghul general reflected, "If the treasury is with the army, the merchants following the army [to supply it] have a sense of security too."

The imperial progress was one of the few occasions when the great mass of Shah Jahan's ordinary subjects, living in the countryside, had a chance to glimpse their emperor. It must have been an amazing spectacle to people whose rhythm of life was defined not by the complex rituals of the court but by the changing of the seasons and the coming of the monsoon. Living mostly in mud-walled thatched huts in villages shared with goats, chickens and big-boned, ambling water buffalo, they cooked over fires fueled by cattle dung and tended fields of rice, wheat, barley and millet. Their prosperity varied widely depending on the fertility of the land, but the French doctor François Bernier, writing later in Shah Jahan's reign, thought their lives bleak: "Of the vast tracts of country constituting the empire of Hindustan," he wrote in his account, "many are little more than sand, or barren mountains, badly cultivated and thinly peopled; and even a considerable portion of the good land remains untilled from want of labourers; many of whom perish in consequence of the bad treatment they experience from the Governors. These poor people, when incapable of discharging the demands of their rapacious lords, are not only often deprived of the means of subsistence, but are bereft of their children, who are carried away as slaves." He noted, even then, a drift from the land: "Thus it happens that many of the peasantry, driven to despair . . . abandon the country, and seek a more tolerable mode of existence." Some went to the towns, but others seized the opportunity of a new life with the passing Moghul forces "as bearers of burdens, carriers of water or servants to horsemen."

Shah Jahan sometimes rode, protected from the sun by a silken parasol, on fine horses kept in peak condition by a special diet that included butter and sugar. When he tired of riding, he would mount his own imperial elephant, "richer adorned than the rest," and sit beneath a canopy of cloth of gold. To awestruck foreigners, this was "by far the most striking and splendid style of travelling, as nothing can surpass the richness and magnificence of the harness and trappings." Alternatively, he was borne along in a "field throne . . . a species of magnificent tabernacle, with painted and gilt pillars and glass windows . . . the four poles of this litter are covered either with scarlet or brocade, and decorated with deep fringes of silk and gold. At the end of each pole are stationed two strong and handsomely dressed men, who are relieved by eight other men constantly in attendance."

Moghul noblewomen sometimes rode on horseback, especially in mountainous regions, concealed from public view by a linen garment covering them from head to toe, with only a small, letter-box-shaped piece of netting to look through. More usually, hidden behind brocade or satin curtains, they reclined full-length in palanquins suspended from curved bamboo poles resting on the shoulders of four or six bearers trained to run smoothly over uneven ground and thus avoid jolting the dozing occupant. Bent bamboos were specially cultivated at great expense for the purpose. Women could also lie in sumptuously upholstered ox-drawn carts or in capacious litters slung between two powerful camels or two small elephants. Peter Mundy described how the litter's sides were covered with "a certain hard, sweet smelling grass . . . just like our thatch in England, making fast therein a little earth and barley, so that throwing water on the outside, it causes the inside to be very cool . . . and also in a few days causes the barley to spring out, pleasant to see."

Mumtaz and her daughters traveled in yet greater luxury and dignity as befitted their rank. Sometimes they were carried on men's shoulders in roofed and gilded litters resembling sedan chairs and covered with magnificent silk nets of many colors, enriched with embroidery, fringes and tassels. Often they rode in richly decorated howdahs—small, swaying, glittering canopied castles—secured to the backs of docile female elephants by means of pulleys and ropes. Through screens of golden mesh the empress could look out on the passing world, a task made easier by the water sprinkled on the road ahead to subdue the dust that would otherwise have risen in choking clouds around her.

Strict protocol was preserved throughtout. When Mumtaz wished to travel by elephant, the beast was led into a specially erected tent where it knelt down. The mahout, or elephant driver, covered his head with a piece of coarse cloth to ensure he caught no glimpse of his royal passenger as she climbed into her howdah. She seldom traveled with Shah Jahan. Instead the imperial harem followed about a mile behind, surrounded closely by armed female guards and by eunuchs who drove off flies with jeweled peacock-feather fans.

Eunuchs also rode or walked ahead, lashing out with their sticks at any man daring to get too close. François Bernier, who later watched the extravagant cavalcade bearing one of Mumtaz's daughters to Kashmir, wrote, "Woe to any unlucky cavalier, however exalted in rank, who, meeting the procession, is found too near. Nothing can exceed the insolence of the tribes of eunuchs and footmen which he has to encounter, and they eagerly avail themselves of any opportunity to beat a man in the most unmerciful manner." Nevertheless, the fairy-tale spectacle of the imperial harem, howdahs "blazing with gold and azure," enchanted Bernier so that he "should have been apt to be carried away by such flights of imagination as inspire most of the Indian poets, when they represent the elephants as conveying so many goddesses concealed from the vulgar gaze."

The royal kitchens moved en masse with the emperor, the imperial gold and silverware and porcelain wrapped and stowed in panniers and supplies of food and water for the imperial family carefully guarded for fear of poisoners. Tandoors—the hot clay ovens used by the Moghuls in their nomadic days and introduced by them into India—were an efficient means of cooking food quickly while on the move, especially meat, lentils and bread.*

Given its enormity, the progress of the imperial court and armies was stately and steady, often covering no more than ten miles a day. Officials measured and documented the length of each day's march with a piece of rope. The Venetian Niccolao Manucci, who observed the process some years later, described how "they begin at the royal tent upon the king's coming forth. The man in front who has the rope in his hand makes a mark on the ground, and when the man in the rear arrives at this mark he shouts out, and the first man makes a fresh mark and counts 'two.' Thus they proceed throughout the march, counting 'three,' 'four,' and so on. Another man on foot holds a score in his hand and keeps count. If perchance the king asks how far he has travelled, they reply at once, as they know how many of their ropes go to a league." Manucci also noted how the passage of time was calculated: "There is another man on foot who has charge of the hourglass, and measures the time, and each time announces the number of hours with a mallet on a platter of bronze."

Sometimes, when the emperor wished to make a detour to visit a local fort or curiosity or perhaps a shrine, the harem took a shorter route, reaching the camp in advance of the emperor. Mumtaz was thus ready to welcome Shah Jahan with the customary greeting, *"mubarak manzil"* (happy be the journey), as he entered the royal enclosure to the beating of kettledrums and the metallic fanfare of trumpets.

The setting for this ritual had changed little since the time of Timur. The imperial camp was laid out to a predetermined plan with well-defined streets like a small city, which, in its huge scale, it resembled. It even had its own bazaars. Within the encampment, every nobleman had his allotted place to pitch his tents, which did not vary from one camp to the

---

* The fact that the Moghuls did not penetrate the far south of India explains why tandoori cooking is not widely found there.

next, so that people could easily find their way. Nobles always took care when erecting their tents to keep them lower than the imperial ones, knowing that they would otherwise be pulled down and they themselves perhaps ruined. The ordinary soldiery and camp followers inhabited the perimeter, cooking their meals over fires of cow and camel dung. The life of the camp reflected that of any large mass of people. A Moghul noble wrote, "Though there was much praying and fasting in the camp, gambling, sodomy, drinking and fornication were also prevalent."

Mumtaz and Shah Jahan occupied a large, fortlike enclosure in the center of the camp, separated by a wide space from the tents of their nobles and well protected by artillery and palisades from the teeming life of their soldiery. The outer walls consisted of panels of wood draped with scarlet cloth and fastened with leather thongs, with a handsome gatehouse. A selection of the emperor's swiftest horses was kept saddled and ready by the gatehouse in case of any emergency. Within the enclosure were all the facilities of the royal court—tented halls of public and private audience shimmering with fabrics shot through with gold and silver thread. In the center of each hall was a gorgeously decorated stage, where Shah Jahan held court beneath a canopy of velvet or flowered silk. There was even a portable wooden two-story house with a *jharokha* balcony so that Shah Jahan could, as usual, display himself to his people to assure them he still lived. The well-screened, spacious and sumptuous harem quarters lay close by. Bathhouses and privies were accommodated in special tents—an emphasis on cleanliness that went back to Timur's time. His nomadic warriors had been accustomed to rinse off the sweat, dust and blood of battle in mobile public bathhouses using water heated in boilers.*

Transporting the massive imperial tents with their protective awnings of waxed cloth was an immense exercise, especially since there were two sets of everything. Abul Fazl recorded that in Akbar's time the task required one hundred elephants, five hundred camels and four hundred

* Jahangir traveled with a five-foot-high, six-foot-wide bath shaped like a giant teacup and carved from a single lump of rock. When he wished to bathe, his attendants filled it with warmed rosewater. Steps up the outside and down the inside helped him climb in and out. Today the bath sits in a courtyard of the Agra fort.

carts. The duplicates made it possible for one camp to be pitched while the other set of tents was dispatched ahead with the superintendent of the royal household, who would select a suitable site for the next night's encampment and ensure everything was in place to receive the emperor and empress.

Lighting, as elaborate as in the royal palace, was designed to make the Moghul camp shine gloriously—and conspicuously—from afar. Servants erected a giant pole more than 120 feet high, anchored by sixteen ropes, on top of which sat a giant bowl filled with cotton seed and oil, which they lit at sunset, sending flames shooting into the night sky. It was called Akash-Diya, the "Light of the Sky." Nobles, summoned to wait on the emperor at night, found their way with flambeaux. Bernier wrote that the camp "is a grand and imposing spectacle on a dark night, to behold, when standing at some distance, long rows of torches lighting these nobles through extended lanes of tents."

Although the imperial court was marching to war in November 1629, life for Shah Jahan and Mumtaz was as festive as at Agra. Singers, dancers and musicians entertained the imperial family, and a menagerie of exotic animals, from lions to rhinoceroses, accompanied the camp so that fights could be staged. Shah Jahan also went hunting. There is no evidence to suggest that Mumtaz was, like her aunt Nur, a crack shot or that she accompanied him, but Shah Jahan certainly relished hawking and hunting tigers and lions—a royal prerogative. He also stalked deer using trained leopards, carried hooded to the chase, jeweled collars around their furry necks. The Dutchman Francisco Pelsaert, who witnessed the leopards at work, thought it a remarkable form of sport, writing: "These brutes are so accustomed to men that they are as tame as cats, whether they are reared from cubs or tamed when full grown. They are very carefully fed, and each has two men to look after him, as well as a cart, in which they sit, or are driven out, daily. When they come to a place where they sight buck, the leopard is released from the cart and he creeps on his four feet until he gets a view, taking cover behind trees, plants or thickets, until he sees that his first quick rush and spring will be successful, for that is his only chance. Most are so well trained that they never, or very seldom, miss."

BY EARLY 1630 Shah Jahan, Mumtaz and their retinue had passed
through the ranges of the Vindhya Mountains and were journeying
through shady, wooded hills toward the city of Burhanpur on the Tapti
River, 450 miles southwest of Agra. Shah Jahan and Mumtaz knew the
Deccan well; they had spent a third of their seventeen years of married
life there, some of it in Shah Jahan's years of triumph as a victorious
young prince, some of it in perilous circumstances. They also knew well
the palace fortress in Burhanpur, where Mumtaz had given birth to two
daughters and where one of her sons had died. Shah Jahan's half-brother
Khusrau had met his mysterious end in the fortress, while another half-
brother, Parvez, had died there of alcoholism. As Shah Jahan and Mumtaz entered Burhanpur, it must have stirred memories for them both.

Mumtaz, however, had little time for reflection. Moving into her
chambers in the royal apartments, she began preparing for the birth of
her thirteenth child. Barely a month later, on 23 April 1630, she gave
birth to a daughter but, as the court chronicles reported simply and
without comment, the child died shortly afterward.

AS THE SKIES grew heavy with the approaching monsoon rains, Shah Jahan reviewed his strategy for subduing Khan Jahan Lodi and the forces of
Ahmednagar. On this occasion, he did not intend to fight in the field
himself, but his presence as overall commander in the Deccan was vital
since, as one of his historians wrote, "discord and dissension existed
among the chiefs and leaders of the army to such an extent, that they
constantly sought to undermine each other's enterprise." Impatient of
such displays of ego, Shah Jahan acted swiftly to quell internal rivalries,
recalling some of his military commanders and appointing others in
their place. One of those dismissed was Mumtaz's ambitious brother
Shaista Khan, who had argued with another leader. However, over the
coming months the emperor would rely increasingly on the military competence and diplomatic skills of his father-in-law, Asaf Khan.

Even with their great superiority in men and weaponry, the progress
of Shah Jahan's forces was slow. The rebels wisely avoided pitched battles, relying instead on guerrilla tactics in a terrain which they knew far
better than their imperial adversaries. On one occasion ten thousand

rebel horsemen ambushed a rear guard of imperial troops that had become separated from the main force, killing some and forcing the imperial commander to ignominious flight. However, by the end of 1630, the ruler of Ahmednagar had had enough and made terms. His decision signaled the end for Khan Jahan. Abandoned by his former allies, he fled toward the Punjab, but Moghul patrols caught and killed him. His severed head was delivered to Shah Jahan at Burhanpur and mounted on the city gates.

Shah Jahan still planned to subdue Bijapur and Golconda and to punish the host of minor Deccani rulers who had joined with Khan Jahan and rebelled against their Moghul suzerains. However, his campaign stagnated into a succession of sieges as his enemies retreated to their strongholds. As a chronicler wrote, "The fortresses were strong, the garrisons determined." Matters were made worse by the most severe and protracted famine seen in the region for a century. Across great tracts of land not a blade of grass was to be found, making it impossible for Moghul forces to forage.

The drought had started three years earlier and by 1630 extended from the Arabian Sea far inland. European merchants described "desperate multitudes, who setting their lives at nought, care not what they enterprise so they may but purchase means for feeding." Streets and highways were "a woeful spectacle" filled with "dying and dead in great numbers." Peter Mundy, who journeyed from the coast to Burhanpur at this time, witnessed people fighting each other for animal excrement, from which they hungrily plucked pieces of undigested grain. He saw desperate parents selling their children or even giving them away "to any that would take them . . . that so they might preserve them alive, although they were sure never to see them again." The sweet stink of death hung in the air. On some nights Mundy could find nowhere to pitch his tent because of the piles of naked, skeletal bodies dragged out of the starving towns and villages by those who still had strength, and abandoned to the jackals.

Shah Jahan understood the seriousness of the situation, which had even reached the streets of Burhanpur, though its citizens could at least draw on the dwindling waters of the Tapti. His historian recorded: "During the past year no rain had fallen . . . and the drought had been

especially severe . . . dog's flesh was sold for goat's flesh, and the pounded
bones of the dead [people] were mixed with flour and sold [to make
bread] . . . Destitution at length reached such a pitch that men began to
devour each other, and the flesh of a son was preferred to his love." To
aid his stricken subjects, Shah Jahan remitted taxes and ordered his officials to open feeding stations in Burhanpur and other cities, where bread
and broth were doled out to the hungry. He also ordered five thousand
rupees to be distributed among the poor every Monday, "that day being
distinguished above all others as the day of the Emperor's accession to
the throne."

IN THE MIDST of death and desolation, replete with kites and vultures
arcing over the barren landscape, Shah Jahan and the fertile Mumtaz
conceived another child. Mumtaz spent some of her pregnancy planning
the marriage of her eldest son, the fifteen-year-old Dara Shukoh. The
bride she proposed to Shah Jahan was Dara's first cousin, the daughter of
Shah Jahan's half-brother Parvez. It was a dynastically sensible alliance,
and perhaps Mumtaz also hoped to heal rifts within the imperial familiy.
Whatever the case, her husband and son welcomed the suggestion, and
Shah Jahan dispatched messengers to Agra with instructions to his officials to prepare for a magnificent ceremony.

As she awaited the birth of her child, Mumtaz could enjoy the com-
forts of the palace-fortress. The three-story building containing her
apartments overlooked the river on one side and sunken gardens on the
other. There was the diversion of her husband's war elephants stabled in
the nearby Hati Mahal on the riverbank, from which they could be led
down to bathe in the Tapti. Mumtaz herself bathed in a suite of marble
hammams beneath domed ceilings painted with interwined flowers and
leaves. Cool scented water ran down one marble shoot, while warm water, heated by perpetually burning oil lamps, rippled down another.

In the intense summer heat of June 1631, Mumtaz went into labor.
Her daughter Jahanara was by her bedside, and Shah Jahan waited in an
adjacent chamber. The court astrologers predicted the birth of yet another Moghul prince, but after an agonizing thirty-hour struggle a daughter, Gauharara, was born. Various disputed accounts, said to be based on

copies of long-disappeared Persian manuscripts, relate what occurred in these, the final moments of the thirty-eight-year-old empress's life. According to one persistent tale, as Mumtaz lay exhausted in the throes of labor, she heard her baby cry out from within her womb. Alarmed by the thin, eerie sound, she told Jahanara to run and fetch Shah Jahan. The baby was born just as her anxious husband hurried to her side. Mumtaz barely had time to ask him to keep their children safe before whispering good-bye and dying in his arms. It was three hours before dawn.

According to a similar but more elaborate version, the heavily pregnant Mumtaz was playing chess with her husband when both heard the cry of a baby. Surprised, they looked around them but could see no child nearby. After a while, they again heard the sound of weeping and realized with horror that it was coming from within Mumtaz's womb. Fearing this was a bad omen, they hurriedly summoned doctors, astrologers and other learned men to interpret the meaning. While Shah Jahan distributed money to the needy in frantic attempts to secure divine intervention, the physicians tried to save his empress, now in terrible and growing pain. Despairing of her life and with tears in her eyes, she gasped out her last words of love to Shah Jahan: "Today is the time of departure; it is the time to accept separation and embrace pain. For some time, I was fascinated by the beauty of my beloved, now [I] shed blood because today is the time of separation." As she grew weaker, Mumtaz sought Shah Jahan's promise not to have children by any other. She also told her tearful husband that the night before she had dreamed of "a beautiful palace with a lush garden, the like of which she had never imagined" and begged him to build her tomb just like it. A further account suggests yet more lyrically that the dying Mumtaz's parting words were "build for me a mausoleum which would be unique, extremely beautiful, the like of which is not on earth."

Shah Jahan's official court historians relate a simpler though no less touching story. The long, wracking labor and final agonizing delivery of her daughter had been too much for Mumtaz. "Weakness overtook her to the highest degree," and aware that she was dying, Mumtaz sent Jahanara to fetch Shah Jahan. "Moved beyond control," he rushed to her bedside for a brief, final farewell. The weeping Mumtaz, "with heart full of pain," begged him to care for their children and took her final leave of him.

Mumtaz Mahal's temporary tomb in Burhanpur

Soon after, "when three watches of the said night still remained . . . she passed on to the mercy of God."

According to Islamic custom, Mumtaz was buried quickly. The traditional method of preparing a woman's body for burial was for a female washer first to bathe it in cold camphor water and then to wrap it in a shroud made of five pieces of white cotton. Next, because of a deep-seated fear of ghosts, the body was carried out headfirst through an opening newly made in the palace wall. This procedure was intended to hinder the spirit from finding its way back inside the building where the death had occurred. Mumtaz's body was then borne on a bier to a walled Moghul pleasure garden originally built by Shah Jahan's uncle Daniyal as a hunting ground on the opposite bank of the Tapti River. There she was laid in a temporary tomb, her head pointing northward and her face turned toward Mecca.

CHAPTER TEN

"Dust of Anguish"

MUMTAZ'S SUDDEN DEATH CRUSHED SHAH JAHAN. For nineteen years she had been the "light of his nightchamber" from whom he could never bear to be apart. Yet their transcending passion and her remarkable fecundity had been their undoing. As one of Shah Jahan's historians wrote, Mumtaz had been "the oyster of the ocean of good fortune, who most of the years became pregnant," so that

> She brought from the groin of the exalted king
> Fourteen royal issues into the world.
>
> Of these, seven now adorn Paradise,
> The remaining seven are the candles of government.
>
> When she embellished the world with these children,
> She waned like the moon after fourteen.
>
> When she brought out the last single pearl,
> She then emptied her body like an oyster.

Fourteen pregnancies in nineteen often itincrant, sometimes perilous, years had simply been too much for Mumtaz.

The court historians also captured Shah Jahan's despair at the fleeting nature of human happiness, even for emperors: "Alas! This transitory world is unstable, and the rose of its comfort is embedded in a field of thorns. In the dustbin of the world, no breeze blows which does not raise the dust of anguish; and in the assembly of the world, no one happily occupies a seat who does not vacate it full of sorrow." According to their accounts, Shah Jahan lamented the futility of his privileged existence without Mumtaz: "Even though the Incomparable Giver had conferred on us such great bounty . . . yet the person with whom we wanted to enjoy it has gone." In the first throes of grief, he even contemplated renouncing the throne, telling his courtiers, "If the World-Creating God had not charged us with . . . the custodianship of the world and the protection of all humanity . . . we would have abandoned kingship and taken up sovereignty over the world of seclusion."

Shah Jahan went into deep mourning, exchanging his "night-illuminating gems and costly clothes" for "white garb, like dawn," which he would wear for the next two years and thereafter on every Wednesday—the day of Mumtaz's death. The most celebrated poet of Shah Jahan's reign wrote:

> *running tears turned his garments white*
> *In Hind, white is the colour of mourning.*

Black and blue had been the mourning colors of the early Moghuls, but by Shah Jahan's time they had adopted the symbol of austerity and mourning of their Hindu subjects: white. The rest of the court followed suit, donning plain white clothes in place of their brilliant robes. The emperor also renounced "all kinds of pleasures and entertainments, particularly listening to songs and music." He struggled to control his emotions, but "there constantly appeared involuntary symptoms of grief, sorrow and distress" on his face, while "from constant weeping he was forced to use spectacles."

Mumtaz's death very visibly marked the end of Shah Jahan's youth. His historians recorded that "his auspicious beard, which before this grievous event had not more than ten or twelve grey hairs, which he used to pluck out, within a few days turned more than one-third grey: and he gave up the practice of plucking out grey hair. And he used to say the fact that at his age the august beard had become white so quickly was due to the excess of affliction and pain on account of this soul-consuming event."

For a full week the emperor made neither his customary appearances on the *jharokha* balcony nor in the Halls of Private and Public Audience. At the end of that week, on 25 June 1631, he took a boat across the Tapti River to the gardens where Mumtaz was buried, where he "poured oceans of lustrous pearls of tears" over his wife's grave. A few days later, on 4 July, the usually joyous Rosewater Festival took place, but although he presented the traditional jeweled flasks of rosewater, essence of hyacinth and essence of orange flowers to his and Mumtaz's children and her father, Asaf Khan, the celebrations were curtailed and the mood somber.

Mumtaz had died an immensely rich woman. Her personal estate was valued at more than 10 million rupees in gold, silver, gems and jeweled ornaments. Shah Jahan gave one half of this fortune to their eldest daughter, the seventeen-year-old Jahanara, and distributed the remainder between the other surviving six children (Their youngest son, Daulat Afza had died some months earlier). Despite her youth, tellingly it was the beautiful, clever, accomplished Jahanara, and not one of Shah Jahan's other two neglected wives, who now assumed Mumtaz's place as first lady of the Moghul Empire with the title Begum Sahib. Several months later, Shah Jahan ordered Jahanara to take charge, as her mother had done, of the imperial seal so that "from that date, the duty of affixing the great seal to the imperial edicts devolved upon her." As her mother had also done, she soon began issuing orders in her own right.

SHAH JAHAN NEVER intended Burhanpur to provide Mumtaz's permanent grave. Her body was disinterred, and in December 1631 a melancholy procession set out to bring the dead empress home to Agra. Jahanara did not accompany it but stayed to comfort her grieving father, who remained for a short period in the Deccan to oversee his military campaigns. The task of escorting the golden casket in which Mumtaz lay fell to the fifteen-year-old Shah Shuja and to Mumtaz's friend and chief lady-in-waiting, Satti al-Nisa. As they traveled slowly northward, holy men recited verses from the Koran, and imperial servants distributed

food, drink and silver and gold coins to the poor. As the cortege neared
Agra, a court poet described how a great wailing arose.

> The world became dark and black in the eyes of its people.
> Men and women of the city, from among the subjects and
>   attendants,
> Applied the indigo of grief to their faces.

Mumtaz was quickly interred in a small domed building on the banks
of the Jumna. Yet even this second grave would not be her final resting
place. Though still at Burhanpur, Shah Jahan had already planned an illumined tomb, a fitting monument to his Queen of the Age.

AT LEAST THREE motives inspired Shah Jahan's plans for the building,
which would almost immediately become popularly known as the Taj
Mahal from a shortening of Mumtaz Mahal's name. Foremost was his
abiding love for Mumtaz and his desire to commemorate her, but his perception of buildings as symbols of imperial power and prestige and his
love of architecture and design for their own sake were subsidiary factors.

Some historians have in recent years tried to diminish Shah Jahan's
love for Mumtaz Mahal, but this runs counter to all we know about the
relationship between a couple who were both friends and lovers. Shah
Jahan, highly conscious of his imperial image, was careful to ensure that
what his court historians wrote reflected his views, and he approved their
every word, making changes where necessary. He would therefore have
explicitly sanctioned comments about his overwhelming sorrow, the "constant" signs of grief which appeared "involuntarily" on his face and his
disdain for his appearance. He would also have endorsed statements that
his other wives "enjoyed nothing more than the title of wifeship" and
that "the intimacy and deep affection" he had for Mumtaz he did not
have "for any other" in the glowing eulogy of Mumtaz Mahal. Its final
paragraph encapsulates their relationship: "She always had the glory of
distinction and honour of pre-eminence of the felicity of constant company and companionship and fortune of closeness and intimacy with His
Majesty. The friendship and concord between them had reached such an

extent the like of which has never been known between a husband and wife from among the classes of sovereigns, or the rest of the people and this was not merely out of carnal desire but high virtues and pleasing habits, outward and inward goodness, and physical and spiritual compatibility on both sides had been the cause of great love and affection and abundant affinity and familiarity."

Such sentiments are particularly striking given that Shah Jahan was from a society in which men outwardly dominated, polygamy was common and admission of feelings for an individual wife—and such overwhelming grief at her loss—would have been seen as a weakness in a sovereign, not a virtue. Of course, other rulers in both East and West had expended some of their greatest and most expensive architectural and artistic efforts on commemorating the dead; examples include the pyramids in Egypt, the buried terra-cotta army at Xian and the Ming tombs near Beijing in China, and the elaborate tombs commemorating dead shoguns built at Nikko in Japan from 1616 to 1636. However, these memorials usually commemorated rulers, rather than their consorts.

The Moghuls, and Shah Jahan in particular, were undoubtedly also conscious of the power of buildings to impress and overawe the public and to demonstrate the insignificance of the subject and the futility of resistance to imperial power. Abul Fazl wrote, "Mighty fortresses have been raised which protect the timid, frighten the rebellious and please the obedient . . . imposing towers have also been built . . . and are conducive to that dignity which is so necessary for earthly power." Shah Jahan's chronicler Lahori wrote of the emperor's architectural projects, "Construction of these lofty and substantial buildings which, in accordance with the Arabic saying, 'verily our relics tell of us,' [will] speak with mute eloquence of His Majesty's God-given aspiration and sublime fortune." He described the Taj Mahal itself as "a memorial to the sky-reaching ambition" of Shah Jahan. Yet, though Shah Jahan's passion for fine buildings and his appreciation of the image they created would coalesce nicely in the huge project on which he was about to embark, they were secondary to his determination to celebrate a matchless love. Otherwise he would not have placed Mumtaz at the center of his greatest concept.

IN PLANNING A mausoleum for Mumtaz Mahal, Shah Jahan was working
within a long tradition of tomb building among his ancestors both in
central Asia and in India. Admittedly, an order from Ghengis Khan that
no one who viewed his funeral procession should live to tell the tale is
said to have been carried out, and certainly there is no surviving record
of where he is buried. However, his descendants left ample evidence of
their vigor and sophistication as tomb builders, such as the over 160-
foot-high octagonal tomb surmounted by an egg-shaped dome and
ringed by eight minarets the Mongol prince Uljaytu had built for himself
in his imperial capital of Sultaniya in Persia in the early fourteenth century. It embodies many elements that would emerge in more polished
form in Moghul architecture.

Prince Uljaytu's octagonal tomb in Sultaniya

The squinch (shaded) is an arch across the angle of two walls

One of the technical limitations overcome by the time of Shah Jahan was how to place a dome on a building whose interior size exceeded that of the dome itself. The problem had been solved as early as the third century AD by builders of the Persian Sassanid dynasty, who pioneered the use of a simple arch across the angle of two walls—the squinch—to support the dome. This turned a square into an octagon. If required, further small arches could be added across the corners of the octagon, thus producing a sixteen-sided structure almost approximating the circle of the dome. The invention of the squinch coincided with the development in Syria of the pendentive—a kite-shaped vault supported by a pier over the angle of the square. Designs of squinch and pendentive developed rapidly as builders experimented with construction techniques and artistic possibilities and learned how to place a dome on buildings of any shape and size. The techniques spread westward as well as east, to be realized in St. Sophia at Constantinople, Santa Maria del Fiore in Florence and St. Peter's in Rome, although spires and towers, not domes, remained the most usual high point of churches in western Europe.

Timur, the Moghuls' ancestor of choice, had been a great builder and constructed a series of royal mausolea, of which his own, in Samarkand, is by far the most imposing. It still stands in the center of what was a madrasa, or Islamic school complex, and has what is known in architecture as a *double dome*. By using a double shell with a void between the

*The pendentive (shaded) is a vault
over the angle of the square*

inner and outer skins, rather than just a very thick, very heavy single shell, designers achieved a much greater difference between the exterior and interior heights of the dome. This enhanced the proportions of the building and also saved considerable weight and structural stress on the rest of the building. Timur's tomb itself has a great, high, bulbous ribbed dome tiled in bright turquoise blue on the exterior and, within, a lower, hemispherical dome emerging from the same drum-shaped base. The outer shell ensures the visibility and exterior magnificence of an imperial monument, while the lower inner one keeps the interior proportions in harmony.*

Islamic rulers struggled with the Koranic prescription that tombs should be open to the sky. Some seem to have used a low inner dome, such as in Timur's mausoleum, as a metaphor for the canopy of the sky, since many such domes are decorated with stars. Others left a gap between the top of the external entrance doors and the lintel to allow fresh air to circulate above the tomb. Babur preferred to leave his own tomb genuinely open to the sky. Akbar, however, built a massive double-domed tomb for his father,

---

* Versions of the double dome design were also adopted in Europe; for example, Filippo Brunelleschi used it for the cathedral dome of Santa Maria del Fiore in Florence and Christopher Wren in his designs for the dome of London's St. Paul's Cathedral.

Humayun. In his own tomb, which Akbar originally designed himself but was altered by Jahangir, his cenotaph sits within an open pavilion, although his actual burial place lies deep below this. Jahangir's large, flat minaretted tomb, built in one of his and Nur's favorite gardens in Lahore, also originally had his cenotaph within a pavilion open to the skies but his burial place below within the tomb. (The cenotaph has since disappeared.)

ONCE HE HAD decided that he wished to commemorate Mumtaz Mahal and the awesome nature of his love for her, as well as the power and prestige of his imperial reign, Shah Jahan had first to choose a suitable site for the complex he envisaged. Among the factors he seems likely to have considered were a wish for the site to be peaceful and away from the bustling city of Agra. It should also be visible from a distance and near enough to the River Jumna to allow easy supply of water for irrigation of the gardens and for its water features, as well as to provide a cooler environment in summer. If the site was to be on the Jumna, it should not be at a point easily subject to flooding or erosion but should allow his architects to make use of the river, whose level was considerably higher than it is today, as a constantly changing reflective backdrop to their design. The emperor may also have wanted to allow for a future tomb for himself nearby. Finally, Shah Jahan would have wished to be able to see the mausoleum from his quarters in the Agra fort. The pleasure gardens where Mumtaz Mahal had been temporarily buried were in direct line of sight from his window in the fortress palace of Burhanpur.

The site Shah Jahan chose, about one and a half miles from the Agra fort, and situated at the end of a series of nobles' gardens and directly opposite one of Babur's gardens, satisfied these criteria. It was, for example, downstream from a sharp approximately right-angled bend in the river at the Agra fort which formed a watershed, thus reducing the thrust of the Jumna at the Taj site. The land in question was owned by his vassal, the raja of Amber (Jaipur), who willingly offered it to the emperor. However, Islamic tradition considers that women like Mumtaz Mahal, who die in childbirth, are martyrs and thus that their burial sites should become places of pilgrimage. Tradition also requires that there should be no perceived element of coercion, whether real or not, in the acquisition of such holy sites. Therefore Shah Jahan gave the raja not one but four separate properties in generous compensation. He had acted quickly and had already acquired the land by January 1632 when Mumtaz's body was returned to Agra. Thus it was here, at the site of the future Taj Mahal, that she had temporarily been laid to rest.

To develop a concept and then a detailed plan for the tomb complex, Shah Jahan would naturally have called on the advice of the experienced team of architects built up to work on his father's and his own previous projects. The account of the building of the Taj Mahal by the court historian Lahori names Mir Abul Karim and Mukamat Khan as the superintendents of construction, who, as their title implies, were the project managers responsible for the organization and carrying out of the work. Mir Abul Karim was already about sixty years old at the time Shah Jahan appointed him and had previously worked on several projects for Jahangir at Lahore. Mukamat Khan had come to India during Jahangir's reign from Shiraz, in southern Persia. Shah Jahan had named Mukamat Khan as his minister of works shortly after his accession, and he seems to have been primarily an administrator rather than an engineer or architect. Shah Jahan continued to promote him frequently. In 1641 he would appoint him governor of Delhi, where he superintended the construction of the Red Fort in the new city of Shahjahanabad.

Lahori does not name the Taj's architect. Neither do any of the other contemporary accounts. For the chroniclers to name the superintendent of construction for a building, but not the architect, was not particularly unusual, partly because architects often worked in teams and partly because they seem to have been considered lower in status than the superintendents of construction. Just as in the West, there was nowhere that aspiring architects could study. They learned "on the job," rising from the ranks of master craftsmen.* However, because Lahori named no architect for the Taj Mahal, his identity has been the subject of much dispute. According to the Portuguese father Sebastien Manrique, who visited Agra in 1640, "[The architect] was a Venetian by name Geronimo Veroneo who

---

* Sir Christopher Wren was unusual in that he moved to architecture from science, the discipline in which he had received his only formal training.

Shah Jahan on the Peacock Throne

Portrait identified as Mumtaz Mahal

Shah Jahan holding a turban jewel in his twenty-fifth year

Semiprecious inlay and floral relief carving on the Taj Mahal

Vibrant floral inlay on the Taj Mahal

Incised "sunburst" painting on the ceiling of the Taj Mahal mosque

Interior of Itimad-ud-daula's tomb including naturalistic floral paintings

Soaring southern gateway of the Taj Mahal

Sunrise on the Taj Mahal

Setting sun on the Taj Mahal

had come to this part in a Portuguese ship and died in the city of Lahore just before I reached it." Europeans chauvinistically attached a great deal of credibility to this claim during succeeding centuries. Their chauvinism derived partly from a wish to claim a share in an acknowledged wonder of the world and partly from a racist sentiment that a non-European could not have designed such a beautiful building.

Manrique's claim has little substance. European influence on Moghul architecture was very limited. If a European had been the architect, he would almost certainly have incorporated in the building at least some European architectural features. There are none.

Also, Manrique is the only person to name Veroneo as the architect, although there are many other contemporary European accounts. In particular, the English clerk Peter Mundy was in Agra when construction of the Taj began. Unlike Manrique, Mundy knew Veroneo personally, but he did not mention him as the architect in his description of how building commenced. Veroneo's body was seemingly brought to Agra from Lahore since he is buried in the Christian cemetery at Agra. The well-preserved Latin inscription on his tombstone reads simply, "Here lies Geronimo Veroneo. Died at Lahore on 2 August 1640." Had he designed the Taj Mahal, it is likely his tombstone would have recorded it. Furthermore, as his place of burial confirms, Veroneo was a Christian, and Shah Jahan would have been unlikely to employ a non-Muslim to design a holy complex, to much of which only Muslims were admitted.

Most significant, Veroneo was a jeweler by trade and not an architect. Peter Mundy mentioned him as a goldsmith in the pay of Shah Jahan, and other European travelers also record him as a highly skilled jeweler. If Manrique's story, which can only have reached him at secondhand, has any kernel of truth, it may be that Shah Jahan consulted Veroneo about the enameled and jeweled golden screen or rail containing forty thousand tolas of gold (about one thousand pounds) which he originally had made to surround Mumtaz's tomb and later replaced with a white marble screen. No paintings or detailed description of the gold rail exists, so the extent, if any, of European influence cannot be determined.

In the middle of the nineteenth century, Colonel William Sleeman, who had attained celebrity by suppressing the murderous cult of Thugees

in India, claimed in his popular book on the country that a Frenchman, Augustin or Austin of Bordeaux, was the architect of the Taj.*
However, the only other reference to Augustin in India occurred 150
years earlier in a book by his fellow Frenchman, the jeweler Jean-
Baptiste Tavernier, which stated unequivocally that Shah Jahan wished
to employ Augustin to cover part of his private apartments in silver but
that Augustin had died before he could do so. This story may possibly
have given rise to Sleeman's account. Most conclusively, in a letter now
in the French National Library in Paris, Augustin of Bordeaux describes himself as "not a draughtsman" and uninterested in architectural matters.

Toward the end of the nineteenth century, a series of manuscripts
surfaced in Agra and elsewhere purporting to be copies of original
seventeenth-century documents written in the court language of Persian
and relating to the construction of the Taj Mahal. Many historians consider these manuscripts entirely spurious and produced to satisfy the
hunger of the British in general, and a British school headmaster in Agra
in particular, for hard facts. These documents named a man called Ustad
Isa as the architect of the Taj Mahal and gave his birthplace as variously
Agra, Persia and Turkey. The doubts about the manuscripts are such that
Ustad's very existence might be questionable had a local Indian historian not found evidence that a family claiming descent from him, who
were themselves draftsmen, lived in Agra until 1947. In that year, being
Muslims, they migrated to Pakistan following the partition of India. The
family were also said to possess a seventeenth-century plan of the Taj
Mahal, though this can no longer be located. The same historian, how-
ever, points out that the word used in the manuscripts to describe Ustad
Isa's position means "draftsman," not "architect," and that therefore while
Ustad may have existed, he was probably, at most, responsible for putting
on paper the builders' plans based on the thoughts of others.

In the end, the most credible name for the architect of the Taj

---

* The Thugees were a sect of highway murderers who infiltrated themselves into
  groups of travelers and after a day or two ritually strangled their companions with
  a yellow silk handkerchief, mutilated their bodies and stole their possessions. In
  English the word *thug* soon came to mean any brutal hooligan.

Mahal is that of Ustad Ahmad Lahori, who died in 1649. During the 1930s a researcher discovered an early eighteenth-century manuscript of a poem written by one of Ustad Ahmad Lahori's sons in which he claimed that his father was the architect of both the Taj Mahal and the Red Fort at Delhi. There is other contemporary evidence, including a court chronicle, that he was, indeed, the architect of the Red Fort but none that he was the architect of the Taj Mahal. It seems incongruous that if Ustad was the architect of both buildings, and not just the Red Fort, that Shah Jahan did not have his chronicler say so. Perhaps Ustad's son was, understandably, simply adding to his family's prestige by claiming for his father, who probably had a part in the project, a greater share of the glory of what was immediately recognized as a masterpiece by his son as well as by the Europeans who fabricated a European architect.

The romantic may wish to believe the story contained in one of the disputed nineteenth-century manuscripts: When Shah Jahan despaired of the poor designs submitted to him, a vision of the completed tomb appeared to a Sufi mystic in a dream. The Sufi gave the design to Shah Jahan so that he could fulfill the dying Mumtaz's wish for "a mausoleum which would be unique, extremely beautiful, the like of which is not on earth."

However, others may find the answer in what his court historian Lahori said about Shah Jahan's personal involvement in how the buildings were designed: "The royal mind, which is illustrious like the sun, pays full attention to the planning and construction of these lofty and substantial buildings, which . . . for ages to come will serve as memorials of his abiding love of constructiveness, ornament and beauty. The majority of the buildings he designs himself and on the plans prepared by skilful architects after long consideration he makes appropriate alterations and amendments." As far as the generality of buildings is concerned, these statements may reflect a patron's or sponsor's exaggerated view of his own role in a project. However, Shah Jahan did have a fine appreciation of architecture. Even in his youth Jahangir commended his skills. In his grief Shah Jahan is bound to have wanted a much greater input into the design of his wife's tomb than of other buildings. He may, indeed, have made such a significant contribution to the initial concept, or made so many changes to plans submitted by others or even redrawn them, that he did not wish to single out for credit any one of the team of architects whom he consulted.

IN JUNE 1632 Shah Jahan arrived in Agra, where he could oversee his great project in person. As one of his official historians wrote, Burhanpur had become "distasteful to the royal mind of His Majesty" as the scene of "the lamentable demise of Her late Majesty the Queen." Indeed, in later years he would avoid the city if he could. Furthermore, his Deccani campaign had not prospered. After more than two years of ineffectual warring, during which he had lost thousands of men to famine and disease as well as to the fighting, the ruler of Ahmednagar had broken the peace he had so recently made with Shah Jahan and was again defying him, as were the sultans of Golconda and Bijapur. Having gained little more than a few forts and an exhausted army, Shah Jahan left the campaign in the hands of his old ally and present commander in chief, Mahabat Khan. However, the complex intrigues of the region would prove too much, even for that old soldier. By his death in October 1634, the region would still be simmering with dissent, and Shah Jahan would be forced to launch repeated military campaigns in an attempt to suppress sporadic outbursts of full-blown rebellion.

As must have been his intention, Shah Jahan reached Agra in time to participate in the Urs—the traditional annual ceremony for the dead— which would mark the first anniversary of Mumtaz's death. Peter Mundy witnessed the return of the imperial court, now minus its empress: "All the face of the earth, so far as we could see, was covered with people, troops of horses, elephants with innumerable flags, small and great, which made a most gallant show." Shah Jahan was riding a dark gray horse, his son Dara Shukoh close by him. On 11 June, six days before the anniversary of his wife's death, Shah Jahan was borne into the fort at Agra in a closed palanquin at midnight—the hour deemed most auspicious by his astrologers.

The Urs was somber but lavish. "The comptrollers of the royal household erected gorgeous pavilions in the gardens around her sacred grave, spread magnificent carpets and laid out a lavish array of foods, beverages, condiments, confectionery and fragrant essences—more than can be imagined. All the learned and pious Shaikhs and divines then congregated together and formed a glorious assemblage." Shah Jahan, in his white robes of mourning, listened to the reciting of prayers then withdrew. The official history states that "His Majesty retired to his private apartments to avoid the dense crowds." No doubt he wished to be alone with the grief that was beginning to find a permanent expression in his great building, for which the foundations were already being dug on the banks of the Jumna.

CHAPTER ELEVEN

"The Builder Could Not Have Been of This Earth"

MUMTAZ'S "ILLUMINED TOMB" WAS, SHAH JAHAN and his architects decided, to be the heart of a much larger complex. The mausoleum itself, at the center of which she would be buried following Islamic tradition, lying north-south with her face turned westward to Mecca, would sit on a terrace or platform by the riverside within a walled garden. A water channel, running north-south on exactly the same line on which Mumtaz's body lay, would form a central axis on both sides of which matching subsidiary buildings and other features would be laid out symmetrically.

Directly to the west of the mausoleum, on the platform, would be a three-domed mosque, where pilgrims could worship. The Koran does not stipulate that a Muslim must visit a mosque to pray; he or she may pray anywhere but to do so must face Mecca. In the mosque the direction of prayer is marked by an alcove in the back wall of the sanctuary known as the mihrab. A building identical in form to the mosque would be built directly to the mausoleum's east. Since the rear wall faced away from Mecca, the building could not be used as a mosque and probably served as a guesthouse for pilgrims, but its main purpose was aesthetic: to balance the mosque opposite or, as the Moghuls themselves put it, to serve as its *jabab*, or "echo." At the other end of the walled garden, facing the mausoleum, would be an ornate gatehouse.

Outside this gateway, to the south, would be an assembly area, or forecourt, known as a *jilau khana* with accommodation for attendants and bazaars around its sides. Finally, beyond that, would be caravanserais, or inns for visitors, and further bazaars, again all laid out symmetrically on either side of a central thoroughfare continuing the north-south axis provided by the main water channel. The whole area beyond the gateway would form a secular counterpart to the mausoleum compound, meeting the physical needs of the workers and visitors for food and accommodation, while the mausoleum complex nourished their spirits. The walled enclosure embracing the mausoleum and the garden would alone measure some 1,000 by 1,800 feet and was intended, in the words of Lahori, to "evoke a vision of the heavenly gardens . . . and epitomise the holy abodes of paradise."

In turning the concept into a detailed design, the Moghul architects had no design manuals or architectural textbooks to call upon. Like other architects in the Islamic world, they were guided by example rather than precept, drawing on the Moghul tradition of tomb building with its strong central Asian and Persian influences. In addition they assimilated much from the strain of Muslim architecture introduced into India by the sultans of Delhi during their three-hundred-year rule and by other Muslim rulers such as those of Gujarat and Mandu. They also drew on the Hindu architectural tradition, from which many of those doing the building work came, for features such as the domed kiosk, or *chattri*, finials and the use of intricate stone carving.

By contrast, Hindu builders had available to them treatises on buildings covering such matters as soil type and its identification by color, scent and smell; techniques of brick masonry; the configuration of buildings and the most auspicious times to undertake various stages of the building work. These textbooks were not among the many Hindu works of all kinds translated on the orders of Akbar and his successors into Persian, and there is no evidence that they were ever used by Moghul architects. However, the Hindus among the builders would almost certainly have consulted them to interpret and implement the plans passed to them by the architects.

In seeking examples that might influence their design, the Moghul architects would have been aware that their predecessors in Persia and central Asia and in the Delhi Sultanate had worked to an octagonal ground plan in many buildings, including both palaces and tombs such as

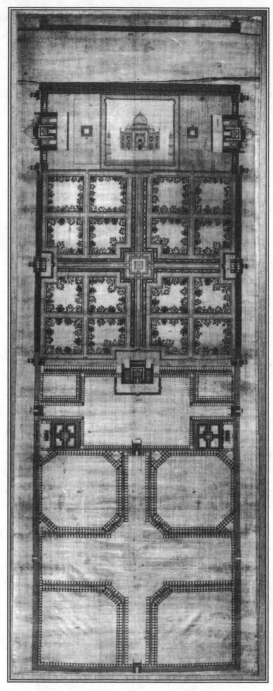

Schematic Plan of the Grounds of the Taj
Mahal; *Agra, c. 1800, opaque watercolor on cloth*

that at Sultaniya. An Italian merchant who visited Tabriz in Persia in the early sixteenth century described a now disappeared palace as called "'Astibisti' which in our tongue signifies eight parts as it has eight divisions." Architectural historians also point to the Dome of the Rock in Jerusalem, bathhouses in Damascus and palaces in Constantinople as conforming to this ground plan. They believe that the plan had its origins in pre-Islamic times, although to the Moghuls and their Muslim ancestors the octagon, which resulted from the squaring of the circle, had become a metaphor for the reconciliation of the material side of man, represented by the square, with the circle of eternity.

Humayun is said by Abul Fazl to have employed an octagonal design in a floating palace, which he had built on the Jumna. The builders joined four two-story palaces, floating on barges, by arches to form an octagonal central pool. (Humayun is even said to have had other barges planted with flowers and trees to provide a garden setting for his floating palace.) The earliest surviving examples of the use of octagonal design in Moghul India are in two tombs built in Delhi, probably between 1530 and 1550. Because their occupants are not known, they are simply designated the Sabz Burj (Green Tower) and Nila Gumbad (Blue Dome) from their original tiling. (The former is particularly important in the genealogy of the Taj Mahal and is disconcertingly now tiled in blue. It is also sited in the middle of a busy roundabout.) Both buildings have eight small chambers surrounding an octagonal central tomb area with a dome above. The eight chambers are said to represent the eight divisions of the Koran.

Variations and developments of such octagonal designs, rather confusingly sometimes known as "the nine fold plan" from the number of chambers including the central chamber, are the basis for many Moghul buildings including palaces and tombs. For example, the tomb of Humayun in Delhi, constructed in the 1560s, is based on an octagonal plan. For the Taj Mahal, the architects chose as their concept for the mausoleum a cube with its vertical corners chamfered to produce an octagon, with the cenotaph in a central octagonal space surrounded by eight interconnecting spaces on each of two levels. For each of the eight exterior façades of the mausoleum, the architects planned two stories of arched recesses. On the four main sides, these recesses would flank massive

The Sabz Burj in Delhi

entrance arches, or *iwans*, similar to those on Humayun's tomb, whose top border would rise higher than the rest of the façade.

The Sabz Burj is also the earliest surviving Moghul building in India to incorporate the double dome used in Timur's mausoleum in Samarkand, although the design, which originated in Persia, had been employed in the tomb of one of the Delhi sultans a few years earlier. In Humayun's double-domed tomb, the half-grapefruit-shaped outer dome and its lower inner one sit on a relatively low drum. In the Taj Mahal, one of the architects' greatest achievements was to produce an elegant double dome design for the mausoleum. The inner dome, which rises eighty feet above the floor, is in harmony with the scale of the rest of the interior and produces a resonant echo. The swelling outer dome sits upon a high drum and is in perfect proportion to the remainder of the exterior of the complex. Shah Jahan's chroniclers described the outer dome as "of heavenly rank" when complete and as "shaped like a guava"—a fruit only recently introduced into India from the New World. Others have likened it to a flower bulb, a ripe pear, a fig, a bead of liquid or even a woman's breast.

The architects surrounded the main dome with four domed kiosks. Although such *chattris* were used in Humayaun's tomb, there they seem too detached from the main dome. In the Taj Mahal the architects placed them so that they cluster around the dome, seeming, from eye level, to be attached to it and softening the outline of the drum. Mindful of Shah Jahan's love of jewelry, some have seen them as the minor stones or even the claws of a ring in which the dome is the major jewel.

The architects also added to the plan a plinth to raise the mausoleum itself above its riverside platform and positioned four circular white marble minarets, one at each corner of the plinth. Built on octagonal bases, the tapering minarets have an interior staircase and three stories, on each of which a balcony supported on brackets casts shadows on the minaret in the sun. The minarets rise to some 139 feet, and each is topped with an octagonal *chattri*. Although minarets have the practical advantage in a mosque of providing places for the call to prayer, they are not essential and, indeed, are not found in early Islamic holy buildings such as the Dome of the Rock. Their first use in a mosque in Damascus in the early eighth century probably resulted from the incorporation of the corner towers of a Roman temple previously on the site. By the seventeenth century, at least a single minaret was general in mosques but not in mausolea or other religious buildings. Among the designs from which the architects may have drawn inspiration were the four towers on the gateway to Akbar's tomb at Sikandra, the towers on Itimad-ud-daula's jewel of a tomb in Agra and those at each corner of Jahangir's mausoleum in Lahore. When they were built, one of Shah Jahan's chroniclers described the Taj's minarets as "like ladders reaching towards the heavens" and another as like "accepted prayers from a holy person ascended to the skies."

One of the Taj Mahal's minarets

Architecture is said to be the marriage between art and engineering, and one of the most pleasing aspects of both the minarets and the dome is their symmetry and proportion in relation to other parts of the complex. Such factors, rather than technical innovation, make the Taj Mahal stand out from all other Moghul buildings. Architects had to have a thorough knowledge of mathematics and geometry. Abul Fazl described them as lofty-minded mathematicians whose designs could only be understood by the scientifically inclined. Moghul miniatures and evidence today preserved in Samarkand show that they used these mathematical skills to calculate the relationships between different features and to lay out their designs on large sheets of gridded paper. At a later stage they often made wooden models to demonstrate how the buildings would look. (The use of such models in the Taj Mahal is mentioned in some later doubtful accounts of the building but, although likely, is not referred to by contemporary sources.) It is therefore no accident, for example, that the architects made the first-story gallery of the minarets level with the first floor of the mausoleum, the third-story gallery level with the top of the drum on which the central dome sits and the cupola of the minarets level with the maximum bulge of the dome.

The perfect balance and proportion of the Taj Mahal complex have been the subject of much detailed calculation and retrospective computation in recent years. One writer suggested that the sight lines converge at a height of five feet six inches above a central point in the entrance gateway. This is just the level at which Shah Jahan's eyes would have been, if the writer's deductions about his height from his clothes are accurate. Others deduced that the key measurement from which nearly all the rest derive is the diameter of the mausoleum's octagonal hall, which is some fifty-eight feet. The octagon, with its symbolic reconciliation of man with eternity, is certainly key to the geometric design for the complex, appearing, for example, in the planning of the mosque, guesthouse, gateway and bases of the minarets as well as in the mausoleum itself.

The Taj's designers also added to the harmony of the whole by their use of uniform architectural features throughout the complex. For example, they employed only one basic design of column, although varying the proportions and degree of decorative detail according to the significance of the location. A variant of what is known as the Shahjahani column, it

The Taj Mahal's Shahjahani columns and cusped arches

is many-sided with a base formed of panels and a capital ornamented with delicate vaulted webbing in what is called the *muqarnas* style. Similarly, the cusped, or "piecrust," arches supported by the pillars and the inset paneling throughout the complex are both of a single basic design.

As SOON AS Shah Jahan had agreed on the plans, construction began. According to the historian Lahori, this was as early as January 1632 while Shah Jahan was still in the Deccan. First the site was cleared and, as

Peter Mundy recollected from the time of his visit, hillocks in the sur-rounding area were "made level not to hinder the prospect." Then thou-sands of laborers excavated the deep foundations, which were key to the stability of the monumental structure to be built above. These founda-tions had to resist erosion by the Jumna's waters and conduct away any floods from the monsoon rains that beset Agra from June to September. Rainfall of more than eleven inches on a single day was once recorded.

Contemporary Moghul miniatures reveal that, just as in India today, the laborers, sweating in temperatures which in May and June can rise to above 110 degrees Fahrenheit, would have included Hindu women as well as men, all of whom had only hand tools to help them in their tasks. Al-though the Chinese had invented wheelbarrows many centuries earlier and Europeans had used them for more than three hundred years, these laborsaving devices were then unknown in India. Both male and female laborers carried away the excavated material in baskets upon their heads. As well as laying drainage pipes, they packed a layer of gravel across the whole of the excavated and leveled site to facilitate water runoff.

To bear the main weight of the construction at the northern end of the site, the workers dug deep shafts, which they lined with bricks and a cement of lime and sand or brick dust and then filled with rubble and more cement. For added strength and adhesion, they added materials such as jute and molasses to the cement. The workers connected these shafts, whose depth they varied to compensate for the slope of the Jumna's banks, with numerous piers, on top of which arched vaults supported the main structure. Along the riverbank itself, they buried large boxes made of ebony in the subsoil and filled them with cement to provide added rein-forcement against the rise and fall of the Jumna's waters. Finally, they fin-ished the foundations with more stones and cement. A Moghul chronicler exulted, "And when the spade wielders with robust arms and hands strong as steel had with unceasing effort excavated down to the water table, the ingenious masons and architects of astonishing achievements most firmly built the foundation with stone and mortar up to the level of the ground."

The next step was the construction along the reinforced riverbank of the vast sandstone-faced platform, some 970 feet long and 364 feet wide, on which the mosque, guesthouse and mausoleum were to be built. By this time, five thousand people a day (some sources even say twenty thousand), were working on the site, both unskilled laborers and masons as well as other craftsmen. Some were local, but others, in the words of one of Shah Jahan's chroniclers, came "from all parts of the empire." They congregated in and around the area of secular accommodation Shah Jahan had ordered to be constructed at the south of the complex. It seems to have taken shape quickly and was popularly known as Mumtazabad. As well as the laborers' sparse accommodation, the four caravanserais or travelers' inns, built around courtyards were soon alive with merchants and carriers bringing materials to the site by road or by boat along the Jumna.

To allow the sandstone from local quarries to be transported by carts pulled by teams of oxen, laborers constructed a ten-mile-long raised road of packed earth. Once at the site, masons cut the stone blocks using a series of small nail-like wedges, which they hammered in straight lines into the stone to split it. The stones were then lifted into place and held there with cement and iron dowels and clamps. The masons took such great care to finish off the facing stones that the chronicler records that they were "so smoothly cut and joined by expert craftsmanship that even close inspection fails to reveal any cracks between them." The precision was achieved by measuring the stones again, marking any further cuts and trimming to the marked line with hammers and ever-finer chisels. Then the masons smoothed the stone by rubbing sharp grit followed by finer grit over them beneath a kind of large, flat iron trowel. Some of the masons were so proud of their work that they incised their marks into the stone. The 250 marks found so far on the Taj Mahal vary widely. Some are in the form of stars or Hindu swastikas (the latter represents the cosmos spreading in four directions). Others are geometric designs such as triangles or squares. There are also arrows and what looks like a lotus flower.

On top of the sandstone platform the masons built the massive square plinth for the mausoleum itself with sides measuring some three hundred feet and standing nineteen feet high. To emphasize its position on the central axis as the focus of the whole complex, Shah Jahan and his architects had agreed that the mausoleum with its minarets and its plinth would be the only structures entirely faced in white marble. The remainder would

The marble-faced plinth on which the Taj Mahal sits

be in sandstone with, in the case of important buildings like the mosque and guesthouse, key features such as domes clad in white marble or decorated with marble inlay.

The marble came from quarries two hundred miles away at Makrana, just southwest of Amber (Jaipur). An imperial instruction of 20 September 1632 from Shah Jahan to his vassal the Rajput raja of Amber, whose quarries they were, commanded: "We hereby order that whatever the number of stone cutters and carts on hire . . . that may be required by the aforesaid [Moghul official] the rajah should make them available to him; and the wages of the stone cutters and the rent money of the carts he will provide with funds from the royal treasurer. It is imperative that the pride of peers and contemporaries should assist in all ways in this regard; and he should consider this a matter of utmost importance, and not deviate from this order."

Peter Mundy was certainly impressed by both the rate of the work and the disregard of the cost, writing, "The building . . . goes on with excessive labour and cost, prosecuted wth extraordinary dilligence, gold and silver esteemed common metal and marble but as ordinary stones." Another

European traveler encountered some of the marble on its journey toward Agra from Makrana. He wrote, "Some of these blocks were of such unusual size and length that they drew the sweat of many powerful teams of oxen and of fierce-looking, big-horned buffalos, which were dragging enormous strongly-made wagons in teams of twenty or thirty animals."

Because the marble was more fragile, less easily available and hence more costly, even greater care had to be taken to avoid cracks and chips when chiseling and smoothing the stones with successive layers of grit to achieve the high polish and meticulous finish that typifies the Taj Mahal. Shah Jahan's court poet praised the precision with which the marble blocks had been joined.

> *Like milk with sugar they are so well blended*
> *Not even a hair's crack is to be found.*

The builders constructed the plinth to rise convexly toward the center, cleverly offsetting the distorting effects of perspective that would otherwise have caused the mausoleum to appear to sit in a slight hollow. Once the builders had finished the plinth, they began work on the mausoleum. Contrary to popular belief, the mausoleum is not solid white marble but brick faced with marble slabs mainly between fifteen and eighteen inches thick. Small flat bricks, on average seven inches long by four and a half inches wide and only one and a half inches thick, were used. They were baked in kilns close to the site to minimize transport problems. Also nearby were the kilns to break down chunks of limestone or *kankar*, earth full of limestone gravel, to make the quicklime for the mortar.

Scaffolding made from bamboo or wood is still used extensively throughout Asia and was the norm at the time the Taj Mahal was constructed. However, for some reason not clear but perhaps related to local scarcity of materials or to the enormous weights involved, the builders are said to have used brick scaffolding for the Taj Mahal. When the work was finished, Shah Jahan was apparently told that the brick scaffolding would take five years to remove, but he had the bright idea of ordering that those who dismantled it could keep the bricks, and as a result, it came down overnight. A myth suggests that this brick scaffolding was used to preserve the Taj from view before completion, and one variant adds that a man who peeped over the wall was ordered to be blinded for his curiosity.

As the building of the mausoleum progressed, the marble and other materials had to be lifted ever higher up the scaffolding. As in the construction of the Pyramids, ramps are likely to have been employed. But at a certain stage, the stones had to be hoisted. A system of beams, ropes and pulleys powered by men, oxen and even elephants, seems likely to have been the solution. To secure the stones during lifting, either ropes were used or, in the case of the heaviest blocks, metal lifting claws were inserted into precut holes in the marble. Once at the required height, the masons employed metal crowbars to fit the blocks into place after any further trimming.

The facing blocks were alternately placed horizontal to the brick core or inserted more deeply into the brick with only the smallest cross-section exposed. This technique, known to masons as *stretcher/header*, together with the use of iron clamps, gave greater strength and adhesion.* The fact that the estimated weight of the dome is some 12,000 tons gives one some idea of the labor and difficulty involved in construction. The load factor transferred from the dome, which functions as a series of arches, to the supporting walls is about 750 tons per square foot. A chronicler described how the builders topped "the heaven-touching dome" with a gold finial "glittering like the sun" and over thirty feet high rising from lotus petals, a common symbol for fertility in India and elsewhere.

The workers faced the interior of the mausoleum about three feet above the floor with marble. Above this level they plastered the brick as they did the other interiors within the complex. The main constituents of the plaster, which was up to two inches thick and sometimes applied over an initial coat of mud and straw, were white lime and marble dust. But the plasterers added other ingredients, such as egg whites, gum and sugar, depending on the level of finish and adhesion required, and built up finer and finer coats, which they polished to produce a white sheen replicating marble. They even used a similar technique on some of the

---

* The iron clamps have proved to be a problem over the years. Rusting and thermal expansion have produced cracks in the stone and let water into the structure.

exteriors. What appears to be marble on some lower parts of the south-ern gateway is, in fact, polished white plaster. The curators recently found that the back of the *iwans*, where they project above the main façade of the mausoleum, are also red sandstone faced with white lime plaster.

Once the main framework of the buildings had been constructed, the next task was their decoration and ornamentation. Although the mau-soleum at a distance looks completely white, the marble is, in fact, ex-tensively decorated with calligraphy, stone carving and inlay both inside and out. Calligraphy—decorative writing—is considered an art form in the Islamic world, as it is in China and Japan. Both the Arabic and Per-sian scripts used in the Taj Mahal's calligraphy are, with their swirling fluid lines and frequent dots, inherently decorative. Fine calligraphy was more prized than painting. One of Shah Jahan's court poets described how "each line" of some beautiful calligraphy was "as heart ravishing as the province of Kashmir." According to Islamic traditions, the words of the Koran—the first known book in Arabic—are divine both in form and in content. Given the prohibitions placed in the eighth century on animal and human images, whether painted or sculpted and however re-ligious their motives, for fear of idolatry or the assumption by man of God's creative function, Koranic inscriptions are a key ornament to many buildings and in particular to mosques.* In the Taj Mahal the cal-ligraphy was designed not only to instruct visitors and to condition their response but also to serve a decorative function.

Persian calligraphers were celebrated for producing imaginative ver-sions of their own and Arabic script, and Shah Jahan appointed a Per-sian, Amanat Khan, as the calligrapher for the Taj Mahal. He was a scholar from Shiraz, a well-known center of Islamic learning, and had come to the Moghul court early in the seventeenth century with his brother, Afzal Khan, who became one of Shah Jahan's most important officials. Amanat was sufficiently well known as a calligrapher by around 1610 to have been appointed by Jahangir to undertake the calligraphy on Akbar's tomb, which, according to his signed inscription, dates from

---

* The Alhambra in Granada in southern Spain is a well-known example.

1022 in the Islamic calendar (1612–13 in the Western calendar). Amanat also undertook such duties as providing official escorts for ambassadors. His inspection seal is found on several manuscripts from the imperial library, where he could well also have had some responsibilities.

Amanat Khan, who was the only person allowed by Shah Jahan to inscribe his name on his work on the Taj, signed his calligraphy in two places, once above the south arch on the interior of the mausoleum, dated 1045 (1635–36), and a second time toward the bottom of the same interior arch in 1048 (1638–39). There is also an unsigned inscription simply recording the date of the work on the bottom left of the arch on the western exterior of the tomb, 1046 (1636–37). These three inscriptions are important beyond proving that Amanat Khan was the calligrapher. They show that the structure of the mausoleum was sufficiently complete for work to begin on interior decoration no more than at most four years after building had started, and that exterior decoration was at an advanced stage only a year later. The positioning of the two interior dates shows that Amanat Khan and his team started at the top of the building and worked down.

Apart from some of the inscriptions on the imperial cenotaphs and the date and calligrapher inscriptions, which are in Persian, all the rest of the calligraphy consists of writings from the Koran in the original Arabic. There are more than twenty-five such passages, a greater number than on any other building including mosques constructed under Shah Jahan. Usually a religious leader would have chosen the text from the Koran, but Amanat, as a scholar and respected member of the Moghul court as well as an experienced calligrapher, is likely to have chosen his texts himself, perhaps in discussion with Shah Jahan.

Once the content and location were decided, Amanat Khan would have designed the calligraphy in his studio, writing it full-size on large sheets of paper. In doing so, he would have tried to meld form and content into a singular intellectual beauty. The resultant design would then have been traced onto the marble, and stonecutters would have chiseled channels into the stone, into which they inserted black stone to form the writing. Particularly interesting, especially to those who cannot read the script itself, is the calligraphy around the entrance arch to the mausoleum and the southern gateway to the mausoleum complex. In both locations Amanat Khan varied by minute amounts the size and thickness of the lettering and the spacing between it to negate the distorting effect of height and thus to ensure that the fluid lettering appears of a uniform proportion from human-eye level, rather than diminishing with height.

As the main entrance to the Taj complex, the southern gateway was designed by the architects to prepare the visitor for what lay beyond. It is, in fact, a large building. Its octagonal floor plan derives, like that of the mausoleum itself, from the chamfering of the square. At the corners are octagonal towers topped with a single white domed octagonal *chattri*. The building is faced with red sandstone but, as one of the complex's main features, sumptuously inlaid with white marble, particularly around the entrances on its northern and southern sides which are set into large *iwans*. On the top of the frame of both *iwans* sits a line of eleven small white marble domed octagonal *chattris*. The entrance door blocks the view of the Taj Mahal until the visitor is admitted. Instead, their eyes are drawn to the calligraphy set into the frame of the southern *iwan*. There are many powerful lines, but the following in particular make clear that the visitor is invited to enter a spiritual place—an earthly equivalent of the heavenly paradise.

> *But O thou soul at peace,*
> *Return thou unto thy Lord, well-pleased, and well-pleasing*
> *unto Him,*
> *Enter thou among my servants,*
> *And enter thou My Paradise.*

Amanat Khan's work moved onlookers. One of Shah Jahan's court historians described how "the inscriptions on both the interior and exterior—comprising chapters from the Koran and verses referring to Divine Mercy—have been inlaid in utmost lavishness and artistry, with the subtlety of genius . . . and the point of the stone-cutting chisel displaying such delicate freshness and color as to surpass the artistic skill of the sky and draw the line of invalidation and sign of cancellation across the calligraphical writing [of others]."

Amanat Khan's calligraphy on the Taj Mahal

In 1632, just after the work on the Taj Mahal had begun, Shah Jahan had increased Amanat's rank, which brought a higher income, and a year later promoted him again, this time to the rank of a commander of one thousand. Both promotions seem to have honored his position as calligrapher of the Taj Mahal. In December 1637, when work on the calligraphy of the main mausoleum was seemingly nearing completion, Shah Jahan gave Amanat an elephant as a reward for the beauty of his inscriptions inside the tomb. Amanat Khan died sometime in the eighteenth year of Shah Jahan's reign (1644–45). How long he worked on the tomb is unknown, but since there is an unsigned inscription on the gateway to the Taj Mahal complex dated 1057 (1647), another calligrapher must have been employed at some time.

"All over the interior and exterior of the mausoleum, especially on the platform containing the illuminated cenotaph, carvers of rare workmanship, with delicate craftsmanship, have inlaid a variety of colored stones and precious gems—the jewels of whose description cannot be contained in the ocean of speech, nor may even the most ordinary degree of whose narration be achieved through the faculty of speech and discourse. And compared to its beautiful execution, which possesses infinite degrees of beauty, the masterpieces of Azrang and the picture galleries of China and Europe have no substance or reality, and appear like mere reflections on water." So wrote Shah Jahan's historian Salih about the remarkable decoration throughout the Taj Mahal.

When he visited the Taj in 1663, François Bernier described how "everywhere are seen the jasper and jade as well as other stones similar to those that enrich the wall of the grand duke's chapel at Florence, and several more of great value and rarity, set in an endless variety of modes, mixed and enchased in the slabs of marble which face the body of the wall. Even the squares of white and black marble which compose the pavement are inlaid with these precious stones in the most beautiful and delicate manner imaginable."

Today the decoration of the Taj Mahal still strikes the visitor not only with its good taste and restraint, which prevent it from overwhelming the architectural form, but also with the skill and sensuous delicacy of its execution. In addition to the inset calligraphy, the Taj Mahal's builders used three main types of ornamentation: intricate stone inlays, relief carvings and, mainly in the mosque and guesthouse, incised, painted decoration. In each case, floral themes dominate. Moghul artists worked away with chisel or inlay to depict flowers such as the iris, lily, lotus and tulip.

In both Asia and Europe there was in the seventeenth century a much more generally understood use of trees and plants as symbols than in the West today, where red roses for love are perhaps the only flowers with such widely appreciated symbolic significance. Persian poets described flowers as springing from the waters of paradise. They were often used in Islamic and, in particular, Persian art and design as symbols of paradise. Their use in the decoration of the Taj Mahal reinforced the message that the complex was intended to evoke an earthly paradise.

However, going beyond symbolism, from Babur onward, the Moghuls all had a special love for the natural beauty of flowers in their earthly manifestations in gardens. Motivated partly by his interest in natural science as well as in gardens, Jahangir had studied "the sweet scented flowers" of India, which he thought exceeded all others in beauty. His passion for painting had led him to receive many Western paintings of plants and blooms, including illustrations from the detailed herbals then appearing in Europe. These drawings inspired the introduction of a more naturalistic representation of flowers in all Moghul decorative arts. For the first time, for example, plants were shown in vases or growing in earth or in pots, as in the tomb of Itimad-ud-daula. Another sign of renewed European influence was the sudden reappearance of acanthus foliage, which had disappeared after India's early contact with the Greco-Roman world.

Shah Jahan added a further ingredient to the mix: his love and knowledge of jewels. According to the French jeweler Jean Baptiste Tavernier, "In the whole empire of the Great Moghul, there was no one more proficient in the knowledge of stones than Shah Jahan." His passion for jewels can be seen in the nature and value of the gems inlaid in the Taj Mahal and in the attention to decorative detail and finish. Indeed, the extraordinary craftsmanship led the nineteenth-century British bishop Heber of Calcutta to make a widely quoted remark that the Taj Mahal was built by giants and finished by jewelers. Others have seen the Taj Mahal itself as a white marble jewel set in a sandstone casket formed by the rest of the complex.

As exemplified by the comments of Bernier and Salih, the influences on, and origins of, the inlay work have been the subject of a somewhat sterile and chauvinistic controversy over the years. Some have claimed that the technique derives solely from the Italian hard stone inlay work, known as *pietra dura* and practiced particularly in Florence under the Medici, and that travelers brought it to India. Others have pointed out that, long before Europeans arrived, the Indians had developed the technique of stone inlaying known as *panchi kura*, meaning "driven-in work," which was used for both calligraphy and decoration. While the latter is certainly true, semiprecious stones, which are of an even greater hardness than the inlays previously used in India, were not employed before the arrival of the Europeans. Therefore, just as European painting had an effect on Moghul painting, it seems quite likely that either the Europeans or the objects they brought with them to the imperial court as gifts influenced Shah Jahan and his craftsmen to extend *panchi kura* to incorporate the jewels so beloved by the emperor.

Such a debate is much less important than the stupendous beauty of the inlay, which led a court poet to write:

> *They set stone flowers in the marble*
> *That by their color, if not their perfume*
> *Surpass real flowers.*

Two centuries later, the Russian theosophist Madame Helena Blavatsky enthused that some of the flowers "look so perfectly natural, the artist has copied nature so marvellously well, that your hand involuntarily reaches to assure yourself that they are not actually real. Branches of white jasmine made of mother of pearl wind around a red pomegranate flower of cornelian . . . while delicate oleanders peep out from under rich green foliage . . . every leaf, every petal is a separate emerald, pearl or topaz."*

More than forty different types of gems are used in the Taj Mahal. Shah Jahan had them transported from throughout Asia. Caravans brought jade along the silk route from Kashgar in China; beautiful, deep-blue, gold-flecked lapis lazuli was mined in the high mountains of northeastern Afghanistan; yaks carried turquoise on the first stage of their journey from upper Tibet; coral came from Arabia and the Red Sea; yellow amber from upper Burma; deep green malachite from Russia and rubies across the sea

---

* Madame Blavatsky founded theosophy in 1875, perhaps the first "new age" teaching. Theosophy was in some ways similar to Akbar's new religion. It saw truth in all religions and incorporated Hindu and Buddhist elements into a philosophy emphasizing the individual's need to understand their own karma and for direct, intuitive communion with the divine in mystic trances.

from Sri Lanka. Lahsunia, the cat's eye stone, is said to have been brought from as far as the Nile Valley in Egypt. The choice of a particular stone for an application or location was influenced not only by its color or transparency but also by its astrological associations. Sapphires, for example, were considered to have inauspicious connotations for many purposes and were therefore rarely employed.

When the gems reached Agra, "wonder working . . . magic making" artisans polished them and cut them to size with a small bow saw. These saws had up to five copper strings set at various distances apart to allow slices of stone of different thicknesses to be made. Stonecutters, probably using patterns prepared by artists to guide them, chiseled grooves into the white marble, into which they inserted the inlays and fixed them in place with a putty made of oil, lead oxide and wax. Gem experts have counted up to sixty slices of stone, each cut and matched with precision, to form a single flower of only an inch in size. Craftsmen showed great skill in using the variations of color within a single stone to suggest the shade variation within a single petal. They did not confine the art of *panchi kura* to the main buildings. Instead they used it extensively throughout the complex, thus adding to the unity of the whole. They reserved their finest work for Mumtaz Mahal's cenotaph at the heart of the mausoleum, and for the mausoleum itself, but even decorated the crenelations of the sandstone battlements, topping the complex's walls with white marble inlay in a flower pattern to which they added a black marble center.

A series of carved dado panels runs around the bottom of the walls on both the outside and inside of the mausoleum. The panels depict sprays of flowers such as tulips and irises, which rise in relief from the white marble.* Each panel has an inner frame of black marble and then a broad frame of stone inlay in stylized flower patterns. When the sun

---

* The tulip is native to central Asia, the word deriving from the Persian word *dulband*, meaning "turban" or "turban-shaped." At the very time when the carvers were portraying tulips on the Taj Mahal, tulip mania was sweeping Europe. It reached its height in Holland in early 1637 when a Dutch merchant paid 6,650 guilders (twenty-five times the annual wages of a carpenter) for a few dozen bulbs, not for planting but as an investment. A few days later the bubble burst, with prices falling to less than a tenth of what he had paid.

falls through the screens into the interior, it throws the flowers into even deeper relief, highlighting the three-dimensional effect. To make these carvings, known in India as *manabbat kari,* artists painted the design onto the white marble with henna. Carvers then used a series of ever finer chisels to remove successive layers of surrounding marble, thus allowing the flowers and plants to emerge in all their beauty.

The incised painting found mainly on the mosque and the guesthouse has, by its very nature, proved less durable than the carving and the inlay. However, the beauty of its plant and geometric designs is still clear on both their walls and ceilings. The method of producing the incised painting was simple and can be seen in folk art in many places in India. Artists began by painting a red earth wash over the white plaster on which they drew the designs. They then delicately scraped away the red overlay from within the drawings to reveal the white plaster once more and to make the flowers and geometric patterns appear to stand out from the red background.

CHAPTER TWELVE

"This Paradise-Like Garden"

THE TAJ COMPLEX, SO EXQUISITELY ORNAMENTED with jeweled, carved and painted plants and flowers crafted by the hand of man, would not have been considered complete without a correspondingly lovely natural setting—a garden of paradise.

The English word *paradise*, which first appeared in a Middle English text of 1175, is a simple transliteration of the old Persian word *pairidaeza*, meaning "a walled garden." But the linking of gardens to an eternal idyll is much older and is common to both Christianity and Islam with their shared roots in the Old Testament and the arid Middle East.

Paradise is closely associated with the Garden of Eden lost by Adam and Eve. In his epic poem *Paradise Lost*, written at the end of Shah Jahan's life, John Milton described how, in the Garden of Eden,

> *Rose a fresh fountain, and with many a rill*
> *Watered the garden; thence united fell*
> *Down the steep glade . . .*
> *And now, divided into four main streams,*
> *Runs diverse . . .*

Water has always been the stuff of life to desert dwellers. Oases in the Arabian Desert were perhaps the forerunners of the garden, and the bright, verdant green of their vegetation became a sacred color to the Arabs and

subsequently the color of Islam. When the prophet Muhammad proclaimed Islam, the Koran stated that the Islamic eternal dwelling, or paradise, was a series of terraces, each containing ever more splendid gardens
irrigated by four watercourses. Part of the description from the Koran
reads:

> With o'erbranching trees in each:
> In each two fountains flowing:
> In each two kinds of every fruit:
> On couches with linings of brocade shall they recline.
> And the fruit of the two gardens shall be within easy reach:
> Therein shall be the damsels with retiring glances,
> Whom nor man nor djinn hath touched before them:
> Like jacinths and pearls:
> Shall the reward of good be aught but good?
> And beside these shall be two other gardens:
> Of a dark green:
> With gushing fountains in each:
> In each fruits and the palm and the pomegranate.

When the Arabs invaded Persia in the seventh century, bringing with
them the Koran, they encountered another thriving garden tradition
stretching back more than one thousand years. Xenophon wrote of how
the great Persian ruler Cyrus had, in the sixth century BC, planted a garden with his own hands. One of Cyrus's successors, Xerxes, was so trans-
fixed by the beauty of a plane tree that he adorned its branches with gold
amulets. The melding of Arabic and Persian cultures with their common
love of horticulture produced gardens which their creators designed to
be an earthly counterpart to the heavenly paradise.

The designers used a simple basic plan. Paradise gardens are almost invariably walled, providing privacy and a protection for the peaceful order
within from the dusty chaos and swirling discord without. Watercourses
intersect in the center of the garden and represent the four rivers of life
and perhaps also symbolize the irrigation essential to living in the desert.
Some take the cross where the water channels meet as representing the
meeting of the human and the divine, but beyond any symbolic meaning,

the Persians used the water for the very practical purpose of irrigating the four sections of the garden, which they stocked with flowers and trees. The gardens thus became known as *char baghs*, "four-fold enclosed gardens." (*Bagh* is another Persian word for "garden.")

When Timur invaded Persia in a series of campaigns in the 1380s, he took back to central Asia much from the cultural reservoir the country and its people provided. As well as craftsmen, he borrowed ideas from the "paradise garden" and incorporated them into the gardens with which he surrounded his capital city of Samarkand. Because their kingdoms were hillier, and often better provided with water, Timur and his nobles made more use of running water in fountains and waterfalls cascading down through terraced gardens. From the limited pictorial and descriptive material available, they seem to have planted their gardens with fruit trees such as pomegranate, peach, quince and cherry, together with other trees such as plane and poplar. They filled the beds with flowers like the iris, rose, violet and narcissus. Interestingly, because of the local climate they apparently used clover, not grass, for ground cover. Timur gave his vast gardens encircling Samarkand romantic names such as World's Picture and Meadow of the Deep Pool. As he moved his nomadic encampment from garden to garden, Timur, who was tall and broad with a long white beard, had his throne placed on a platform above the spot where the watercourses representing the four rivers of life crossed, to emphasize his domination of the four quarters of the world.

Babur brought with him to India the Timurid garden tradition. One of his first acts was to build cooling gardens in his hot new capital of Agra. These were essentially pleasure grounds; in time, though, his successors were to make their gardens the setting for their tombs. Emperors and their nobles would create *char baghs* to enjoy and live in while alive, and in which they would be buried when they died. The Moghuls introduced other developments, including broader water channels and a greater use of large sheets of still water to reflect the tombs or pavilions built at the channels' intersections. Shah Jahan usually built pavilions of white marble, sometimes with a counterpointing pavilion in black, as, for example, in the black pavilion that in 1630 he ordered to be constructed in the Shalimar Gardens in Kashmir.

The Moghuls made even more use of running water in their gardens than their Timurid forebears. They incorporated fountains producing spouts of water and a romantic, cooling mist that brightened into a prismatic rainbow when struck by the rays of the sun. They added water shoots and embellished water channels by causing water to run down sheets of marble carefully carved in fish-scale patterns to produce ripples and reflections. As dusk fell and bats swooped down to drink, servants lit oil lamps kept dry in niches behind the falling water to enhance the velvet beauty of the night.

Such was the importance of the garden to the Moghuls that they frequently used it as a metaphor for the state. Abul Fazl described Akbar's motive in punishing wrongdoers as being to improve the world for all: "As gardeners adorn gardens with trees and move them from one place to another, and reject many, and irrigate others, and labour to rear them to a proper size, and extirpate bad trees and lop off rotten branches, and remove trees that are too large . . . and gather their various fruits and flowers and enjoy their shade when necessary, and do other things which are established in the science of horticulture, so do just and far-seeing kings light the lamp of wisdom by regulation, and instructing their servants, and thus appear the standard of guidance."

Whatever the symbolism they employed in their garden design, and however cleverly they manipulated the garden as a metaphor, Babur and his successors enjoyed their gardens profoundly for their natural beauty, designing them to appeal to all five senses: sight, scent, sound (through the sound of water and of birds and insects attracted to the fruit and pollen), touch (the texture of leaves, the smoothness of marble and the coolness of water) and taste (through the consumption of the fruit.) Like Timur, the Moghuls often conducted their business in the open air. In one miniature painting Babur sits in his garden enthroned beneath a canopy and surrounded by blossoming trees and flowers to receive ambassadors. Other paintings show emperors and nobles besporting themselves with their scantily clad concubines in secluded bowers within their gardens, bright flowers in full bloom, fertile trees laden with ripe fruit ready to drop and phallic fountains shooting plumes of water skyward.

In one of the best-known portraits of Shah Jahan, he is surrounded by flowers, among them irises, tulips, daffodils, hollyhocks and campanula. To him, the design of the gardens of the Taj Mahal would have been as

Babur enthroned in one of his gardens in India

important as that of the buildings and would have combined with them
to create a coherent, exquisite whole. A court poet wrote of the emperor's
desire to create in the Taj Mahal complex a perfection that would endure

> *So long as the words flower and garden remain,*
> *So long as there are residues of cloud and rain.*

SHAH JAHAN AND his planners designed the Taj Mahal garden as a classic
walled garden to be laid out on the *char bagh*, or quadripartite, plan. Two

marble water channels, one of which is the north-south channel that forms the central axis of the whole complex, cross at right angles in the middle of the garden, halfway between the tomb and the gateway, and divide it into four squares. The water channels are raised, as in most Moghul gardens, to allow them to irrigate the surrounding planting. To reaffirm the bilateral symmetry, the architects designed identical red sandstone pavilions to be built into the boundary walls at the two ends of the east-west cross channel. They topped each pavilion, where musicians are said to have played, with an octagonal *chattri*. At the intersection of the channels they placed a large square white marble pool, perfectly positioned to reflect the Taj in its waters. Such pools, which were a feature of Moghul gardens, apparently have their origins in the ablution tanks of mosques where the Islamic faithful undertake a ritual cleansing prior to prayer.* The designers set the pool in a marble platform sixty-four feet square decorated with lotus patterns. At certain times of day, five fountains within the pool shot jets of water into the air. Around the edge of the pool were twenty-four more fountains with another twenty-four playing on each side of the pool in the broad central channel running between the gateway and the mausoleum. The gardeners stocked the pool with lotus flowers, the symbols of fertility, and with goldfish.

The designers further subdivided the garden, quartered by the channels, into four equal squares, producing sixteen in all. What the Moghuls planted in the Taj gardens is not clear in detail. Today's arrangements are much influenced by British planting just over a century ago. For example, although the Moghuls introduced to India the cypress, which originally came from Persia and Asia Minor, as a symbol of eternity, including the eternity to which the dead were destined, the avenue of cypresses now leading to the tomb from the gateway is unlikely to have been original. Cypresses did, however, probably feature among "the trees and rare aromatic herbs" that the court historian Salih mentions being planted. Perhaps, as often in their gardens, the Moghuls originally alternated cypresses with fruit trees. The latter provided shade as well as symbolizing

---

* Some architectural historians argue that the positioning of ablution tanks in mosques may, in turn, originate from the placing of fire pits in Zoroastrian temples, from which many early mosques in Persia were converted.

Satellite photo of the Taj Mahal and the Mahtab Bagh, separated by the Jumna River, October 10, 1999

earthly life renewed each spring, in contrast to the more sober associations of the cypress. Some garden historians think that the gardens of the Taj Mahal were originally much lower than they are today to the extent that those walking along the raised water channels would have been so high above the gardens that they would have been able to pluck the luscious fruit from the trees with ease.

When François Bernier, the French doctor, visited the Taj Mahal, he found the gardens "full of flowers." Unfortunately, he did not name them, but they probably included the roses (so essential to the attar of roses invented by Mumtaz's grandmother), as well as irises, crown imperials and other spring bulbs featured in the tomb's inlay work. As for other flowers, Jahangir mentions among his favorite bushes jasmine—another source of perfume—and the flowers of the pagoda tree. Among the fruit trees would have been the mango and the orange. The Moghuls also loved apples and pears. Although easier to cultivate in the more temperate climate of Kashmir, if carefully watered, they grew in Agra for the dry three quarters of the year.*

As everyone who has ever visited a construction site knows, the actual

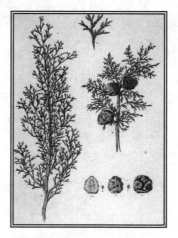

Botanical illustration of cypress

---

* Amid all their opulence and prodigality, the Moghuls showed some economic prudence when they sold excess fruit and flowers from their imperial gardens, including the Taj Mahal, to offset their running costs.

planting of the Taj Mahal's garden would have had to await the completion of the remainder of the complex and the removal of all the rubble,
scaffolding and other building paraphernalia. However, the architects
would have drawn up the detailed plans for the gardens at the same time
as those for the rest of the complex, not only because the garden was an
integral part of the overall concept but also to allow the builders to construct the garden features, such as platforms and paths, and, in particular,
the system for supplying water to the Taj's pools and fountains from the
Jumna River.

The scale and sophistication of these waterworks, built to the west of
the site, again show that the Taj was an immense engineering achievement
as well as an artistic one. West of the Taj, where the land slopes down to
the Jumna, the builders diverted the river's waters into a settlement tank,
in which silt and other debris would sink to the bottom, and then into a
channel parallel to the western wall of the Taj and some 250 feet from
it. Alongside this channel's western edge the workers constructed a tall
arched brick aqueduct, whose top was wide enough to contain not only
another water channel but also a system of thirteen *purs* to raise the water up to it.

Each *pur* consisted of a roller placed at the edge of the aqueduct overlooking the water channel below. A large leather bucket was attached to
a rope wound around the roller, and water was raised by an attendant
leading a pair of oxen away from the roller down a gentle slope. (The
buckets were made from the skins of oxen tied together at the four
extremities—an ominous indication to the oxen of their eventual fate.)*

Once the *purs* had raised the water to the aqueduct, it flowed along the
channel into a storage tank and then, once that was filled, onward into
another. Alongside the southern end of this latter tank the builders constructed a final aqueduct, some thirty feet high, at right angles to the other

---

* The Moghuls had continued to use the system of *purs*, which was native to India,
  despite Babur's condemnation of it as "laborious and filthy . . . it takes one person
  to lead the ox and another to empty the water from the bucket. Every time the ox
  is led out to pull up the bucket and then led back, the rope is dragged through the
  ox's path which is sullied with ox urine and dung." Presumably attendants washed
  the roof down regularly.

Remains of the Taj Mahal's aqueduct

one and to the Taj's western walls. When a second series of *purs* had raised the water to this level, a channel conducted it to a series of three connecting tanks built into the end of the aqueduct close to the wall of the Taj complex by the western pavilion, at the terminus of the Taj's main east-west water channel. The first tank—the one farthest from the Taj wall—was four and a half feet deep, the next six feet and the one nearest the wall nine feet. These progressively deeper tanks produced the necessary head of water pressure to feed the Taj's garden. Pipes took the water down underground into the complex where the builders buried the main pipe in masonry beneath a paved walkway.

To make sure that the fountains went off uniformly, and not randomly, however far they were from the header tank and however inconsistent the water flow, the engineers designed an ingenious system of copper pots placed beneath the fountains. They connected the water supply to the pots, rather than directly to the fountains, so that the water first filled the pots and only when all were filled did it rise simultaneously from the fountainheads.

By 1643, the year that the main tomb complex was completed, the Taj's gardens were yet to reach their full maturity but were already stocked with bright, fragrant flowers and luxuriant trees. They were, in the words of Shah Jahan's historian Salih, like "the black mole on the forehead of all the world's pleasure spots and each of its bounty-laced flowerbeds is pleasing and heart-captivating like the flowerbeds of the garden of the keeper of Paradise. Its attractive green trees are perennially fed with the water of life and the stature of each . . . surpasses that of the celestial lotus tree . . . light-sprinkling fountains gush forth sprinkling pearls of water . . . In short, the excellent features of this paradise-like garden such as its pathways fashioned entirely of red stone, its galaxy-indicating water channel and its tank of novel design which has materialised from the crystal of purity from the world of illumination have reached a stage surpassing imagination, and the smallest particle of its description cannot be accommodated by the faculty of speech."

CHAPTER THIRTEEN

The Illumined Tomb

ON THE NIGHT OF 6 FEBRUARY 1643, SHAH Jahan mourned his dead wife
in the luminous tomb he had created for her. It was almost complete, although embellishments would continue until 1648 and subsidiary parts
of the complex would not be finished until around 1653. The occasion
was the twelfth Urs, or "death anniversary"—the first time the ceremonial feast had been held in the Taj itself.*

Guests approaching through the flower-scented gardens at dusk must
have been awed by the sheer scale of the domed mausoleum rising up
against the backdrop of the sky. As one of Shah Jahan's poets wrote:

> *The back of the earth-supporting bull sways to its belly,*
> *Reduced to a footprint from carrying such a burden.*

Yet despite its great size, it appeared ethereal, even spectral, so that
according to the poet, "The eye can mistake it for a cloud." He also captured its radiance.

> *Light sparkles from within its pure stones,*
> *Like wine within a crystal goblet.*

---

* The Urs was of course celebrated on the anniversary of Mumtaz's death according
to the Muslim lunar calendar and not the Western solar one.

When reflections from the stars fall on its marble,
The entire edifice resembles a festival of lamps.

The mourners passed through the great portal on the south side of the mausoleum, framed by Amanat Khan's fluid calligraphy, and through a grilled door into the central octagonal chamber. The marble floors were carpeted with richly colored rugs of intricate design, and the walls were hung with costly velvets and silks gleaming in the soft light from enameled golden chandeliers—during Urs ceremonies tombs were especially illuminated as emblems of the "shining excellencies and perfections" of the departed. Mullahs chanted prayers "for the repose of the soul of Mumtaz residing in the gardens of Paradise," the sound rising and echoing in the void beneath the dome.

In the center of the chamber was an octagonal latticed marble screen more than six feet high, "highly polished and pure . . . with an entrance fashioned of jasper after the Turkish fashion, joined with gilded fasteners," according to the court chronicler Lahori. The screen, or *jali*, was a replacement for the bejeweled solid gold rail Shah Jahan had originally commissioned, but which he ordered to be removed for fear of thieves and vandals. Carved from a single block of marble to resemble filigree, the screen veiled the slender white marble cenotaph within. This cenotaph, inlaid with bright jeweled flowers, their curving fronds suggesting vitality and renewal as if they were truly growing over the marble, lay directly beneath the dome. The top and sides of the cenotaph bore gracefully swirling Koranic inscriptions and an epitaph inlaid in black marble at its southern end told the onlooker that here was

THE ILLUMINED GRAVE OF ARJUMAND BANU BEGAM,
ENTITLED MUMTAZ MAHAL, WHO DIED IN THE YEAR 1040

Mourners that night probably also saw the fabulous "sheet of pearls," which, according to one of his historians, "Shah Jahan had caused to be made for the tomb of Mumtaz Mahal, and which was spread over it upon the anniversary and on Friday nights." Directly beneath in the crypt a second white marble cenotaph containing Mumtaz's body rested on a marble platform. It was as lavishly inlaid and bore the same epitaph to Arjumand Banu, but its inscriptions also included the ninety-nine Islamic names for God.

The chief mourner, Shah Jahan, probably reached the Taj by boat from the Agra fort. However he journeyed there, that first marking of Mumtaz's death in the Taj itself must have seemed particularly charged with meaning. As well as reviving tender memories, it marked a crucial stage in the achievement of his ambition: the creation of a perfect, paradise-resembling tomb as Mumtaz's final resting place

The realization of that ambition had not been cheap. No complete, detailed accounts have survived whose authenticity is above question. Shah Jahan's historian Lahori recorded the cost of constructing the Taj to be "fifty lakhs" of rupees—5 million rupees. However, this number is thought to have covered only direct labor costs and to exclude many items including all materials. Using data from some of the later disputed manuscripts, some historians put the figure as high as 40 million rupees. The construction itself had been funded by the imperial treasury and by the treasury of the province of Agra. Shah Jahan had also ordered a deed of endowment to be drawn up, including the revenue from thirty villages, to ensure that his beloved Taj would be properly maintained and guarded in future years. He intended his great creation to endure. As a court poet eloquently expressed it:

> *When the hand of perpetuity laid that foundation,*
> *Impermanence ran fearfully to hide in the desert.*

SHAH JAHAN'S GREATEST consolation over the twelve years since Mumtaz's death had been Jahanara, the oldest surviving child of the fourteen Mumtaz had borne him. As well as filling Mumtaz's role as first lady of the Moghul Empire, Jahanara had cared for the younger brothers and sisters for whose safety and security the dying Mumtaz had pleaded. Like her mother, Jahanara was highly educated, with interests ranging from music and architecture to religion and literature. She knew the Koran by heart, was well versed in Persian and Arabic and was an accomplished writer. As with her beautiful mother, no formally attributed likeness of her exists, although a portrait in an album prepared for her brother Dara

Shukoh in about 1635 may be Jahanara. A graceful young woman rests one hand lightly on the trunk of a pink-blossomed tree, while in her other hand she holds a spray of flowers. Narcissi and lilies bloom at her feet.

Dara Shukoh, only one year her junior, was Jahanara's favorite brother. He shared her love of the mystic Muslim creed of Sufism, and both had become devotees of the Sufi Mullah Shah. Jahanara wrote that "of all the descendants of Timur, only we two, brother and sister, were fortunate enough to attain this felicity. None of our forefathers ever trod the path in quest of God and in search of the truth. My happiness knows no bounds, my veneration for Mullah Shah increased and I made him my guide and my spiritual preceptor." Jahanara had lovingly made the arrangements for Dara Shukoh's wedding to his cousin in early 1633—originally planned by Mumtaz and postponed because of her death—and spent huge sums on the festivities. The English traveler Peter Mundy witnessed some amazing pyrotechnics: "great elephants whose bellies were full of squibs, crackers, etc; giants with wheels in their hands, then a rank of monsters, then of turrets, then of artificial trees [and other] inventions, all full of rockets." For the first time since Mumtaz had died, Shah Jahan permitted singing and dancing at court.

Shah Jahan's affection for Jahanara "exceeded all that he felt towards his other children." In 1644, the year after Mumtaz's twelfth Urs, according to his historian, the thirty-one-year old princess almost died. On the night of 4 April, she "was proceeding to her own sleeping apartment when the border of her chaste garment brushed against a lamp left burning on the floor in the middle of the hall. As the dresses worn by the ladies of the palace are made of the most delicate fabrics and perfumed with fragrant oils, her garment caught fire and was instantly enveloped in flames. Four of her private attendants were at hand, and they immediately tried to extinguish the fire; yet as it spread itself over their garments as well, their efforts proved unavailing. As it all happened so quickly, before the alarm could be given and water procured, the back and hands and both sides of the body of that mine of excellence were dreadfully burned."

Fire was a perennial risk. The fabrics worn by the imperial women were indeed light and sheer to the point of transparency and very flammable.

A portrait said to be of Jahanara

Jean-Baptiste Tavernier described a particular muslin so prized that "the merchants are not allowed to export it, and the Governor sends all of it for the Great Mogul's seraglio and for the principal courtiers. This it is of which the sultanas and the wives of the great nobles make themselves shifts and garments for the hot weather, and the King and the nobles enjoy seeing them wearing these fine shifts and cause them to dance in them."

An anguished Shah Jahan, cast into "deep gloom," did not appear the next day but remained in the harem. He ordered holy men in the mosques to recite prayers for his daughter's recovery, released prisoners from their captivity and donated enormous sums to the poor. He summoned dozens of doctors and surgeons, even foreign physicians, and tended Jahanara himself, "administering her medicine and diet, and applying and removing her bandages with his own hand." He neglected his duties so that "owing to His Majesty's being constantly occupied in tending the invalid, he repaired to public audiences and private conferences very late and quitted them early."

Two of the attendants who had tried to help Jahanara died of their burns—one after seven days, the other after eight. The princess herself, however, started slowly to respond to treatment by a Persian doctor, and for a while her condition improved. However, she began to deteriorate again, causing Shah Jahan to despair until a royal page devised a dressing which after two months caused the wounds to close. In gratitude, Shah Jahan ordered the imperial kettledrums to be sounded and Jahanara to be weighed against gold—"an observance hitherto limited solely to the person of the Emperor." However, not until late 1644 did Shah Jahan feel sufficiently confident of her complete recovery to stage a great eight-day festival of thanksgiving during which he lavished "rare gems and ornaments" on his convalescent daughter from "130 virgin pearls of the purest water" to "a tiara formed of one immense diamond." He also bestowed on her the revenues of the port of Surat once enjoyed by her great aunt, the empress Nur. Surat was then the principal port where European trading nations conducted much of their business, and the revenues were large. The celebrations ended with a magnificent fireworks display on the riverbank "to the great delight of the bedazzled spectators." "In fact," added Shah Jahan's historian, "not since His Majesty's auspicious accession had a jubilee such as this been celebrated."

These events reveal Shah Jahan's intense, even obsessive love for his daughter. Foreigners, observing from the sidelines and eagerly receptive to rumor, saw something more sinister in the relationship: incest. They pointed out that, unlike the other royal princesses, Jahanara lived independently in her own palace outside the fort at Agra. They also noted the custom introduced by Akbar that prevented imperial princesses from marrying. Had Jahanara, they speculated, replaced Mumtaz in everything, finding in Shah Jahan a husband, and had he found a way of reincarnating his dead empress?

The Dutchman Joannes de Laet, writing in the very year of Mumtaz's

death and who, though not a traveler to India himself, collated the reports of others, claimed that "to so many murders of his relatives he
[Shah Jahan] added incest also; for, when his beloved wife had died . . .
he took to himself as wife his own daughter by that dead woman." Just a
few months later Peter Mundy took up the theme: "The Great Moghul's
or King's daughters are never suffered to marry (as I am informed), being
an ancient custom. This Shah Jahan, among the rest, hath one named
Chiminy Begum [Jahanara], a very beautiful creature by report, with
whom (it was openly bruited and talked of in Agra) he committed incest, being very familiar with her many times."

The stories persisted, cropping up in earnest letters home to England
from clerks based in Agra and Surat. François Bernier, who arrived in the
Moghul Empire toward the end of Shah Jahan's reign and doubtless lapped
up tales that had lost nothing in the intervening years, made the most
explicit claims. Jahanara was, he wrote, "very handsome, of lively parts"
and had been "passionately beloved by her father. Rumour has it that his
attachment reached a point which it is difficult to believe, the justification of which he rested on the decisions of the Mullahs . . . According to
them, it would have been unjust to deny the King the privilege of gathering fruit from the tree he had himself planted."

He also accused Jahanara of taking other lovers: "I hope I shall not be
suspected of a wish to supply subjects for romance," he wrote piously.
"What I am writing is a matter of history, and my object is to present a
faithful account of the manners of this people. Love adventures are not
attended with the same danger in Europe as in Asia. In France they ex-
cite only merriment; they create a laugh, and are forgotten; but in this
part of the world, few are the instances in which they are not followed by
some dreadful and tragical catastrophe." He went on to describe an incident poised between farce and revenge tragedy. Jahanara, he suggested,
had begun an affair with a young man "of no very exalted rank" but handsome. The jealous Shah Jahan, alerted to his daughter's liaison, entered
her apartments "at an unusual and unexpected hour," causing her lover
to hide in a big cauldron used to heat water for baths. After conversing
with his nervous daughter "on ordinary topics," he observed that "the
state of her skin indicated a neglect of her customary ablutions, and that
it was proper she should bathe. He then commanded the eunuchs to

light a fire under the cauldron, and did not retire until they gave him to understand that his wretched victim was no more." Bernier also reported that Shah Jahan slew another of his daughter's lovers by smilingly handing the unfortunate youth poisoned betel to chew.

Not all Europeans, though, were convinced. The Venetian Niccolao Manucci dismissed Bernier's stories of boiled and poisoned lovers as "founded entirely on the talk of low people." He attributed the charge of incest to the fact that Jahanara served her father "with the greatest love and diligence in order that Shah Jahan should accede to her petitions. It was from this cause that the common people hinted that she had intercourse with her father." Manucci claimed to have firsthand knowledge of happenings within Jahanara's mansion. He described how "the princess was fond of drinking wine, which was imported for her from Persia, Kabul and Kashmir. But the best liquor she drank was distilled in her own house. It was a most delicious spirit, made from wine and rosewater, flavoured with many costly spices and aromatic drugs. Many a time she did me the favour of ordering some bottles of it to be sent to my house, in sign of her gratitude for my curing people in her harem . . . The lady's drinking was at night, when various delightful pranks, music, dancing, and acting were going on around her. Things arrived at such a pass that sometimes she was unable to stand, and they had to carry her to bed." As if anticipating questions he added, "I say this because I was admitted on familiar terms to this house, and I was deep in the confidence of the principal ladies and eunuchs in her service."*

The official Moghul sources are silent on any incestuous behavior, portraying Jahanara as an adored daughter, nothing more. Since Shah Jahan approved every word of the court histories, this is not surprising. At this distance in time, allegations of incest are as hard to prove as they are to dismiss. The close bonds between Shah Jahan and Jahanara clearly provoked comment. It is plausible that an emperor disorientated by a terrible grief found physical solace in a daughter who closely resembled the young Mumtaz. It is also possible that a young princess passionately

---

* The family weakness for alcohol had clearly been inherited by both Jahanara and her younger sister Raushanara, and, as imperial princesses, they were free to indulge it within their private quarters.

devoted to her father, perhaps fearing for his reason, acquiesced. However, it seems more likely that, while Shah Jahan may have harbored sexual feelings, conscious or unconscious, they were not fulfilled. In later years, rebellious sons would accuse him of many things but not of incestuous relations with their sister.

Also, Shah Jahan's obsession with Jahanara fitted a pattern that was not necessarily sexual. His deepest feelings seem to have been reserved for the women in his life. He had been broken by grief when his mother died, and his enduring, exclusive love for Mumtaz had been as much about companionship and empathy as about sex.

Whatever the reality of their relationship, Jahanara's influence over Shah Jahan was beyond question. Manucci was only one of many to observe that "she obtained from her father whatever she asked." In 1644, the year of her recovery from the near-fatal fire, Jahanara interceded on behalf of her brother Aurangzeb, who, soon after her accident, had clashed with Shah Jahan.

Until this time, Aurangzeb had been the very model of a martial Moghul princeling. In 1635 Shah Jahan had sent the then sixteen-year-old Aurangzeb to war. The enemy was the wealthy raja of Orchha, Jujhar Singh, whose territory lay in a richly forested region about one hundred miles south of Agra. The raja had rebelled at the start of Shah Jahan's reign but had been pacified shortly before the much bigger campaign that had taken Shah Jahan and Mumtaz to the Deccan in 1629. However, the raja had subsequently shown unwelcome signs of independence, prompting Shah Jahan to appoint Aurangzeb to lead an army against him. Although this was Aurangzeb's first appointment in the field, his forces overpowered the raja, who fled in panic into the forests, where he was murdered by wild Gond tribesmen. Aurangzeb pursued the remainder of his family and captured them before the women had time to commit the rite of *jauhar*, burning themselves on great funeral pyres, which, a court historian disapprovingly observed, "is one of the benighted practices of Hindustan."

Tellingly, Shah Jahan ordered the Hindu temple built by Jujhar Singh's father—the man who had so obligingly murdered Akbar's friend and chronicler Abul Fazl at Jahangir's request—to be pulled down and replaced by a mosque. This was a signal of Shah Jahan's drift away from the religious tolerance of his father and grandfather. The balanced pragmatism of his younger days was yielding to a bleaker, more rigid, regimented outlook. The first signs had come in the immediate aftermath of Mumtaz's death. In early 1632 he had ordered the destruction of all newly built Hindu temples and was especially adamant that his orders be enforced in that "great stronghold of infidelity," the Hindu holy city of Benares. He also banned any further temple building. His actions may have been prompted by grief and a sense that Mumtaz's death had been a punishment for his leniency toward unbelievers. They may also have been in response to pressure from orthodox mullahs. Though a Sunni Muslim himself, Shah Jahan had, on his accession, dismissed certain hard-line Sunni clerics and perhaps felt the need to placate them.

Also in 1632 Shah Jahan had ordered the first full-scale attack on Christians in the Moghul Empire. His target was the Portuguese in their long-established trading settlement on the River Hugli in Bengal, northwest of present-day Calcutta. Shah Jahan had always been more suspicious of foreigners than his father, Jahangir, as the English ambassador Sir Thomas Roe had complained bitterly. The Portuguese, as well as being "unbelievers," had according to Shah Jahan's historian compounded their sins by fortifying their town "with cannon and matchlocks and other instruments of war" and attacking neighboring villages, forcibly converting people to Christianity and selling others into slavery.

If this was not enough, Shah Jahan had personal motives for attacking these particular "heretics." During his rebellion against his father, the Portuguese had refused to help him and indeed had aided the imperial forces fighting against him. On Shah Jahan's accession they had conspicuously failed to offer the traditional congratulations and gifts. Some accounts also suggest a link between Shah Jahan's vendetta against the Portuguese and Mumtaz. They describe how, when Shah Jahan and Mumtaz were fleeing through Bengal, the Portuguese took advantage of their plight as they passed close to Hugli. According to Niccolao Manucci, "Some Portuguese sallied forth and seized two beloved female slaves of [Mumtaz Mahal]. This lady sent word to them that it would be better for them to help a prince then seeking refuge in flight than to attempt to rob him. Therefore she urgently prayed them to send her the two slave girls.

But the Portuguese paid no heed to her request, an act which cost them dear."

The reckoning was indeed expensive. On Shah Jahan's order the governor of Bengal besieged the settlement, placing a string of boats across the river to prevent the Portuguese from escaping by boat and then detonating a huge mine beneath the fortifications. In the ensuing panic, "warriors of Islam" overran the settlement, capturing more than four thousand people, mostly women and children, who were dispatched on an eleven-month march to Agra. François Bernier described their fate: "The handsome women, as well married as single, became inmates of the seraglio; those of a more advanced age, or of inferior beauty, were distributed among the Omrahs [nobles]; little children underwent the rite of circumcision, and were made pages; and the men of adult age, allured, for the most part, by fair promises, or terrified by the daily threat of throwing them under the feet of elephants, renounced the Christian faith." According to Lahori, those who refused to convert were imprisoned and "such of their idols as were likenesses of the prophets were thrown into the Jumna, the rest were broken to pieces." Shah Jahan also ordered the demolition of churches in Agra and Lahore erected during his father's reign. The loud chiming of the clock in the steeple of the Agra church had been heard in every part of the city. Perhaps Shah Jahan did not wish the infidel sound to penetrate Mumtaz's resting place.

Shah Jahan's punitive actions against Christian communities did not, in fact, continue. The Jesuits in Agra, themselves harassed in the early years of Shah Jahan's reign, managed to rehabilitate themselves and even to intercede for some of the captive fathers from Hugli. However, Shah Jahan's gestures toward fundamentalism had been welcomed by the young Aurangzeb, whose religious vision of the world was more bleakly austere than that of any of his Moghul forebears and who would be relentless in his pursuit of it.

At this early stage in his life Aurangzeb was in high favor. The year after his successful campaign against the raja of Orchha, Shah Jahan appointed him governor of the Deccan, a post he would hold for eight years. The presence of Aurangzeb with an enormous army in this still troublous region was sufficiently threatening to persuade Bijapur's ruler to sign a treaty with the Moghuls and to induce the ruler of Golconda to

Aurangzeb

make a token submission. In the following years Shah Jahan promoted Aurangzeb twice more, increasing his rank and his allowances.

In May 1644, learning of the accident that had befallen Jahanara, Aurangzeb had hastened from the Deccan to her bedside in Agra. However, something occurred during that visit which soured his relationship with his father and lost Aurangzeb both his rank and governorship. The historian Lahori says that the prince had fallen "under the influence of ill-advised and short-sighted companions" and "had determined to withdraw from worldly occupations." However, more specific clues are offered in a bitter letter written by Aurangzeb ten years later to Jahanara in which he stated, "I knew my life was a target [of rivals]."

The rival Aurangzeb feared but did not name was his handsome, charismatic elder brother, the Sufi-following Dara Shukoh. Dara was frequently by his father's side, the object of constant signs of his love and affection, and in 1633 Shah Jahan had marked him out as his chosen successor, conferring on him the district of Hissar Firoza, traditionally awarded to the heir apparent, together with the right to pitch a crimson tent. Aurangzeb resented these marks of favor to Dara. As he grew up, he also came to disapprove thoroughly of Dara's wide-ranging religious interests, which, though they mirrored the tolerance and curiosity of Jahangir and Akbar, smacked to him of heresy. Dara in return disparaged Aurangzeb as a narrow-minded fundamentalist.

According to a courtier, the tensions between the two brothers were dramatically and publicly exposed during Jahanara's convalescence when Aurangzeb accompanied his father to inspect Dara's new riverside mansion in Agra. While they were touring the building, Dara invited Aurangzeb to enter an underground chamber, but he refused, convinced that Dara meant to kill him there. Instead, he remained obstinately in the doorway, defying even his father's order to enter.

This story seems too melodramatic to be true, but the suggestion of some kind of showdown is valid. Certainly Aurangzeb was jealous of Dara and felt neglected by his father. Unable to contain his feelings any longer, he must have complained to his father, but instead of winning Shah Jahan's sympathy incurred his anger. In the ensuing row either Shah Jahan stripped him of his rank and office, or, as some accounts suggest, Aurangzeb himself resigned his position out of pique.

Whatever the case, Aurangzeb soon regretted the breach but needed seven months to regain Shah Jahan's favor. Even then, as a court historian recorded, this was only "due to the urging of his royal sister." Jahanara chose the celebrations for her recovery as the moment to make her plea, and Shah Jahan indulged her, reinstating Aurangzeb in his former rank and a few months later, in February 1645, appointing him governor of wealthy Gujarat. All appeared well again, but the episode held disturbing echoes of past jealousies within the imperial family, in particular Shah Jahan's own rivalry with Khusrau. Shah Jahan and Khusrau had, of course, been only half-brothers while Dara Shukoh and Aurangzeb were full brothers, but over coming years this would count for nothing at all.

CHAPTER FOURTEEN

"The Sublime Throne"

IN LATE 1645 NEWS REACHED SHAH JAHAN from Lahore of the death of his ally turned adversary, the sixty-eight-year-old Nur Jahan. The bazaars hummed with lurid rumors of murder, but it seems more likely that, as the official histories recorded, she had died of natural causes. Since the death of her husband she had lived the secluded life of a widow with little scope for intrigue, so that Shah Jahan had no cause to order her death. His policy toward Nur had been to ignore her personally and systematically to remove traces of her once pervasive influence, withdrawing from circulation all coins stamped with her name and purging his court of officials once loyal to her. Moghul historians would be divided in their view of her, depending, of course, on their political loyalties. Many deplored her power over Jahangir, but none could deny her remarkable career, which owed as much to her abilities as to Jahangir's weaknesses.

Unlike the elaborate ceremonials marking Mumtaz's death, Nur's funeral was modest. Her body was placed in a marble sarcophagus in the tomb she had built for herself close to that of her husband, Jahangir. Nur had begun to construct her tomb in 1641, the year that her brother and political rival Asaf Khan died. As Shah Jahan's chief minister and father-in-law, Asaf Khan had also studiously ignored Nur. Despite the death of his daughter Mumtaz, the bonds between father and son-in-law had remained strong. The Portuguese friar Sebastien Manrique claimed to have witnessed a banquet where Asaf Khan entertained Shah Jahan in a chamber adorned with "rich carpets of silken, silver, and golden embroidery" and "large perfume-holders and braziers of silver, of wonderful workmanship, ranged all around the hall, in which the sweetest perfumes were burnt." Scented water played from a seven-spouted fountain, and beautiful girls laid golden ewers on a white satin tablecloth so that the emperor could wash. "Eunuchs richly attired in Hindustan style, with trousers of different coloured silks and white coats of the finest transparent muslin," served dinner. During the meal Shah Jahan addressed Asaf Khan's wife, Mumtaz's mother, as Mother and invited her to sit on his right in the place of honor.

ALTHOUGH THE TAJ Mahal was largely complete, Shah Jahan absorbed himself in other elaborate, expensive and ambitious building projects. In 1647 he began construction of the exquisite Moti Masjid (the Pearl Mosque) in the Red Fort at Agra. However, he reserved his grandest plans of all for Delhi, building an entire new metropolis—Shahjahanabad—on the west banks of the Jumna. It would be the last of the so-called seven cities of Delhi built by successive Islamic dynasties as their capital from the twelfth century onward. Shah Jahan's historian Inayat Khan described his quest for "some pleasant site, distinguished by its genial climate, where he might find a splendid fort and delightful edifices . . . through which streams of water should be made to flow, and the terraces of which should overlook the river." As well as desiring to found a city as an expression of his power, Shah Jahan, who found the heat of Hindustan just as oppressive as his forebears had, wished to escape Agra's hot, searing winds and, perhaps, also memories of Mumtaz.

Shah Jahan began work on Shahjahanabad in 1639, and, as with the Taj, progress was swift. An army of workmen constructed a massive citadel, the Red Fort, encircled by high sandstone walls with twenty-seven towers and eleven great gates. This new fortress-city was twice the size of the Red Fort at Agra. Grand avenues connected the different sectors: the bazaars, administrative offices, courtiers' residences, the imperial chambers of state and the harem with its pavilions decorated with gold and inlaid jewels.

Fountains and watercourses sparkled throughout. François Bernier

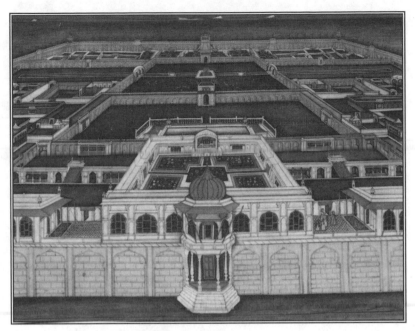

The Red Fort at Delhi

marveled at the urban planning: "Nearly every chamber has its reservoir of running water at the door; on every side are gardens, delightful alleys, shady retreats, streams, fountains, grottoes, deep excavations that afford shelter from the sun by day, lofty divans and terraces, on which to sleep coolly at night. Within the walls of this enchanting place no oppressive or inconvenient heat is felt." A water channel, the River of Paradise, flowed past the imperial quarters. As with nearly all Moghul water courses, the gradient was as shallow as possible—just enough to keep the water moving, but imperceptible to the human eye. The main harem building, the Rang Mahal, was a palace of shimmering white marble with, at its four corners, small chambers whose surfaces sparkled with tiny mirrors. But most elegant of all was Shah Jahan's Hall of Private Audience—an open marble pavilion inlaid with precious stones in floral designs to create a jeweled garden beneath a ceiling of silver and gold.

Ten days of gorgeous ceremonials marked the inauguration of Shahjahanabad. Three thousand workers labored for a month with powerful cranks and hoists to erect in the courtyard of the new fort a giant velvet canopy woven on the looms of Gujarat, embroidered in gold and large enough to shade ten thousand people. On 18 April 1648, at the exact moment deemed favorable by the court astrologers and to the beating of kettledrums, Shah Jahan arrived by royal barge and mounted his Peacock Throne.

The gem-studded golden throne surmounted by its brilliant-eyed birds stunned those European visitors lucky enough to see it. Friar Manrique was positively transported by its brilliant diamonds, glowing emeralds and "celestial" sapphires: "So, if what is most perfect disturbs our feelings, just as the glowing rays of the sun confronting us obscure our vision; if the roar of dashing, clashing waters hurling themselves from a lofty rock stuns and deafens our hearing; if the scent of aromatic drugs and oriental spices confounds our sense of smell; if the sweetness of the honey of Hybla vitiates our sense of taste; if the effect of frost numbs and destroys the sense of touch;—what wonder is it that, when my senses were distracted at the sight of so remarkable and surprising an object as that throne, I could not well grasp the precious nature of its constituent materials?"

The throne was an appropriate symbol for the Great Moghul, probably the seventeenth century's richest monarch. His annual income was 220 million rupees, while his treasure houses were heaped with rare jewels and precious metals worth many millions more. Yet the throne was also emblematic of the empire's growing financial ossification. Although imperial revenues were three times what they had been in Akbar's day, this had not been achieved by expansions in territory or by making the existing Moghul lands more productive through improved agricultural techniques and nurturing trade. Instead Shah Jahan had squeezed his subjects, allowing imperial tax collectors to levy increasingly oppressive taxes. Consequently, as his reign wore on, many of Shah Jahan's subjects were putting their wealth into gems and precious metals and secreting them from the tax collectors—a recipe for financial stagnation, not dynamism. And while revenues had trebled, imperial expenditure had quadrupled since Akbar's reign.

Shah Jahan had, like Jahangir, followed Akbar's administrative system of awarding ranks and salaries to his nobles and officials in terms of the numbers of soldiers they were required to support. Expediency and political pressure to satisfy powerful factions had led him to award ever-higher ranks, and consequently incomes, to them. Such pressures had also forced him to ignore the fact that his supporters rarely maintained the numbers of troops that their rank required of them. Sometimes they maintained a mere fraction, borrowing horses and men from each other when it became time for an imperial inspection. Sometimes they bribed corrupt officials to turn a blind eye to their failings by, in turn, disregarding the same officials' squeezing of the population to enrich themselves.

Aware that his spending was increasing much faster than his income, Shah Jahan tried to arrest this rising inflation in ranks and salaries. However, in practice too severe an economy would have alienated his supporters, so his limited measures had little effect on the outflow of funds. Undeterred, Shah Jahan continued pouring his passion and the decreasing resources of his treasury into his grand architectural designs. In 1650 he ordered the construction of the Jami Masjid in Shahjahanabad, the largest mosque in the empire, which over the next six years grew to dominate the city with its three sandstone and marble domes and two soaring minarets. It would be his last major project.

The prophet Muhammad is reported to have once described architecture as "the most unprofitable thing that eats up the wealth of the believer." The full costs of Shah Jahan's building projects throughout his reign are difficult to quantify because figures in the chronicles sometimes omit the costs of items such as the materials, as seems to be the case for the 5 million rupees quoted by Lahori for the Taj Mahal. However, conservative calculations indicate that an average of between 10 and 20 percent of the annual expenditure from the Moghul treasury (another figure difficult to estimate accurately) was spent on buildings. Such expenditure was directed to enhancing the imperial image of the Moghul court and to beauty for its own sake, rather than to the construction or improvement of military defenses or supply and communication routes. Therefore the projects seriously depleted the treasury as well as distracting the emperor and his officials from the business of governing the empire, increasing its prosperity and strengthening it against internal dissent and external aggression. The consequences of this expensive distraction would become clear over the next few years for the emperor personally and over the next few decades for his empire.

BEREFT OF MUMTAZ, his companion of nearly two decades, Shah Jahan also sought distraction by indulging in frenetic, loveless couplings in a fruitless attempt to find physical compensation for his emotional loss. He suffered terrible pains for three weeks, which, according to his historian, were brought on by his overenthusiastic use of aphrodisiacs. Although he took no further wives, European visitors were quick to report of his many sexual partners. While the various accounts may be exaggerated and designed to titillate, their frequency and detail suggest a basis of truth. Equally, they suggest that rumors of Shah Jahan's sexual obsession with Jahanara were unlikely to have been true. Had she become Mumtaz's surrogate in a physical sense, he would not have been so promiscuous.

The Venetian Manucci described the opportunities afforded to Shah Jahan by the Meena Bazaar, the event at which he reputedly first saw the young Mumtaz: "In those eight days, the king visited the stalls twice every day, seated on a small throne carried by several Tartar women, surrounded by several matrons, who walked with their sticks of enamelled gold in their hands, and many eunuchs, all brokers for the subsequent bargaining; there were also a set of women musicians. Shah Jahan moves past with his attention fixed, and seeing any seller that attracts his fancy, he goes up to the stall, and making a polite speech, selects some of the things and orders whatever she asks for them to be paid to her. Then the king gives an agreed-on signal and having passed on, the matrons, well-versed in these matters, take care that they get her; and in due time, she is produced in the royal presence. Many of them come out of the palace very rich and satisfied, while others continue to dwell there with the dignity of concubines."

Manucci also painted a raucous, raunchy picture, worthy of the Restoration court in England, of Shah Jahan's dalliances with the wives of some of his courtiers. As these women passed in state through the streets, people would boldly call, "O breakfast of Shah Jahan! Remember us! O luncheon of Shah Jahan! Succour us!" Manucci also claimed that "For the greater satisfaction of his lusts Shah Jahan ordered the erection of a large hall twenty cubits long and eight cubits wide, adorned throughout with great mirrors. The gold alone cost fifteen millions of rupees, not including the enamel work and precious stones, of which no account was kept. On the ceiling of the said hall, between one mirror and another, were strips of gold richly ornamented with pearls. At the corners of the mirrors hung great clusters of pearls, and the walls were of jasper stone. All this expenditure was made so that he might obscenely observe himself with his favourite women. It would seem as if the only thing Shah Jahan cared for was the search for women to serve his pleasure."

Bernier wrote of how his troupe of dancing girls diverted him "with their antics and follies," which, he carped, "transgressed the bounds of decency." Sometimes Shah Jahan was so taken with one of these low-born girls that he ordered her admission to the harem, justifying his passions with the excuse that "a good article may be from any shop."

Shah Jahan had, however, no further children to rival those he had with Mumtaz, and Europeans speculated whether some form of abortion was being practiced within the harem. Shah Jahan certainly found no fulfilling relationship to rival that between himself and Mumtaz in its mix of sublime sexual compatibility interleaved with friendship and trust. Perhaps his incessant pursuit of loveless sex and his debauching of his courtiers' wives and daughters represented a fervid quest to prove that Mumtaz Mahal had been unique and worthy of a unique love.

PREOCCUPIED WITH HIS building schemes, his sexual athletics and the complex daily ritual of court life, Shah Jahan increasingly left the conduct of military campaigns to his four sons. In earlier years he had usually chosen to be close to the action, albeit not fighting himself, but by now he preferred to issue his orders from afar. By 1648, when he took up residence in Shahjahanabad, all his sons were mature men; Dara Shukoh was thirty-three, Shah Shuja thirty-one, Aurangzeb twenty-nine and Murad Bakhsh twenty-three. Dara, open-minded, aesthetic and liberal, was a scholar rather than a warrior, with the intellectual curiosity about religion of some of his Moghul forebears, especially Akbar. In his writings he compared elements of Hindu doctrine with Sufism, the mystical branch of Islam. In addition, he translated the *Upanishads*, the major expression of Hindu philosophy, into Persian and persuaded his father to donate a stone railing to a Hindu temple. Dara composed elegant poetry and was a talented calligrapher. However, as Bernier observed, though polite and open-minded, "he entertained too exalted an opinion of himself; believed he could accomplish everything by the powers of his own mind."

Shah Shuja, according to Bernier, resembled Dara but was more politically astute. While Dara disdained advice and did not bother to cultivate important nobles, feeling court politics beneath him, Shah Shuja was an accomplished intriguer who knew how to acquire useful friends. At the same time, he was "a slave to his pleasures; and once surrounded by his women, who were exceedingly numerous, he would pass whole days and nights in dancing, singing and drinking wine."

Aurangzeb lacked the courtly urbanity of his elder brothers. Contemporary accounts depict a focused, capable, sometimes melancholy man who was, according to Bernier, "reserved, subtle and a complete master of the art of dissimulation." The Frenchman accused him of affecting "contempt for worldly grandeur while clandestinely endeavouring to pave the way to future elevation." Aurangzeb was certainly cunning and ambitious but also insecure and paranoid, hence his extraordinary row with Dara when he accused him of plotting to murder him. Like Dara, he was religious, but instead of his brother's open, inquiring, all-embracing mysticism, which he thoroughly despised, Aurangzeb was a fierce advocate of austere orthodox Sunni Islam. While governor of Gujarat, he had attempted to seize premises belonging to a Jain temple until prevented by Dara.

Of all the brothers, Aurangzeb had the most difficult relationship with Shah Jahan, whom he strove to please but who frequently rebuffed him. His letters to Jahanara reveal his despondency that his father found him "undeserving [of] confidence and trust." "Alas! alas! unhappy, disgraceful, and unfortunate are my stars," he lamented. The Venetian Manucci put his finger on the cause of Aurangzeb's alienation when he observed that the prince knew his father "did not love him." Aurangzeb's position echoed previous sourings of relationships between Moghul fathers and sons. Jahangir had felt unloved and unappreciated by his father, Akbar, while Shah Jahan had grown resentful and distrustful of Jahangir.

Murad Bakhsh, Shah Jahan and Mumtaz's youngest surviving son, was an engaging, swashbuckling playboy whose "constant thought," again according to Bernier, "was how he might enjoy himself." He loved hunting, despised political intrigues and claimed that "he trusted only to his sword and to the strength of his arm." It was to him that Shah Jahan turned in 1646.

Like his predecessors, Shah Jahan yearned to recapture the peacock blue–domed city of Samarkand—"the home and capital of his great ancestor Timur"—from the Uzbeks. Vicious infighting among the Uzbeks gave him his chance, and he dispatched Murad with a force of fifty thousand cavalry and ten thousand musketeers, rocket-men and gunners to pursue his cherished dream. Local rulers fled at the advance of such a force, leaving the way clear to the River Oxus. Murad seized the ancient city of Balkh, but here he paused, although Samarkand lay just 170 miles northward.

An exasperated Shah Jahan urged his son onward, promising him the governorship of Samarkand, but the pleasure-loving Murad lacked his father's romantic attachment to the wild, arid regions of their ancestors and refused, returning unbidden to Lahore. Shah Jahan angrily stripped him of his rank and banned him from the imperial court. However, others in the Moghul army shared Murad's distaste for central Asian adventuring; an imperial force of Rajputs retreated back to the Indus only to be ordered to retrace their steps. As Lahori wrote, the region seemed too alien: "Natural love of home, a preference for the ways and customs of Hindustan, a dislike of the people . . . and the rigours of the climate" weakened their resolve.

Aurangzeb did not lack resolve. Shah Jahan recalled him from Gujarat and gave him command of the expedition, but even he fared no better. Harassed and harried by Uzbeks and Turkomans, he could make no effective progress, though he won the amazed admiration of his troops for his bravery and piety when, in the thick of battle, he unfurled his mat to prostrate himself at the hour of evening prayer. By late summer 1647 he was pulling back to Kabul before winter snows cut off his retreat but, even so, lost thousands of men in the chill mountains. The campaign had cost 20 million rupees, and not an inch of territory had been added to the Moghul Empire. It was the first serious military setback of Shah

Jahan's reign and an unwelcome call on a treasury already under pressure from the emperor's building projects.

Other yet more serious and expensive failures followed, further stretching Shah Jahan's resources. A decade previously Shah Jahan had retaken Kandahar on the empire's western borders from the Persians. However, the shah of Persia took advantage of the Moghuls' Samarkand campaign to recapture Kandahar. In February 1649, after a siege of only fifty-seven days, the Moghul garrison of seven thousand, as the chroniclers put it, "from want of spirit" surrendered to the Persians in return for their lives.

Unaware that his garrison would capitulate so tamely, Shah Jahan had already, on hearing of the attack on the city, sent Aurangzeb at the head of fifty thousand men to defend Kandahar. Prevented by harsh winter weather from a rapid crossing of the mountains, Aurangzeb did not reach Kandahar until mid-May, three months after the Persians had jubilantly occupied the city. Aurangzeb besieged Kandahar but, lacking heavy artillery, could not breach the walls and in early September gave up. Three years later, in 1652, he tried again, and again he failed, retreating on Shah Jahan's orders after just two months. Shah Jahan blamed the failure squarely on Aurangzeb, writing resentfully to his son that "with such resources it was wonderful the fort was not reduced." When Aurangzeb begged to be allowed to try again, his father bit back that had he judged Aurangzeb capable of taking Kandahar, "the troops should not have been recalled."

In December of that year, while passing through Agra, Aurangzeb went to his mother's tomb to obtain "the blessings of visitation" and perhaps to remember the parent whose love had been unconditional. He was dismayed to discover that the Taj Mahal was letting in water and wrote at once to Shah Jahan: "The buildings of these sacred precincts are as stable as they were when completed in the imperial presence. However, the dome over the blessed tomb leaks on the north side during the rainy season, and the four portals, most of the second-storey alcoves, the four small domes, the four northern vestibules . . . have got damp. The marble-covered roof of the large dome has leaked in two or three places during this season. It has been repaired, but we will have to wait and see what will happen next rainy season." He added disconsolately that

Aurangzeb's letter to Shah Jahan describing the damage to the Taj Mahal

the builders "admit their inability to come up with a plan for the large dome. Blessed saint, extend your hand! Such magnificent buildings have been afflicted so by the evil eye!" He also reported that the garden across the Jumna from the Taj, known as the Mahtab Bagh, had been "completely inundated, and therefore it has lost its charm," although the octagonal pool and the pavilion around it were still in good condition. He begged Shah Jahan to act, urging that "if a ray of imperial attention is cast to remedy the situation, it would be appropriate." Major works to strengthen the foundations and waterproof the dome were clearly put in hand.

In 1653 Shah Jahan mounted a third attempt to reclaim Kandahar, this time entrusting his forces to Dara Shukoh. His eldest son, who spent much time with his father, rarely went into battle but had unwisely boasted that he could take Kandahar in a week. Shah Jahan gave the prince an army of seventy thousand, huge amounts of artillery and experienced European mercenary gunners to make good his claim. Even so, during a five-month onslaught Dara too failed to breach walls of dry clay that in places were nearly thirty feet thick. The Moghuls would never hold Kandahar again.

The three abortive attempts to retake Kandahar had cost a colossal 120 million rupees, over half Shah Jahan's annual revenue. But loss of prestige was even more wounding than loss of money. Shah Jahan, who as a prince had known many military victories, resented failure. Yet his disappointment did not dent his affection for his eldest son, and he gave Dara increasing powers. In 1654, during the celebrations for his sixty-fifth lunar birthday, Shah Jahan bestowed a special title on Dara reaffirming him as heir apparent and ordered him "to seat himself on a golden chair near his own sublime throne." Portraits of Dara at this time depict him with a soft halo about his handsome head, further emphasizing his status.

None of this was lost on Aurangzeb, whom Shah Jahan had meanwhile appointed governor of the Deccan for the second time, and who had departed for the south. Neither father nor son could know that, although each had many years left to live, they would not meet face-to-face again. The strained relations between them contrast sharply and poignantly with the grief-stricken scenes when, thirty years earlier, Shah Jahan and Mumtaz had been forced to surrender Aurangzeb and Dara to the uncertain care of Nur Jahan following Shah Jahan's rebellion. Now, just as when Jahangir dispatched Shah Jahan to the Deccan, Shah Jahan showed Aurangzeb little affection, routinely slighting him, even pettily accusing him of failing to send him the best mangoes from his favorite tree. When Aurangzeb asked for additional funds to finance his administration of the region, his father refused, urging him to raise the money through more efficient tax gathering and by improving cultivation.

The Sons of Shah Jahan Enthroned, by Amal-i-Bhawani Das. Top: Shah Shuja and Dara Shukoh; middle: Murad Bakhsh and Aurangzeb; bottom: Azam Shah, son of Aurangzeb, and an unidentified figure, possibly another of Aurangzeb's sons.

Aurangzeb instead decided to refill his coffers through conquest. The wealthy kingdom of Golconda, which in 1636 had grudgingly yielded suzerainty to the Moghuls, seemed a promising target with its fabulous gold and diamond mines and indolent, luxury-loving sultan. Aurangzeb's excuse for attack was that the tribute due from Golconda under the treaty of 1636 was late and further that Golconda had invaded the Carnatic—a region of small principalities between the Krishna and Kaveri rivers south of the Deccan—without Moghul approval.

In early 1656 Aurangzeb dispatched an army into Golconda under his sixteen-year-old son Mohammed Sultan and followed at the head of another large force. The fact that the nervous sultan of Golconda had by then acceded to all his demands did not affect Aurangzeb's plans. His orders to his son were to kill the sultan if he could or, as he more gracefully expressed it, to "lighten his neck of the burden of his head." The terrified sultan fled from his glittering new city of Hyderabad westward to the fort of Golconda and sent gifts, conciliatory messages and even his mother to seek Aurangzeb's mercy. He also sought help from Dara Shukoh, who, by nature pacific and forgiving, as well as disliking Aurangzeb, intervened to frustrate his brother.

Aurangzeb was also busily lobbying his father, writing temptingly of Golconda's fat riches and urging the kingdom's annexation. "What shall I write about the beauty of this country," he wheedled, "its abundance of water and population, its good air, and its extensive cultivation? . . . Such a money-yielding country!" Despite the many demands on his depleted treasury, Shah Jahan was not, however, tempted. Instead he listened to Dara, who argued that it would be both more prudent as well as more just to reach a peaceful settlement with the sultan. Consequently, Shah Jahan refused to allow Aurangzeb to annex the kingdom, ordering him to accept the sultan's offer of indemnity and quit Golconda at once. He also accused Aurangzeb of seizing jewels belonging to the sultan, refused him any of the Golconda indemnity and rebuked him for exceeding his orders.

Slighted as he must have felt, Aurangzeb believed he had no option but to obey his father, and he reluctantly withdrew. However, he did so only after pressuring the sultan to marry one of his daughters to his own son, Mohammed Sultan. He also exacted a secret promise that the sultan would appoint his new son-in-law as his heir. As he looked around for another victim, Aurangzeb's ambitious gaze fell on Bijapur, which, like Golconda, had made terms with the Moghuls in 1636 and which, also like Golconda, had grown yet richer in the intervening years. The pretext for the invasion was internal strife following the death of Bijapur's ruler in November 1656.

This time Shah Jahan allowed Aurangzeb to have his way. One reason for the emperor's change of mind was the arrival at his court of an ambitious, wealthy Persian adventurer, Mir Jumla, who had recently been vizier to the sultan of Golconda until falling out with him. Mir Jumla artfully presented Shah Jahan with diamonds, rubies and topazes from Golconda and Bijapur.* The glittering mounds convinced the emperor that the kingdoms were worth seizing rather than, as previously, merely imposing Moghul overlordship on them and milking them for tribute. He appointed Mir Jumla to high office and sanctioned Aurangzeb to mount a full-blown invasion of Bijapur. If he was successful, Shah Jahan wrote to his son, he also had imperial permission to annex Golconda.

In early 1657, with Mir Jumla by his side, Aurangzeb advanced slowly and methodically, offering bribes of two thousand rupees to every Bijapuri officer who defected with one hundred men. Aurangzeb was just as personally courageous a fighter as his father. (At the age of fourteen, he had coolly and famously faced a rampaging elephant about to trample him, hurling his spear at the enraged beast.) However, his slow, systematic approach to campaigning was not Shah Jahan's dashing, storming military style. Fearing the monsoon would begin before Aurangzeb had achieved his objectives and influenced again by Dara, Shah Jahan changed his mind and ordered his son quickly to conclude a treaty whereby Bijapur agreed to pay the Moghuls a huge indemnity and to surrender some

---

* Manucci reported that Mir Jumla also presented Shah Jahan with "a large uncut diamond which weighed three hundred and sixty carats," and Bernier wrote of a "celebrated diamond which had been generally deemed unparalled in size and beauty." This was probably the Koh-i-Nur, which had somehow come into Mir Jumla's possession from Persia.

forts, and then to withdraw, leaving Bijapur its independence. Once again Aurangzeb reluctantly acceded.

AURANGZEB'S DECCAN CAMPAIGNS had not been spectacular, but they had further subdued the region and were some compensation for the central Asian misadventure and the disastrous attempts to regain Kandahar. With a brood of sons to conduct any further military actions that might be necessary, this should have been a period of tranquillity for Shah Jahan as he coasted toward old age, allowing him to pursue his grand architectural schemes and, during visits to Agra, to pray for Mumtaz in the marble mausoleum he had created. Instead, in September 1657, the sixty-five-year-old emperor fell dangerously ill. It was the sign of imperial mortality for which his three younger sons had been waiting and the end of his hopes of a contented, graceful old age.

CHAPTER FIFTEEN

"Sharper Than a Serpent's Tooth"

THE STAGE WAS SET. A JACOBEAN TRAGEDEAN would have struggled to create a more convincing central character than the elderly, flawed, Lear-like Shah Jahan. After three decades on the throne he believed in his divine right to rule and in the grandeur and invulnerability of the imperial image he had created. However, he had neglected the detailed running of his state, leaving it to his nobles, who had greater interest in their personal position and prosperity than that of the empire overall. He had not gone into battle, delegating the command of his military adventures to his sons, particularly the three youngest. He had also not pursued his goals with the single-minded vigor of his grandfather Akbar, whose philosophy that "a monarch should be ever intent on conquest, otherwise his neighbours rise in arms against him" had been as useful in suppressing internal dissent as in subduing external threats.

Above all, in a kind of emotional withdrawal, he had grown increasingly impervious to the lessons of Moghul history neatly expressed in the saying *taktya takhta?* (throne or coffin?). Successive generations of ambitious sons had challenged their fathers: Jahangir had rebelled against Akbar, and he himself had revolted against Jahangir. Half-brother had fought half-brother. The gentle Humayun had struggled to subdue Kamran, Hindal and Askari. Shah Jahan had gone yet further, eliminating his half-brothers Khusrau and the hairless Shahriyar as well as, to be on the safe side, an assortment of nephews and cousins. But despite this bloody

233

heredity, Shah Jahan fondly convinced himself that his sons would remain obedient and loyal. That they were full brothers, the offspring of a devoted couple not of an assortment of contending wives and concubines, must have strengthened his conviction.

Had Mumtaz lived, he might have been right. She had been a loving, caring mother to her children, and in the early years their unity as a family had been fashioned by danger and sustained through hardship. With Mumtaz by his side as their children grew up, Shah Jahan would have had more appetite for the business of ruling and no brooding, corroding grief from which to seek consoling distraction in architectural projects or elsewhere. He might still have had his favorites, but Mumtaz's affection and maternal empathy might have mitigated Aurangzeb's sense of alienation and defused the dissatisfactions of Shah Shuja and Murad Bakhsh. The relationships between the three surviving sisters might also have been closer. Instead, Jahanara's assumption of Mumtaz's place as first lady of the empire had, in particular, left Raushanara, three years her junior, extremely jealous. Raushanara was, according to the Venetian Niccolao Manucci, who had recently entered Dara's service, not especially good-looking but "very clever, capable of dissimulation, bright, mirthful, fond of jokes and amusement." He also claimed she was "libidinous." In the family tragedy about to be enacted, she would be Aurangzeb's ardent partisan, a curious ally for a puritan, yet there was common ground. Each had for years felt outshone—Aurangzeb by Dara and Raushanara by Jahanara. In the same way, the youngest girl, Gauharara, whose birth had accompanied Mumtaz's death, would find common cause with her youngest brother, Murad.

Mumtaz, had she survived, would also have had the power to intercede at times of family crisis. The Moghuls had a long tradition of powerful matriarchs who, though living behind the veil, had successfully intervened and whose views were respected. Babur's grandmother had guided him through the early years of his reign while Hamida, Jahangir's grandmother, had brokered his reconciliation with his father, Akbar. Among Mumtaz's Persian antecedents, the close bonds between husbands and wives—her grandfather Itimad-ud-daula and his wife, her father Asaf Khan and her mother, to say nothing of her aunt Nur's hold on Jahangir—had also allowed the senior women an important say in family business.

Jahanara, of course, did have influence. Aurangzeb had written to her many times over the years, addressing her as his "patroness" and asking her to intercede with their father on his behalf. But a sister could not command the respect and obedience of a mother. With his own mother and Mumtaz dead and no other wife or senior female close to him, Shah Jahan, for better or for worse, had had to manage his large, energetic, talented family alone. He would discover that the seven surviving children born to him by Mumtaz—from Jahanara and Dara Shukoh, as close in tastes and temperament as they were in age, to the younger more disaffected siblings—had formed their own alliances. He would also discover, like Lear, which, if any of them, truly loved him.

The crisis began in Delhi on 16 September 1657 when, according to his chronicler, "the emperor fell seriously ill from constipation and strangury."* French physician François Bernier wrote that Shah Jahan "was seized with a disorder, the nature of which it were unbecoming to describe. Suffice it to state that it was disgraceful to a man of his age who, instead of wasting, ought to have been careful to preserve the remaining vigour of his constitution." Manucci was yet more explicit, claiming that Shah Jahan had brought his illness on himself because, yearning for the sexual energy of his youth, he had taken aphrodisiacs.

For three days, Shah Jahan could not urinate and disappeared from the view of his subjects—unable to appear even briefly on the *jharokha* balcony. Dara, fearing how his three brothers would react when they learned of Shah Jahan's decline, forbade the sending of reports to them, far away in the provinces they governed—Shah Shuja in Bengal, Murad Bakhsh in Gujarat and Aurangzeb in the Deccan. In the ensuing vacuum, rumors multiplied that the emperor was dead, even that Dara had usurped and murdered him. As panic spread, Delhi's merchants closed their shops, fearing rioting and looting. The reality was that, nursed by Jahanara, Shah Jahan began slowly to recover, reviving himself with mint and manna soup and making a brief appearance to his worried

---

* Strangury is an extremely painful condition of the urinary tract. Sufferers can only urinate slowly, stinging drop by stinging drop.

people at the window of his bedchamber on 24 September. But one of his court historians recorded how, weakened and fearing death was near, Shah Jahan "turned over much of the management of the affairs of state" to Dara, "requesting the nobles to pledge their fealty to him as the designated heir-apparent." The irony was that, of all the brothers, Dara was not particularly anxious for the throne. As Shah Jahan's favored successor, he would have been content to await the death of the father he loved, but events had forced responsibility upon him. In mid-October Shah Jahan left Delhi by imperial barge for Agra, where, close to the Taj Mahal and the long-dead, still-cherished Mumtaz, he could compose his mind to whatever fate awaited him

In the absence of official reports, Shah Jahan's three younger sons relied for information on messages from their supporters, including in Aurangzeb's case their sister Raushanara and in Murad's their sister Gauharara. The brothers concluded that their father had to be dead and, rejecting Dara's right to succeed him, each plotted to claim the throne. None allowed emerging proof that Shah Jahan was, after all, alive to destroy their momentum. According to Manucci, who was admittedly highly partisan toward Dara, Aurangzeb ordered any letters reaching the Deccan suggesting that Shah Jahan still lived to be burned and their bearers immediately beheaded.

Shah Shuja was the first to act openly, proclaiming himself emperor, ordering the *khutba* to be read in his name and issuing coins to mark the start of his reign. After killing his own finance minister, who was loyal to Shah Jahan, Murad Bakhsh also proclaimed himself emperor and sacked the city of Surat to finance his bid. Aurangzeb, equally ambitious but more cunning, quietly bided his time. Also, he had suffered a recent bereavement: His favorite wife had died in childbirth. He would build a tomb for her that, while seeking to emulate the Taj, would be a pale, spindly shadow of it.

Dara, however, suspected correctly that Aurangzeb, the brother he derided as a "bigot and prayer-monger," was the real threat and ordered senior Moghul commanders nominally under Aurangzeb's control back to Delhi. These included Mir Jumla, the powerful Persian adventurer who had fought with Aurangzeb in the Deccani campaigns and whose forces Dara was especially anxious to keep out of Aurangzeb's hands.

Correctly interpreting Dara's motives, Aurangzeb thwarted him, colluding with Mir Jumla to imprison the Persian on a fake charge. Aurangzeb also secretly contacted Murad Bakhsh. According to some Moghul accounts, he wooed him with assurances that his own sole ambition was to lead a retired, religious life, arguing that Dara's religious heresies made it unthinkable that he should be emperor and promising to support Murad, whom he lauded as a devout orthodox Muslim, for the throne. While this may be true—Aurangzeb was a master of such duplicitous stratagems—he and Murad drew up a written agreement, partitioning the empire between them with two thirds going to Aurangzeb and the remaining third—Afghanistan, Kashmir, the wealthy Punjab and Sind—going to Murad. There is also evidence that some years earlier the two brothers had agreed to divide the empire with Shah Shuja and that, since the crisis began, each had been seeking an alliance with him. Whatever the case, none of the three showed any fraternal compassion for their father's favorite, the haughty Dara, whom they had long envied and whose death was integral to their schemes.

With Shah Shuja already marching toward Delhi, Dara dispatched a huge imperial force under his son Suleiman Shukoh, who, in February 1658, caught his indolent uncle unawares in an early morning attack near Benares and roundly defeated him. Horrified at the idea of his family in armed, open conflict and underestimating the deadly rivalry between them, Shah Jahan still hoped to resolve matters peaceably; he had therefore ordered Shah Shuja to be treated with mercy. Suleiman dutifully permitted his uncle to escape but could not resist giving chase—a decision that would prove disastrous. Dara, meanwhile, had also sent armies south to block the advance of Aurangzeb and Murad, now on the move as well, but this time his forces lost the ensuing battle. Realizing the acute danger, Dara hastily recalled Suleiman but, on the chase, his son was by then many hundreds of miles march from Agra.

Meanwhile, all three rebel princes continued to write unctuous, flowery letters to their father, assuring him of their loyalty and of their desire to pay their respects after his recent illness. They reminded him how, when Jahanara had been badly burned, they had hurried to court out of the same family love. Their armies only accompanied them because they feared Dara was their enemy. Shah Jahan, belatedly and bemusedly grasping the seriousness of what was happening, tried to mediate between his sons, urging that their disputes be debated in the imperial council, even that Aurangzeb and Murad should visit him in the Agra fort so that he could broker a peace. At Shah Jahan's request, Jahanara made a desperate attempt to avert the coming tragedy, writing to Aurangzeb: "The emperor has recovered and is himself administering the state. Your armed advance is therefore an act of war against your father. Even if it is directed against Dara, it is no less sinful." Aurangzeb, however, insisted he had only taken up arms to save himself and that he was loyal to his father, whom he insisted on seeing. "I shall not brook any obstacle to this loving design," he added.

Dara believed the only way to deal with Aurangzeb was to humble him on the battlefield, and persuaded a sorrowful Shah Jahan to agree. On 18 May 1658, Dara left Agra, marching south to seize the fords over the River Chambal and thus prevent Aurangzeb and Murad from crossing until the arrival of imperial reinforcements under his son Suleiman Shukoh from the east. According to his chronicler, Shah Jahan parted from his son "with the greatest reluctance . . . the distraught emperor held his son in a close embrace unaware that fate had decreed that this was to be their last meeting." Then, raising his hands in prayer, Shah Jahan called on God to grant Dara victory.

Niccolao Manucci, about to participate in the battle as a mercenary artilleryman with Dara's troops, described how: "We began the march in such great order that it seemed as if sea and land were united. Prince Dara amidst his squadron appeared like a crystal tower, resplendent as a sun shining over all the land. Around him rode many squadrons of Rajput cavalry whose armour glittered from afar, and their lance-heads with a tremulous motion sent forth rays of light . . . A marvellous thing was it to behold the march, which moved over the heights and through the vales like the waves of a stormy sea." Yet despite the splendor of the ranks of war elephants clad in shining steel armor with swords fitted to their tusks, and the martial cacophony of trumpets and kettledrums, Manucci could see that the army was not all it should be.* The best of the

---

* An elephant's armor consisted of chain mail and over eight thousand overlapping steel plates, two thousand just to cover the head alone.

imperial troops were with Suleiman, and some of Dara's forces, on closer inspection, proved "not very warlike; they were butchers, barbers, black-smiths, carpenters, tailors and such-like."

The other problem was the speed of Aurangzeb's and Murad's advance. By a forced march, they got their army across the Chambal before Dara could stop them, using a little-known and unguarded ford. Instead of engaging his brothers' troops while they were still exhausted from their efforts, Dara hurried back toward Agra. On the great Plain of Samugarh, just eight miles southeast of the city, he paused and prepared for battle. There was still no sign of Suleiman.

On 29 May 1658, the two forces engaged in literally blistering heat: Men's skin was seared by the hot metal of their armor. The fighting was bitter. Murad, riding on an elephant, was hit in the face by arrows, and his howdah was studded with them. After three hours, Dara's troops appeared to be in the ascendant, but at a critical moment Dara paused and dismounted from his elephant. "This was," wrote Manucci, "as if he had quitted victory." In fact, Dara was only transferring to a horse to give him greater speed of maneuver, but the psychological damage was done. Unable to see their commander, panic spread through the inexperienced ranks, and within minutes the whole imperial army was fleeing "like dark clouds blown by a high wind." An attendant grabbed Dara's bridle and hurried him away.

Dara galloped back to Agra, where Shah Jahan, anxiously awaiting news with Jahanara, implored his disconsolate son to come to him, but Dara was too ashamed. He remained in his mansion until the early hours, when he set out for Delhi with his wife, children and grandchildren and a small retinue on horse and elephant. The distraught Shah Jahan sent mules loaded with gold to Dara and orders to the governor of Delhi to throw the imperial treasury open to him, while Jahanara sent him valuable jewels.

The prince had fled just in time. The following day, riding out of Agra to join Dara, Manucci found his road blocked by Aurangzeb's victorious troops, who forced him to turn back. "The government had already changed hands," they told him, "and Aurangzeb was the victor." They were right; Aurangzeb was in effective control. As events would show, the battle of Samugarh had been as pivotal as a Culloden, Yorktown or

Waterloo. Dara would never regain the initiative from his more aggressive, intolerant and battle-seasoned younger brother, and the history of
the Moghul Empire, and of India, would, as a result, take a different, di-
visive and ultimately disastrous course.

ON 1 JUNE Aurangzeb and Murad arrived outside Agra. Jahanara visited
her two brothers, and Shah Jahan sent a conciliatory message to Aurangzeb inviting him to the fort. He also sent him a famous and glittering
sword, Alamgir, Seizer of the Universe. Aurangzeb's curt response was
that he would only enter the fort if his father surrendered it. Predictably,
Shah Jahan refused, at which Aurangzeb, abandoning any pretense of
concern for his father's welfare, laid siege to it. When attempts to blast
its stout walls with cannons failed, Aurangzeb resorted to a simpler plan:
cutting off the fort's water supply from the Jumna. Forced at the height
of the summer heat to drink the brackish, bitter water from the fort's defunct old wells, rather than the "molten snow" of the Jumna, after only
three days, Shah Jahan, lacking the determination that had fueled his
own rebellion with Mumtaz against Jahangir, meekly gave in and opened
the gates.

Aurangzeb ordered his father and Jahanara to be confined to the
harem. The only woman allowed to leave the fort was Raushanara, who,
according to Manucci, departed "with great pomp." Three days later Aurangzeb made a pretense of setting out to visit his father. However, as he
made his triumphal progress toward the fort atop a richly caparisoned
elephant, convenient warnings reached him, or so he claimed, that the
female Tartar guards of Shah Jahan's harem intended to slay him. His attendants also produced a supposed intercepted letter from Shah Jahan in
which he promised his beloved Dara his continued support. Aurangzeb
at once turned around and returned to his quarters.

A fanciful tale, circulating some years later among the European community and probably the result of hindsight, claims that Shah Jahan had
long feared Aurangzeb. According to the story, during one of Mumtaz's
many pregnancies she had longed for apples, which were not then in season. Shah Jahan, anxious to find some for her, encountered a fakir who
gave him two of the fruits. He also told the grateful Shah Jahan that if

ever he felt ill he should smell his hands. So long as they retained the scent of apples he would recover, but when they lost that fragrance "it would be a warning that he had reached the term of his life." Anxious for further insights into his future, Shah Jahan pressed the fakir to tell him "which of his sons would be the destroyer of his race." The fakir answered that it would be Aurangzeb.

AURANGZEB'S IMMEDIATE OBJECTIVE was to rid himself of Murad, whose usefulness as an ally was over. His opportunity came a few days later after both brothers had marched out together in pursuit of Dara. On the night of 25 June, while their armies were camped at Mathura, Aurangzeb invited Murad to his tent and plied his naive and self-indulgent sibling with heady wines that he himself, as a devout Muslim, naturally refused to touch. An inebriated Murad gave himself happily into the hands of a skilled girl sent to "shampoo" him.* As the skillful masseuse went to work, Murad fell into contented sleep. Soon after, the heavily muscled, heavily-armed eunuch whom he had brought to guard him was lured outside the tent and strangled. When Murad finally woke up, he found himself a defenseless prisoner. Later that night, four elephants bearing identical howdahs departed from the camp north, south, east and west. Few knew that the hapless Murad was trussed up on the elephant tramping slowly north. It was carrying him to imprisonment on an island in the Jumna near Delhi.

Aurangzeb decided the moment had come to declare himself emperor. The simple ceremony took place on 21 July 1658 in a garden outside Delhi. The reason for its brevity was that Aurangzeb still had two brothers to deal with: Dara in the west and Shah Shuja to the east. Judging that the problem of Dara was more pressing, he resumed his pursuit of his detested eldest brother. After taking what treasure he could from Delhi, Dara had withdrawn first to Lahore, then southwest along the Indus toward Sind, retreating along the same route taken by his great-great-grandfather Humayun when he had fled the seizer of his throne,

---

* *Shampoo* is a Hindi word in origin, meaning not "to wash the hair" but "to massage."

Sher Shah. Several times Dara could have turned and fought but chose
not to. Although he had amassed another large army, it was inexperienced, and he doubted its loyalty. Aurangzeb skillfully nourished these
doubts through a string of counterfeit letters that his agents smuggled
into his brother's camp, and that falsely appeared to implicate some of
his officers in schemes to betray Dara. At the same time, Aurangzeb sent
genuine letters to Dara's supporters, offering them bribes to change sides.
As a result, Dara's army began to fall apart. Manucci, who caught up with
Dara near Lahore, related a telling incident. Dara's wife had wooed a
powerful raja by assuring him that he was as a son to her. In confirmation
of her words she did something "never done before in the Moghul's empire—she offered him water to drink with which she had washed her
breasts, not having milk in them." The raja drank and promised fealty,
but after extracting money to enlist men to fight for Dara he quietly disappeared back to his lands.

Convinced that he had pushed his demoralized eldest brother far
enough away to pose no immediate danger, Aurangzeb left the problem
of Dara to others and turned his attentions to Shah Shuja, who, by late
September 1658, was advancing on Agra with the declared intention
of liberating his father. With his old ally Mir Jumla, by then "released"
from his pretended imprisonment, Aurangzeb confronted Shah Shuja at
Khajwah, halfway between Benares and Agra on the Ganges. The fighting was fierce, and, as a result of the defection of one of Aurangzeb's
commanders, Jaswant Singh, raja of Marwar (Jodhpur), Aurangzeb
nearly lost. However, he retained his customary coolness, once more dis-
mounting at the prescribed hour to kneel in prayer amid the mayhem of
battle, before rising to steady his men and direct them to victory.* Shah
Shuja fled down the Ganges with Mir Jumla in pursuit, the start of fifteen months of cat and mouse that would see Shah Shuja and his family
pushed into the lands of the pirate king of Arakan, east of Bengal. Here,
amid "impenetrable jungles and mighty rivers full of alligators," as
Manucci shudderingly described the marshy region which he knew by
repute, the fugitives disappeared. They were probably murdered.

---

* This contrasts with the disastrous effect when Dara dismounted at the Battle of
  Samugarh; Aurangzeb's forces clearly had confidence in their leader.

Dara meanwhile had rebuilt his army in Gujarat, and the raja of Marwar sent messages promising that if he would advance toward Agra he would meet him with twenty thousand Rajputs for a showdown with Aurangzeb. Dara agreed, but as he journeyed north there was no sign of the raja, whom Aurangzeb had coaxed, threatened and bribed back to his side. As Dara approached Ajmer, the city some three hundred miles west of Agra where Mumtaz had given birth to him, and with Aurangzeb marching rapidly toward him, he prepared for a stand, choosing a good defensive position in a narrow pass. He held out for three days, but on the night of 14 March 1659, Aurangzeb's forces overwhelmed him.

Dara once more escaped, traveling southward with his fifteen-year-old son Sipihr Shukoh and a handful of attendants. In the confusion he failed to rendezvous with his wife, concubines and eunuchs waiting anxiously nearby with his baggage and treasure. They were reunited with Dara the next day, but only after they had been plundered by their own servants and the women stripped of their jewels. The bedraggled fugitives hurried south toward Ahmedabad in Gujarat, harried by robbers, but even then found no refuge. The nervous citizens of Ahmedabad thought it too risky to admit the refugees. Perhaps Dara was reminded of another bitter journey, decades before, when he, his parents and siblings, including Aurangzeb, had been hunted like foxes and could find no shelter. Bernier, who had run into Dara's fleeing party by chance, described how "the shrieks of the females drew tears from every eye." Dara himself seemed "more dead than alive" and was clearly uncertain what to do. Demoralized and completely lacking his previous self-confidence and hauteur, he was "stopping and consulting even the commonest soldier." At last he concluded that their only safety lay over the wide saline marshes and deserts of the Rann of Kutch in Sind. As one of his women had a badly injured leg, he wanted Bernier to go with him but could not even provide an animal to carry the doctor. Bernier made his excuses.

Dara succeeded in crossing the Rann of Kutch and hoped to find sanctuary to the west in Persia, but at this point his beloved wife Nadira Begum, weakened by dysentery and fatigue, collapsed and died. Sending her body for burial in Lahore, the dazed Dara found refuge with an Afghan chieftain for whom, some years earlier, he had interceded with Shah Jahan and saved from being trampled to death by elephants. The chieftain was neither as grateful nor as honorable as Dara expected and after a few days took Dara and his family captive. He dispatched Dara and Sipihr in a closed howdah to Delhi, where Aurangzeb had, just a few weeks earlier, ascended the Peacock Throne amid scenes of unparalelled magnificence, even by Moghul standards, as if to compensate for the earlier, modest ceremony.

The captives reached the city on 23 August 1659, and, six days later, Aurangzeb paraded them in rags on a filthy elephant through the streets of Delhi. Dara, sitting stoically with bowed head, had been popular, and people in the crowd cried openly and threw ordure and insults at the chieftain who had betrayed him. Bernier, who had returned to Delhi and witnessed the "disgraceful procession," feared that some dreadful act was about to take place.

He was correct. Aurangzeb was, in fact, determined on murder, but he had to find a justification. Convening his council, he maintained that Dara had deposed Shah Jahan in order to suppress Islam. His brother, he insisted, had "revived the customs of infidelity and atheism throughout the empire" and "had not even the resemblance of a Muslim." Aurangzeb's scorn for Dara's religious eclecticism was genuine and longstanding. He despised Dara's interest in Hinduism, and his pursuit of his brother had in some ways been a holy war. However, Dara's "heresies" were also extremely convenient. Aurangzeb so managed the debate in the council that he was able to give the appearance of wishing only for his brother's exile while leaving the difficult decision to others. Thus he was later able to claim, not unlike Elizabeth I over the execution of her cousin Mary Queen of Scots, that Dara's death was forced upon him by others. The council concluded almost unanimously that Dara deserved death, and among those most vociferously demanding his execution was his uncle, Mumtaz's brother Shaista Khan, who had secretly abetted Aurangzeb from the start.

The execution came quickly. The day after the shameful parading of Dara, slaves entered his prison cell, dragged his young son Sipihr from his side, and cut off Dara's still-handsome head. The prince's bleeding torso was borne through the bazaars on an elephant and dispatched for burial in Humayun's tomb. His head was sent to Aurangzeb. Stories quickly spread. Manucci, who had been left behind by Dara to defend a fortress and was not in Delhi at the time, claimed that an exultant Aurangzeb had hacked at the severed head with his sword and then sent it to Agra to be served up to Shah Jahan in a dish. More plausible than this act of Grand Guignol are Moghul accounts of Aurangzeb's dismissive remark that, since he had had no wish to look upon this infidel's face in his lifetime, he had no wish to do so now.

Aurangzeb dealt swiftly with any remaining potential claimants to the throne. In the case of his imprisoned brother Murad, he made use of the fact that, in the early stages of his own bid for the throne, Murad had murdered his finance minister. Aurangzeb blandly invited the minister's family to seek justice, which, under Muslim law, allowed them to demand either financial compensation or, if they so insisted, a life for a life. While the minister's eldest son refused to seek any compensation, either financial or physical, the second son, doubtless bribed, refused money but demanded Murad's death, and on 4 December 1661 Murad was executed. Aurangzeb characteristically rewarded the elder brother for "not enforcing his claim of blood."

Dara's eldest son and Shah Jahan's favorite grandson, Suleiman Shukoh, had sought refuge in the Punjab, but, just as his father had been, he was betrayed into Aurangzeb's eager hands by his host. Aurangzeb forced Suleiman to drink a daily draft of *pousta*—an extract of poppies—which sapped his body and mind and after reducing him to a zombie, killed him. Suleiman Shukoh's own young sons had already been murdered on Aurangzeb's orders. This left Dara's other son, the young Sipihr Shukoh, whom Aurangzeb locked up behind the high sandstone walls and stout elephant gate of the fortress of Gwalior. Fourteen years later, Aurangzeb would marry the prisoner to one of his daughters. Aurangzeb also took action against his own son, Mohammed Sultan, who had briefly and ill advisedly deserted his father's forces to join his uncle Shah Shuja. Aurangzeb confined him to prison for the remaining fourteen years of his young life.

The news of Dara's death left Shah Jahan inconsolable with grief. It must have been a bitter thought that the great love between himself and Mumtaz had not translated itself to their children. Instead, hatred

Shah Jahan's quarters while imprisoned in the Red Fort at Agra, with the Taj Mahal in the distance

and jealousy had transcended family feeling to culminate in the pitiless executions of two of their sons, the disappearance of a third and the destruction of beloved grandsons and great-grandsons. Perhaps Shah Jahan blamed himself for singling out Dara and neglecting his other sons. Perhaps he believed the fault lay with the tradition that, instead of clearly embracing primogeniture, tacitly invited any imperial prince with ability and ambition to make a play for the throne. After all, had he not done so himself?

Shah Jahan passed his final years confined in the marble pavilions that he himself had built in the Agra fort overlooking the Jumna. From there he could gaze across the curve of the river at the Taj Mahal. His best view was from the copper-domed Octagonal Tower built on a bastion projecting out over the river. With walls and pillars inlaid with jewels, superbly carved dados of waving irises and a graceful, sculpted marble pool, it was the loveliest of all the apartments he had created.

He was consoled by Jahanara, his constant and devoted companion, who shared his confinement, but there was no softening of Aurangzeb's resentment. The new emperor imposed a series of petty restrictions on his father, sometimes even forbidding him access to writing materials. He sought to make his father surrender his beloved jewels, asserting that a prisoner leading a retired life had no need of such things, and, in particular, tried to obtain Shah Jahan's pearl rosary. Shah Jahan responded that he would rather grind the one hundred perfectly matched pearls to dust than yield them up. He kept the rosary.

During the first year of Shah Jahan's incarceration, father and son also exchanged letters, full of reproaches on Shah Jahan's side and pious self-justifications on Aurangzeb's. In one letter, however, Aurangzeb cut straight to the point, stating with the deep hurt of a neglected child, "I was convinced that your majesty loved not me." He also taunted his father with Shah Jahan's own commission of fratricide: "By what names does not your majesty still call Khusrau . . . who departed to the place of non-existence long before the days of your accession to empire, and from whom to you no injury or offence occurred?"

As the years of his imprisonment passed, accounts of the conditions in which Shah Jahan was kept conflicted. According to Bernier, Shah Jahan was allowed not only the company of Jahanara but "the whole of his female establishment, including the singing and dancing women, cooks and others." However, Manucci claimed Aurangzeb continued his acts of spite, including the bricking up of a particular window from which the old emperor had loved to watch the quiet flow of the Jumna and, no doubt, contemplate Mumtaz's tomb.

In early 1666 Shah Jahan fell ill with fever, strangury and dysentery—symptoms very similar to those that had precipitated his sons' fight for the throne. A European account attributed the cause, once again, to aphrodisiacs: "The Great Moghul, seeking by artificial means to stir up lust, which was naturally decaying in him, being 73 years of age, wrought his own death." Shah Jahan failed to respond to massages with oil or to an operation to unblock his urinary tract. His fever grew and with it a desperate thirst. According to some accounts, realizing that he was dying, Shah Jahan asked to be carried to an adjoining balcony from where he could more easily see the Taj. There, wrapped in soft Kashmiri blankets and with the weeping Jahanara by his side, he died in the early hours of 22 January 1666. Attendants bathed his body in camphor water,

The tomb chamber of Shah Jahan and Mumtaz Mahal; Shah Jahan's tomb was squeezed in by Aurangzeb

wrapped it in pale shrouds and laid it in a sandalwood coffin. The next morning he was taken out headfirst, as custom demanded, through a newly reopened basement gate down to the riverbank and rowed across the Jumna accompanied by a small party of mourners.

Jahanara had planned "a grand and honourable funeral," but this was not to be. Aurangzeb had not sanctioned a state funeral. Instead, to the chanting of prayers, the old emperor was quickly and quietly laid beside Mumtaz in the marble crypt of the Taj Mahal.

In due course, a white marble cenotaph, inlaid with glowing flowers fashioned from semiprecious stones and bearing a brief epitaph, would be placed there. In the main tomb chamber directly above, another flower-inlaid cenotaph would also be placed. Following Muslim tradition, carved pen boxes standing proud on the lids of both cenotaphs signified that they belonged to a man, just as the slender, inlaid forms of writing slates on Mumtaz's denoted that there lay a woman.

CHAPTER SIXTEEN

Fall of the Peacock Throne

AURANGZEB, WHO HAD ASSUMED THE WHITE garb of mourning, did not begin his journey from Delhi to the tomb of his parents in Agra until two weeks after his father's death. Perhaps he wanted to check that there would be no political backlash. Once arrived, he visited the Taj Mahal, distributed alms and gave every appearance of grief.

He was also reunited and swiftly reconciled with his eldest sister, Jahanara. She had seemingly forgiven Aurangzeb for his treatment of their father. Such was the fifty-one-year-old princess's charm and ability that she quickly became his trusted adviser, supplanting Raushanara. Jahanara felt secure enough in her position to argue against Aurangzeb's increasingly strict regulation of public life in accordance with his fundamentalist Sunni religious beliefs. Aurangzeb had banned court music, court poetry and the keeping of an official chronicle of his reign—the latter on the grounds that it was vainglorious. He abandoned the emperor's morning appearance before his subjects on the *jharokha* balcony as tending toward idolatry. He prohibited cannabis, alcohol and sex out of wedlock with as much success as other rulers who have tried such courses.

In some ways the religious orthodoxy and prescriptions of Aurangzeb are comparable to the Puritanism of Oliver Cromwell, who, just a few years earlier in England, banned merriment or religious festivities at Christmas as well as theater and maypole dancing. Like Cromwell, in his hatred of idolatry Aurangzeb defaced religious statues and sculptures. His main targets were the statues in Hindu temples. To symbolize the domination of Islam, Aurangzeb built mosques at major Hindu pilgrimage sites. In 1669, at Mathura near Agra, sacred to Hindus as the birthplace of Lord Krishna, he constructed a three-domed fortresslike mosque virtually over the Hindu shrine. At the holiest Hindu city of all, Benares on the Ganges, he built a vast mosque on the foundations of a Hindu temple. Its 225-foot-high minarets dominated the city and the ceremonial cremation ghats.

Jahanara's most passionate protest was against her brother's reversal in 1679 of Akbar's abolition of the *jizya*, the poll tax on "infidels," 115 years previously. She threw herself at her brother's feet, arguing it would divide his kingdom by alienating the majority Hindu population. According to Niccolao Manucci, Aurangzeb justified himself by quoting from the Koran and then "bade her goodbye and turned his back upon her, a movement that cut the princess to the very quick."

That same year, Aurangzeb departed from Delhi on a military campaign against some of the Moghuls' greatest Hindu allies: the Rajputs. Although he would live another twenty-seven years, he would never return to his capital. Jahanara died eighteen months later in September 1681, at the age of sixty-seven. Aurangzeb awarded her the posthumous title Sahibat-uz-zamani, "Mistress of the Age." Mumtaz's favorite daughter was buried in a simple tomb close to the grave of a Sufi saint in Delhi. Grass was sewn over her marble sarcophagus, just as she had requested in a poem she had composed in Persian.

> *Let green grass only conceal my grave;*
> *Grass is the best covering of the grave of the meek.*

Aurangzeb's invasion of Rajasthan had been prompted by his wish to impose more direct rule on the Rajputs. He used as a pretext the power vacuum created in Marwar (Jodhpur) by the death of the raja, leaving as his heir an infant son born posthumously. He quickly occupied Marwar and much increased the inhabitants' opposition by destroying several Hindu temples. The neighboring state of Mewar (Udaipur) had only acknowledged Moghul overlordship reluctantly and nominally following defeat by the young Shah Jahan. The conquest of Marwar now led to cross-border friction with Mewar, and fighting broke out once more between the Moghuls and this most independent of Rajput states. Although peace of a sort was soon restored with Mewar, the turmoil and sporadic guerrilla fighting in Marwar did not subside finally until nearly thirty years later, when, after the death of Aurangzeb, the Moghuls finally recognized the raja of Marwar's posthumous son as ruler.

The conflicts in Mewar and Marwar, combined with Aurangzeb's religious policies, had one inevitable consequence: the breaking of the Hindu Rajputs' alliance with the Moghuls, which had been a mainstay of Akbar's and his successors' rule, supplying them with some of their best troops and generals and demonstrating their religious tolerance. Additionally, the war in Rajasthan led to the revolt of Aurangzeb's fourth son, the twenty-three-year-old Akbar. According to Manucci, he was "the boldest and most turbulent" of Aurangzeb's sons. He was also his father's favorite. Nevertheless, Aurangzeb had removed Akbar from command of the army fighting in Mewar because of his lack of success. While Akbar was suffering his father's displeasure, the Rajputs contacted him and suggested that it might be in their joint interests for Akbar to replace his father and to institute a new, more tolerant reign much more akin to that of his great great grandfather and namesake the emperor Akbar. According to a leading unofficial chronicler of Aurangzeb's reign, "the inexperienced prince was led astray from the path of rectitude, and through his youth and covetousness he fell into the snares of the Rajputs."

At first Akbar's rebellion seemed destined to succeed. He and the Rajputs had a greatly superior force, but Akbar dallied, overconfident that the prize was already his. Aurangzeb employed his familiar stratagem of letting fall into Rajput hands, as if by chance, a letter to his son, in which Aurangzeb falsely congratulated Akbar on ingratiating himself with the Rajputs, "as he had been instructed," and added "that he should crown his service by bringing them into a position where they would be under the fire" of the Moghul armies. The letter, as it was designed to, broke apart Akbar's forces. Akbar fled to the Deccan.

Aurangzeb followed with the twin aims of finally quelling that troublesome region and of capturing his errant son. Pausing only to give orders for the permanent imprisonment of his eldest daughter, the poetess

Zeb-un-Nissa, for secretly writing letters of support to Akbar, Aurangzeb marched his armies down to the south. There he was to eat up the remaining twenty-six years of his life and reign in continual warfare.

Akbar had sought refuge with the Marathas in their Deccan mountain hideouts. The martial and Hindu Marathas had long been a problem for Aurangzeb. Under their previous chieftain, Shivaji, they had fought extensive guerrilla wars against the Moghuls. In 1663 Shivaji had tricked his way into Poona, where the brother of Mumtaz Mahal, Shaista Khan, commanded the Moghul garrison. Led by Shivaji himself, the Marathas slipped stealthily and by night into Shaista Khan's compound, broke through a partially bricked-up window into the harem where Shaista Khan was sleeping and attacked him as he struggled from his bed. Before they fled, the Marathas succeeded in cutting off Shaista Khan's thumb and killing one of his sons. Eventually forced to capitulate, Shivaji did so only on condition that after paying tribute to the Moghuls he should retain some of his lands. When taken to Aurangzeb's court at Agra in 1666, Shivaji did not receive the honors he felt he had been promised. He protested volubly before the emperor and was put under house arrest. He soon escaped, carried from the residence hidden in a food basket, before returning to the Deccan mountains disguised as an ash-daubed, seminaked Hindu fakir. In the years that followed, the Marathas' power had increased, and Shivaji's further exploits had made him into one of the first heroes of India's long independence struggle. Shivaji had died a year before Akbar reached the Maratha territories. His son Shambuji, who now ruled in Shivaji's stead, was less martial, preferring, in the words of one European trader, to "divert himself far too much with women and drink." Consequently, he gave Akbar little material support other than protection from the probing raids that Aurangzeb sent into the Deccan hills.

Now free of the parental restraint of his own father, Shah Jahan, which had often stayed his hand in the Deccan, Aurangzeb decided that the best way to deal with the Marathas was first to conquer the neighboring and larger Muslim states of Bijapur and Golconda, the longtime enemies of the Moghuls. Once deprived of their support, the Marathas and their guest Akbar would be easier prey. Aurangzeb attacked Bijapur first, in June 1685, needing fifteen months to conquer the state and open the way to invade Golconda, which by then had a licentious reputation. The capital, Hyderabad, claimed to house twenty thousand prostitutes, many of whom besported themselves before the ruler in the public square every Friday. At the first sign of Moghul attack, the ruler fled from his pleasure dome of Hyderabad to the neighboring mountain fortress called Golconda without, according to a chronicler, "consulting with any of his nobles or even caring anything for his property or the honour of his own women and family." Once inside, he recovered his courage and resisted Aurangzeb's forces bravely. Moghul bribery, not military might, forced open the fortress's gates after a siege of eight months, during which plague had ravaged the Moghul camp. Golconda's dissipated ruler followed Bijapur's into an austere prison as their states were subsumed into the Moghul Empire.

By this time Akbar had fled to Persia with the aid, according to Manucci, of some French merchants, but Aurangzeb remained determined to defeat his son's former hosts, the Marathas. The Moghuls captured the indolent, luxury-loving Shambuji and his chief minister in a lightning raid on the minister's house. Both were hiding in a hole in the ground cut beneath the floor. The Moghuls crowned the pair with bell-bedecked fool's caps, mounted them on camels and paraded them around the roads of the Deccan and into the imperial camp. When brought before Aurangzeb, Shambuji refused to reveal where his treasure was buried, cursed Aurangzeb and blasphemed his religion. Aurangzeb rewarded him with a slow death. First, the Moghuls cut out his blaspheming tongue. Then they blinded him. Further protracted torture followed over two weeks, at the end of which his limbs were hacked off and fed to the camp dogs and his head was stuffed with straw and paraded around the Deccan to show the fate of insolent rebels.

Unsurprisingly, Shambuji's cruel death won loyalty not for Aurangzeb but for the Maratha cause. Aurangzeb stayed in the Deccan, intent on its complete pacification, but guerrilla raids mounted, against which Aurangzeb's 170,000 soldiers and a third of a million camp followers were cumbersomely ineffective. Although with his recent conquests Aurangzeb had extended the boundaries of the Moghul Empire to their largest extent, pushing its borders far down into southern India, the wars in the Deccan became an endless sink for the riches of the Moghuls, which had seemed inexhaustible when Shah Jahan had contemplated his vast and expensive building projects. Aurangzeb's treatment of his Hindu subjects in the Deccan, in Rajasthan and elsewhere had also changed the character of Moghul rule. It was no longer the inclusive, tolerant empire bound together by mutual trust and interdependence established by Akbar. Instead the Moghuls were once again, as in the time of Babur, an occupying power.

Aurangzeb only turned north again sixteen years later, in October 1705. In declining health and at the age of eighty-seven, he reached Ahmednagar, east of Mumbai (Bombay), where he died. The date on the Western calendar was 21 February 1707. As Aurangzeb had wished, it was Friday, the Muslim holy day. He was buried within the confines of a Muslim saint's tomb at Khuldabad, about twenty miles from Ahmednagar. In accordance with his wishes, the tomb of the last of the Great Moghuls was topped by an uninscribed sandstone slab and left open to the skies—an even simpler tomb than that of his great-great-great-grandfather Babur in Kabul, and in complete contrast to his parents' magnificent mausoleum. His resentment toward his father overflowed into his last testament: "Never trust your sons, nor treat them during your life time in an intimate manner; because if emperor Shah Jahan had not [favored] Dara Shukoh, his affairs would not have come to such a sorry pass. Ever keep in view the saying, 'The word of a king is barren.'"

CHAOS SOON FOLLOWED Aurangzeb's death. Akbar had previously died in exile in 1704, but Aurangzeb's three surviving sons—two of whom Aurangzeb had imprisoned at various times—fought for the succession. Two of them and three grandsons died in the conflict. The Moghul Empire quickly disintegrated into a mass of feuding smaller states with a succession of dissipated emperors exercising ever more nominal suzerainty. A raid on Delhi by the Persians, commanded by Nadir Shah, in 1739 led to the city's capture, the payment by the inhabitants of a large indemnity and the carrying off by the Persians of the Peacock Throne and much other treasure. In the nearly 350 years since Timur's raid on Delhi and his roundup of artisans, and in the more than 200 years since Babur had found craftsmen one of the few things he prized in Hindustan, the

reputation of Indian artisans had only increased. Unsurprisingly, therefore, among the Persian booty in 1739 were one hundred masons and
two hundred carpenters to beautify their captor's country.

As the power of the Moghul emperors declined, so did their presence
in Agra, which was relegated to the status of a provincial city. The Taj
Mahal remained a symbol at this time not so much of love but of former
Moghul glories. Its riches and those of the other Moghul monuments
surrounding Agra provided an all too tempting target for plunderers from
near and far, even if their depredations were not on the scale of Nadir
Shah's in Delhi. The Jats, a rising local military power, carried away
much of the wealth of the Moghuls, including, it is alleged, the Taj Mahal's ornate and bejeweled silver gates. They also took marble and sandstone for their own palace complexes. Later in the eighteenth century
when the Marathas, the by then powerful nation once led by Shivaji, occupied the city, they and their French advisers continued to plunder
Moghul buildings, removing semiprecious inlay and more stone for
building projects.

At the end of his embassy to India in 1619, Sir Thomas Roe had advised the English government and the East India Company, "If you will
profit [in India] seek profit in quiet trade; for . . . it is an error to affect
garrisons and land wars in India." The East India Company had, as a trading organization, tried to follow his advice, but as Moghul power had
declined and other European powers, in particular the French, had intervened, it had become drawn into conflict with them and hence into political alliances with local rulers, and finally and reluctantly into the
acquisition of territory and the recruitment of a large army. As late as
1784 the British Prime Minister William Pitt the Younger had declared
territorial expansion in India to be "repugnant to the wish, the honour,
the policy of this nation." Nevertheless, only a few years afterward
under the political leadership of the British governor general Lord
Wellesley, and using the military skills of his younger brother Arthur,
the future Duke of Wellington, the East India Company had fought and
defeated the Marathas and their French mercenaries and annexed their
territories.

By the time the company's army under General Lake occupied Agra
in 1803, most of the valuable fittings, as well as carpets, jeweled canopies

and wall hangings, had disappeared from the Taj Mahal. Although they
took the first steps in surveying the monument and began the first restoration work as early as 1810, the British did not treat it with the respect it
deserved. They rented out the mosque and the guesthouse flanking the
mausoleum as honeymoon cottages. They also held balls at which military bands performed from the plinth of the mausoleum. As Lord Curzon,
the British viceroy at the beginning of the twentieth century admitted,
"At an earlier date, when picnic parties were held in the garden of the
Taj, it was not an uncommon thing for the revellers to arm themselves
with hammer and chisel with which they whiled away the afternoon by
chipping out fragments of agate and carnelian from the cenotaphs of the
emperor and his lamented queen."

The British also used the gardens as a place to indulge in secluded
drinking sessions. An English guidebook of the time sniffed haughtily,
"It would certainly be more in character if no festivities ever disturbed
the repose of a place set aside for sacred memories, but as long as the na-
tives hold constant fairs in the enclosure and throw orange peels and
other debris about the whole place, it is perhaps somewhat hypocritical
to object to a few Englishmen refreshing themselves in a remote corner."

However, the claim that Lord William Bentinck, who was the British
governor in the 1830s, considered tearing down the Taj Mahal and auctioning off its marble, only desisting when news came that the first auc-
tion in London of Indian artifacts had been a failure, is false. His British
enemies in India fabricated the story, which even appeared in an official report. The small kernel of truth upon which they were built was
that Bentinck attempted to sell the remains of a marble bath from another site in Agra, part of which had been shipped to Calcutta sixteen
years previously.

In 1857 both Hindu and Muslim soldiers of the East India Company
army rose in rebellion, which was only suppressed with difficulty by the
deployment of British government troops to bolster the company's remaining forces. At the time of the rebellion there was still formally a
Moghul emperor—an elderly and gentle poet named Bahadur Shah II—
who lived under British protection in the Red Fort in Delhi. After the
rebels captured Delhi, they adopted a very reluctant Bahadur Shah as a

symbolic figurehead of their cause. When the British retook the city, they took Bahadur Shah prisoner, summarily executed some of his sons and subsequently exiled him to Rangoon in Burma (Myanmar), where, in 1862, he died, addicted to opium just as his predecessors Humayun and Jahangir had been. The Moghul Empire was thus ended in name as it had long been ended in power.

An inevitable consequence of the rebellion was that the British government soon assumed authority over India from the anomalous East India Company. Nearly 40 percent of the country was, however, still ruled by independent kings or rajas, such as the raja of Amber (Jaipur), who acknowledged British suzerainty, just as they had that of the Moghuls in earlier times. In 1872 Queen Victoria was proclaimed empress of India.

For Agra, one result of the rebellion was that nervous British commanders destroyed some Moghul palaces to broaden their field of fire in any future rebellion, and drove a railway line to their military encampment—the cantonments—through the main city. The mansion of Mumtaz's father, Asaf Khan, was apparently one of those blown up by the British. However, the Taj Mahal remained intact, and by the early twentieth century Viceroy Lord Curzon was actively restoring it.

Curzon was an aristocrat so haughty that his undergraduate colleagues at Oxford coined the following lines, "My name is George Nathaniel Curzon, I am a most superior person," and the seventeenth Earl of Derby later confessed that Curzon "makes one feel so terribly plebeian." Perhaps his respect for tradition and position led him to remedy the effect of neglect on the imperial Moghul architecture of Agra. He later justifiably boasted of his work and of the skill of the Agra craftsmen. The Taj was "no longer approached through dusty wastes and squalid bazaars. A beautiful park takes their place. Every building in the garden enclosure of the Taj has been scrupulously repaired and the discovery of old plans has enabled us to restore the water channels and flowerbeds more exactly to their original state. The skilled workmen of Agra have lent themselves to the enterprise with as much zeal and taste as their forerunners three hundred years ago. Since I came to India we have spent upon repairs at Agra alone a sum of £40,000. Every rupee has been an offering of reverence to the past and a gift of recovered beauty to the future."*

Curzon had a particular love for the Taj Mahal itself. In a speech from the marble plinth he proclaimed, "The central dome of the Taj is rising like some vast exhalation in the air. If I'd never done anything else in India, I have written my name here and the letters are a living joy." Curzon gave to the Taj Mahal a beautiful brass hanging lamp—modeled on one from an old Egyptian mosque—which was suspended from the center of the interior dome above the imperial cenotaphs, where it still remains.[†]

As THE TWENTIETH century wore on, the British took further steps to survey and record the Taj Mahal, while around them Gandhi and Nehru and others led the movement for Indian independence. Between 1941 and 1943 the Archaeological Survey of India, originally established in the middle of the nineteenth century, undertook a particularly detailed series of studies. Although they found the Taj Mahal was in good structural condition overall, the southwest minaret was tilting by some eight and a half inches and the other three by between one and a half and four and a half inches.

After India regained her independence in 1947, the Archaeological Survey of India quietly continued its work and remains responsible for the care and maintenance of the Taj Mahal, which was listed in 1983 as a UNESCO World Heritage Site. In 1965, when long-standing tensions between India and Pakistan broke out into brief but full-scale conflict, the Agra airfield was an important operational base for the Indian Air Force. Fearing that the white Taj Mahal might on moonlit nights prove

---

* The mention of old plans is, perhaps, the most intriguing point in his statement, but disappointingly they can no longer be found in any British or Indian archive. Possibly these are the same plans said to have been in the possession of the draftsman Ustad Isa's descendants in the first half of the twentieth century. (See chapter 10).

† Curzon may not have understood the sensual passion that was part of the love between Mumtaz Mahal and Shah Jahan since, instructing his wife about lovemaking, he reputedly told her, "Ladies never move."

a useful navigational landmark for Pakistani air attacks on the air base, the Indian government commissioned local tailors to sew a massive black camouflage net to be draped over the white mausoleum and minarets to diminish their visibility from the air. The net was kept in one of the chambers of the Taj complex until about ten years ago, when, almost entirely consumed by mice, it was finally disposed of.

In the first years of the twenty-first century, terrorism has posed a more direct threat to the Taj Mahal, and the Indian government has stepped up security measures. There are sandbagged bunkers at key points around the complex and a barbed-wire fence between the monument and the Jumna. The teams of security guards now familiar throughout the world at airports and government buildings search bags and frisk bodies, accompanied at times of crisis by dogs sniffing for explosives.

However, probably the greatest threat to the monument is man-made pollution from surrounding factories, power stations, railway yards and passing traffic. The Indian government has responded with air pollution measures. It closed 250 factories near the Taj Mahal which lacked equipment to manage their emissions. Such moves, said to have cost up to one hundred thousand jobs, were not universally popular in Agra, where people commented, "Must we make a tomb of the city to preserve a mausoleum?"

Only lead-free gasoline is sold in Agra, and a solar energy power plant is being constructed so that there will be minimal pollution while power is generated for the area. Vehicles powered by electric batteries or human or animal muscle power are the only ones allowed within 550 yards of the Taj complex. The Archaeological Survey of India installed a pollution monitoring system in the tower at the northeast corner of the mausoleum complex, together with a discreet electronic display that informs visitors in real time of the prevailing level of pollutants such as sulphur dioxide. The Survey has made great efforts to remove the yellowing pollutants from the white marble. Some years ago it discovered one of the more successful cleaning agents to be a mixture of clay, cereal, milk and lime, which was recommended by Akbar's chronicler Abul Fazl as an excellent facial cosmetic for women. The conservators applied the paste about one inch thick, and its use produced marked improvements in the color of the minarets and the interior of the mausoleum. The Indian government in 2003 halted construction of an entertainment complex, which had begun six months previously just three hundred yards from the Taj Mahal, following hints from UNESCO that if it did not do so UNESCO would delete the Taj from the World Heritage list.

One of the most pressing concerns is the level and condition of the Jumna. Originally, it flowed beside the Taj Mahal so that Shah Jahan could travel easily by boat from the Agra fort to the landing place on the terrace below the mausoleum. Now the Jumna is a much depleted, heavily polluted river some distance from the terrace. In June 2003 thousands of dead fish were found next to the Taj Mahal, killed by a combination of chemical pollution and raw sewage.

In 2004 two Indian historians warned that the tilt of the minarets had increased considerably since the measurements undertaken in the 1940s, quoting as evidence a UNESCO survey. However, after undertaking further investigations, the Archaeological Survey of India discovered no cracks at the minarets' base or on the plinth and concluded that the tilt was either part of the original design to prevent the minarets from crashing inward onto the mausoleum in an earthquake or the result of subsoil settlement centuries ago. The survey suggested that differences in the measurement of the tilt were within the bounds of statistical error. The historians do not agree. They believe that, in the absence of the counterbalancing pressure of the Jumna's waters, the Taj Mahal and its platform may slowly tilt toward the north and that the increase in the tilt of the minarets is the first instance of this phenomenon. They have proposed, without result so far, damming the Jumna downstream of the Taj Mahal so that sufficient water can be built up to restore the original water level and pressure.

Even though the Taj Mahal is now closed on Fridays to allow time for maintenance and other activities, tourism brings its own difficulties: Condensation from the breath of the Taj Mahal's 3 million visitors a year is one of the biggest problems inside the mausoleum. So many visitors also means that it is difficult to enjoy the Taj Mahal in the seclusion that makes it most evocative. However, it would be impossible, and entirely unjustifiable, to restrict visitor numbers. Increasing the entrance price paid by Indian visitors to the higher sums paid by foreigners would prevent large numbers of Indians from seeing their national heritage. Restrictions by nationality to Indians would mean that foreigners could no longer view a building long celebrated as truly unique. As one of Shah Jahan's poets wrote:

> Since heaven's vault has been standing, an edifice like this
> Has never risen to compete against the sky.

CHAPTER SEVENTEEN

"His Own Tomb on the Other Side of the River"

JUST AS WE WILL NEVER KNOW WHAT LIES behind the *Mona Lisa*'s enigmatic smile, there are unresolved questions about the Taj Mahal. Some may perhaps be solved by further archaeological investigations, but others concern what the grieving Shah Jahan saw in his mind's eye when he planned the monument.

The reason why Shah Jahan and his architects sited the Taj Mahal at the end of its gardens rather than in the middle, as would have been conventional for a mausoleum, has attracted much attention. In the 1970s a respected American historian built on the widely accepted view that the Taj complex was intended to evoke a paradise on earth, by suggesting that the mausoleum itself was a symbolic representation of the throne of God, which sits directly above paradise, and that the whole complex was an allegorical interpretation of the Day of Resurrection as revealed by Sufi mystics. The gardens beneath the Taj would thus represent the plains of assembly for the resurrected upon whom God would look down from his white marble throne represented by the Taj Mahal. The strong Sufi sympathies of Shah Jahan's favorite son and daughter, Dara Shukoh and Jahanara, and his own preoccupation with the creation of extravagant thrones as the symbols of power, give some credence to this suggestion. Others have seen the placement more simply as following the tradition in Agra's riverside gardens of positioning the main pavilion alongside the water to benefit from the views, cool breezes and reflections the Jumna provided.

However, some ten years ago archaeologists from the Archaeological Survey of India and the Sackler Gallery of the Smithsonian Institution in Washington, D.C., began to study the remains of gardens directly opposite the Taj Mahal on the north bank of the Jumna, which are thought to have been among those originally built by Babur and which are known as the Mahtab Bagh (Moonlight Garden). By comparing old drawings and plans of Agra, they found that these gardens seemed to have contained pavilions and to have been directly aligned with the Taj Mahal. When they began their excavations, the site of the Mahtab Bagh was covered in silt from the flooding of the Jumna and choked with grasses and other plants. Most stone and masonry had been removed over the years to construct dwellings in nearby villages. Some of the brickwork fronting the Jumna had fallen into the river.

The archaeologists' careful excavations confirmed that the twenty-four-acre Mahtab Bagh was indeed a nocturnal pleasure garden. The moonlight garden was not a Moghul innovation; Hindu rulers had built such gardens long before their coming. They could be enjoyed in the cool of the evening after the day's heat had subsided, particularly during the nights of the full moon. Gardeners planted them with pale or white flowers to stand out from the dusky background and chose sweet-smelling flowers such as stocks or jasmine to scent the warm, still night air. Another favorite was the champa. The creamy flowers of this member of the magnolia family come out at night and smell richly sweet. Jahangir described how, when in flower, "one would perfume a garden."

The Moghuls enhanced the original Hindu concept, adding running water and splashing fountains. They also lined the gardens' paths with oil lamps and placed them in pavilions as well as in niches behind water features. Often, too, the Moghuls held fireworks parties in their gardens. Miniatures show women in darkened gardens holding in their hands fireworks which spill a shower of golden sparks.

Working in the Mahtab Bagh in temperatures above 120 degrees Fahrenheit and digging down to the planting beds, watercourses and walkways of Moghul times, botanical archaeologists found evidence that

These niches in the Mahtab Bagh once held oil lamps

the champa tree indeed once grew here. They also discovered traces of another sweet-smelling, night-flowering white blossomed tree, the red cedar (a member of the mahogany family despite its name), as well as of cashew, mango, palm and fig trees. In addition, they found carbonized seed from the cockscomb, a red-flowered plant which produces masses of seed attractive to songbirds.*

However, the Mahtab Bagh has a much greater importance for the Taj than this. The archaeologists' work revealed that the garden was square, with towers at its four corners, only one of which is now intact. They also found signs of a gateway in the middle of the northern perimeter wall. Most interestingly, at the southern end of the garden they unearthed the remains of a raised octagonal terrace overlooking the river and opposite the mausoleum itself. A large octagonal pool was set into

Excavations in the Mahtab Bagh

---

* The Mahtab Bagh is today open to the public after being restored. The beds are again filled with flowers, attracting hundreds of bees and butterflies. The Archaeological Survey of India has planted over ten thousand plants and shrubs, including the cockscomb, the mango and the lushly scented champa.

the terrace, and on its north side were the foundations of a small pavilion. The pool had contained twenty-five fountains and was surrounded with lotus leaf designs similar to those used in the Taj Mahal and around pools in other Moghul gardens. When the pool was full, water would have run through a shallow channel at the north of the pool, over a sandstone lip, and fallen down in a small waterfall past a series of niches, in which oil lamps would have been placed by night and flowers by day, into a small sandstone pool at the base.

No water channels remained beyond that point, but in the middle of the garden the archaeologists uncovered another raised pool, about twenty feet square and nearly five feet deep. This led them to conclude that the garden was likely to have been a conventional *char bagh* design with one of the cross channels flowing from the sandstone pool to the base of the octagonal pool to the pool in the middle of the garden, where another channel would have intersected it at right angles. The archaeologists also found outside the garden's walls the remains of its water supply system, in particular a cistern raised on pillars and suggesting, with the remains of other pillars, that the water supply mechanism resembled that of the Taj complex.

The researchers' careful measurements showed that the towers marking each end of the waterfront wall of the Mahtab Bagh were perfectly aligned with those on the opposite bank at the ends of the Taj and that the north-south water channel—the central axis of the Taj—aligned with the putative channel and existing central pool in the Mahtab Bagh. More significant, once it was refilled with water, the octagonal pool perfectly captured the reflection of the Taj Mahal. The archaeologists, on the basis of this work, concluded that the Mahtab Bagh was an intrinsic part of the Taj Mahal concept as a whole and formed a moonlight-viewing garden. From the top of the small pavilion at the north of the terrace, Shah Jahan could have watched the Taj Mahal float above the spray from the Mahtab Bagh's fountains.

Their conclusion that Shah Jahan and his architects had incorporated the Mahtab Bagh within their overall design of the Taj complex, and that they had modified the gardens considerably and added features such as the octagonal pool and pavilions, makes sense of Aurangzeb's linking of the Mahtab Bagh and the Taj Mahal in his letter of 9 December 1652. In this letter he described to Shah Jahan how flooding had caused the garden "to lose its charm" at the same time as he reported on leaks in the Taj Mahal. Most important of all, the research supports the conclusion that Shah Jahan intended the Taj Mahal to sit at the middle of a vast garden, as in the conventional *char bagh* design, with the north-south water channels of the Taj complex and the Mahtab Bagh, both aligned precisely with Mumtaz's body, providing the main axis, but with the River Jumna representing the east-west channel—a truly awe-inspiring if grandiose concept.

Shah Jahan's creation of such a garden also bears on the enduring belief that he had intended the Taj Mahal for Mumtaz alone and wished to build a separate mausoleum for himself across the Jumna from the Taj. In his book about his travels in India, during which he visited Agra in 1640 and again in 1665 (Aurangzeb had imprisoned Shah Jahan by the time of the latter visit), the French traveler and jeweler Jean-Baptiste Tavernier stated that "Shah Jahan began to build his own tomb on the other side of the river but the war with his sons interrupted his plan." In compiling his account, Tavernier would have drawn on his conversations with courtiers and others in Agra. Local oral tradition supports Tavernier's account with the embellishment that the second Taj was to be of black marble and also that Shah Jahan may have intended to link the two with a bridge, perhaps of silver. This story is recounted as firm fact by many guidebooks and most guides, at least as far as it touches on the second black Taj.

Many historians have dismissed the idea of a second Taj because there is no contemporary reference to it other than Tavernier's and because archaeologists found no foundations for such a building during their recent excavations in the Mahtab Bagh. (The octagonal reflecting pool is sited where the black Taj might have been expected to be.) Convinced there is no evidence of any preparations by Shah Jahan to be buried elsewhere, they have gone on to deduce that it was always his intention to be buried in the Taj. They reject the suggestion that he was squeezed into the Taj by his usurping son as an afterthought by citing a precedent: that Mumtaz Mahal's Persian grandfather, Itimad-ud-daula, was buried in the same tomb as his wife. They point out that in each case the woman, who died first, lies in the center, with her husband slightly to one side.

However, before looking at the question of the "black Taj," the argument should be considered the other way around to examine whether there is any evidence that Shah Jahan ever intended to be buried in the Taj Mahal. No court chronicler, no other Indian observer nor European mentions the Taj Mahal as other than the tomb of Mumtaz Mahal until after Shah Jahan's actual interment. The tomb's name, Taj Mahal, generally agreed to be a shortening of Mumtaz Mahal's name, was in popular use well before Shah Jahan's death and suggests that the tomb was then thought of as hers and to be hers alone in future. Mumtaz's cenotaph undeniably occupies the prime position, aligned as it is along the central axis of the whole complex running from the Mahtab Bagh to Mumtazabad—the bazaar and accommodation area at the south of the Taj complex. The placing of Shah Jahan's cenotaph is the only asymmetrical element in the whole complex. If he had intended himself to be buried in the Taj Mahal, would he not have reserved the central position for himself or planned for Mumtaz and himself to be buried symmetrically on either side of the axis?

Furthermore, Shah Jahan's cenotaph does appear squashed both into the main chamber of the mausoleum and into the crypt below. In the former, especially when viewed from above, there seems barely room for it between Mumtaz's cenotaph and the surrounding *jali* screen. If Shah Jahan had intended to be buried near Mumtaz, he would have made the area enclosed by the ornate *jali* screen larger, which there was room to do. Moreover, Shah Jahan's cenotaph encroaches considerably onto the border of black and white floor tiles around Mumtaz's cenotaph while having no such border of its own. In the crypt there is scarcely room for a person to pass between Shah Jahan's grave and the wall, whereas there is some eight feet or so between Mumtaz's grave and the wall on the opposite side. Again, might not Shah Jahan have built a larger crypt if he had intended to be interred alongside Mumtaz?

In addition, the comparison with Itimad-ud-daula's tomb is not as persuasive as it first appears. The small low tombs of Itimad-ud-daula and his wife, who died within three months of each other, are, unlike those of Shah Jahan and Mumtaz Mahal, of the same size and design, and both are contained within a single tiled border on the floor. There is no *jali* screen and plenty of room around the cenotaphs on every side. Bearing this in mind, one could just as well deduce that when casting around for a burial place for his father, Aurangzeb saw the positioning of his great-grandparents' cenotaphs as an inexpensive, inconspicuous precedent for disposing of his father's body with a minimum of fuss, as to suggest that the arrangement in Itimad-ud-daula's tomb supports the argument that Shah Jahan intended throughout to be buried alongside his wife.

On the basis of this evidence it is reasonable to assume that Shah Jahan did not intend to be buried in the Taj Mahal. In that case where did he intend his tomb to be? Although we cannot know for certain, a stronger case can be made for the black Taj than is sometimes suggested, and it has some support including that of a recent director general of the Archaeological Survey of India, M. C. Joshi, who thinks that it must have at least been included at the planning stage. The story not only has contemporary support from Tavernier, but also from the strong local tradition. Shah Jahan was a patron who saw art on a grand scale, and the idea of a counterpointing tomb on the north bank of the Jumna would not have been beyond him. The second tomb would have mirrored the Taj Mahal even more perfectly than any shimmering reflection in the Mahtab Bagh's octagonal pool. Shah Jahan loved to contrast white marble with black. This is exemplified by his building of a counterpointing black marble pavilion in the Shalimar Gardens in Srinagar in Kashmir in 1630, just before Mumtaz Mahal's death. The Taj Mahal also contains much black marble. For example, the joints between each of the white marble blocks of the four minarets are inlaid with black marble, the low wall around the mausoleum plinth is inlaid with the same material and the mausoleum itself has black marble in its framing and calligraphy—what better transition to a black Taj over the water?

By general consent the Mahtab Bagh was a pleasure garden. However, in Timurid and Moghul tradition, rulers and nobles were often buried in the gardens they had built for their own diversion while alive. For example, Nur built Jahangir's tomb in Lahore in one of his favorite pleasure gardens. Jahangir's father, Akbar, was buried in a garden setting that Akbar himself had chosen during his lifetime. At the time in his life when he might have wished to begin work on his own tomb, Shah Jahan had, as Tavernier records, been deposed. The construction of a black Taj, or of any mausoleum in the Mahtab Bagh, was no longer in his power.

While the above argument may not be conclusive evidence that a

The black marble pavilion in the Shalimar Gardens in Kashmir

black Taj was planned, it has the advantage of combining known facts and reconciling competing theories. It also has the merit of appealing to the romantic deep in everyone.

Another debate concerns the purpose of the series of subterranean chambers along the northern riverside end of the sandstone platform supporting the mausoleum on its white marble plinth. Seventeen chambers, linked by short interconnecting passages, are connected to the sandstone platform seventeen feet above by two staircases. The chambers have high ceilings, each arching into a kind of dome fifteen feet high at the apex. The ceilings are plastered and decorated with diamond-cut patterns. The lower parts of the walls have red and green borders up to the dado, similar to those surviving in Shah Jahan's buildings at the royal palace at Burhanpur. Above the dado are arched panels sunk into the walls and outlined in red and green. Along the riverside walls of the chambers these arches seem to have been filled in after construction with the small bricks used elsewhere in Moghul buildings. When the mausoleum is viewed from the river, the only external sign of the chambers' existence is a latticed ventilation screen near where the eastern staircase descends.

Behind the subterranean chambers to the south, away from the river, is a separate narrow, high corridor. Measurements show that the combined width of chamber and corridor is twenty-six feet, two inches, stopping eight inches short of the foundations of the white marble plinth that supports the mausoleum.

The corridor and subterranean chambers are clearly contemporary with the rest of the building. When Shah Jahan visited the Taj Mahal, he did so by river. (The Archaeological Survey of India identified in 1958 the remains of a platform which would have supported the jetty.) Although some argue that the arched chambers were merely part of the architects' sophisticated system to spread the load of the heavy structure above, the consensus is that when the Taj Mahal was originally built, the arches on the river side of the main subterranean chambers were open and thus the chambers provided a series of verandas for the emperor to walk along as he made his way from the jetty to his wife's grave. He could have looked out from the verandas' shade across the river to the Mahtab Bagh. The reason the verandas were bricked in could have been as a precaution against flooding or more likely as part of work commissioned by Shah Jahan in 1652 to repair the dome of the mausoleum and to strengthen the Taj Mahal's structure, following Aurangzeb's report of cracks and leaks.

However, the purpose of the corridor is not so clear. Some archaeologists have argued that it originally ran around all four sides of the foundations of the marble plinth and that at some point it gave access to a crypt beneath the existing one in which there would have been a third set of graves, the real ones. In support of this theory they quote the fact that the corridor is some nine feet longer than the marble plinth, which allows for four-foot-wide corridors to run off from it at both ends around the foundations. What seem to be filled-in doorways are at each end of the corridor, where it might be assumed to have once turned at right angles around the plinth. The disputed nineteenth-century documents reputedly copied from earlier lost manuscripts speak of the cost of three sets of tombstones. Even if these documents represent only a nineteenth-century setting down of oral tradition, it seems a little odd that such a tradition should support the existence of a third pair of tombs if they did not exist. The reason for blocking access to them could have been to preserve structural integrity during repairs in 1652 or at a later stage to prevent vandalism or looting when the Moghuls' hold on Agra began to slip. However, a definitive view would require further archaeological investigations, and the Archaeological Survey of India says it has no intention to undertake them at present.

CONTROVERSY ABOUT WHETHER the Taj Mahal was originally a Hindu temple rumbles on. Arguments about the comparative achievements of Hindu and Muslim in the architecture of India are not new and have often detracted from an assessment of what the Taj is: a synthesis of the two traditions. For example, Aldous Huxley in the 1920s wrote, "The Hindu architects produced buildings incomparably more rich and interesting as works of art [than] the Taj Mahal." However, in recent decades, some nonmainstream Hindu historians have given such controversies a new twist, suggesting that Shah Jahan did not create the Taj Mahal from nothing; rather he modified a preexisting building—either a Rajput palace or a Hindu temple—built by the raja of Amber (Jaipur).

The claim of these historians, which seemingly seeks to minimize the Moghul contribution to Indian architecture (some have also questioned whether other buildings such as Humayun's tomb were Moghul constructions), has received no support from academic historians of any background, and there is no evidence from contemporary Rajput, Moghul or European sources to justify it. The claim is based on statements by two of the official contemporary chroniclers of Shah Jahan that a much earlier palace existed on the site for the Taj Mahal that the raja of Amber gave to the emperor and for which he was, in turn, rewarded with four other estates. The dissenting historians suggest that Shah Jahan modified this building, while leaving clear traces of Hindu architectural features. Over time, under the pressure of debate, the Hindu writers' descriptions of the original building have varied from that of a palace to a Shiva temple whose name, Tajo-Mahalaya, produced the name Taj Mahal. They have also suggested that the reason for the bricking up of the entrance to the subterranean corridors of the Taj Mahal was that they gave access to a statue of Shiva.

Yet all accounts of the construction of the tomb, whether by court historians or by European observers such as Peter Mundy who were present when building started, make clear that work started from the foundations up. The chronicler Lahori talked of "laying the foundations" by digging down to "the water table." Peter Mundy noted, "The building is begun." Had there been any previous major structure on the site, other observers who had visited Agra before Mumtaz's death would have recorded it. Europeans such as the Jesuit Father Monserrate, who visited Agra several times in 1580–82, or Sir Thomas Roe, who gave such a detailed description of Agra and court life in the early seventeenth century, and Francisco Pelsaert, the Dutch trader who visited Agra in 1620–27 and enumerated the gardens and palaces along the Jumna, made no mention of any preexisting building. Although the royal archives of the raja of Amber, who donated the land for the building, refer to building projects, including temples, elsewhere, they contain no reference to any such construction in Agra. Furthermore, the Hindu architectural features of the Taj, such as the chattris, are more likely to derive from the synthesis of Hindu and Islamic styles so apparent in Moghul architecture from Akbar's time onward.

The claim that the building was a Shiva temple particularly puzzles Indian scholars, both because temples cannot be sold after construction and Shah Jahan would not have committed such an inauspicious act as seizing the land, and because the rajas of Amber belong to a particular branch of the Hindu religion that would not have worshipped at a Shiva temple. Perhaps even more conclusively, no known Hindu temple looks at all like the Taj Mahal.

Coming from the other side of the religious divide, the Wakf Board, a charitable endowment set up after the partition of India in 1947 to look after deserted Muslim graves, recently tried to claim guardianship of the Taj Mahal in order to manage it within the stricter religious guidelines of sharia law. In late 2005 the Indian Supreme Court dismissed its case on the grounds that the Taj Mahal had in both Moghul and British times been considered the property of the crown or state and that legally it had remained national property on the transfer of power to independent India.

Such partisan arguments and controversies will no doubt persist, just as the Taj will remain for everyone what Bernier called it some 350 years ago—"a wonder of the world"—even though the original vision in Shah Jahan's mind's eye will always be slightly mysterious.

Epilogue

BECAUSE WE WANTED TO UNDERSTAND WHO Shah Jahan's and Mumtaz's ancestors were and the influences that shaped them and their sense of art and architecture, we began our research for this book not at the Taj Mahal, nor in India, both of which we had visited many times before, but in Uzbekistan and Iran. Traveling along the shifting, sandy banks of the meandering Oxus and through the red-gold sands of the Kizl Kum, or "Red Desert," dotted with coarse, sprouting camel grass helped us to imagine the Moghuls' nomadic days.

Reaching Samarkand, wrecked by one Moghul ancestor, Genghis Khan, but rebuilt by another, Timur, we discovered many of the shapes and forms found in Moghul architecture, such as double domes. The blue, purple, green and yellow–tiled mosques, tombs and palaces of the Timurids are massive in their ambitious scope and scale, more strident in their bright colors, harsher in their lines than those of the Moghuls. Nevertheless, when we descended a narrow, sloping passage to the crypt in Timur's own double-domed mausoleum, where he lies in a sarcophagus topped by what is said to be the world's biggest slab of jade, we found the austerity relieved by a tracery of flowers that would not be out of place in the Taj Mahal.

In Isfahan, the beautiful Iranian city of Shah Abbas with its mosques and sixteenth–century double-tiered bridges, we discovered not only many shapes of Moghul architecture but also sophistication in design and a delicacy of detail we had not found in Samarkand. The half-grapefruit dome of Shah Abbas's Friday Mosque seemed to have the

Timur's tomb in Samarkand, Uzbekistan

quality of fine china. Naturalistic floral designs, such a striking feature of the Taj's decoration, are everywhere—in painting and tiles.

Yet two great differences with Moghul architecture remain. The beautiful surface decoration of Persian buildings was produced by tiles that softened and sometimes obscured the form. If Uzbek architecture seems more masculine than that of the Moghuls, that of the Persians seems more feminine in its subtlety. Also, the basic materials were different from those in India. Here there was no red sandstone to deepen to ox blood in the sunset as it did in Agra. Many architectural elements were missing, some due to differences in the plasticity or carvability of the material, others derived from the influence of Hindu architecture such as the *chattris* (domed

Shah Abbas's Friday Mosque in Isfahan, Iran

kiosks) and the great brass finials rising from the lotus flowers on top of the domes. Many of these we later found in the palaces and fortresses of Rajasthan and the temples there and elsewhere in Hindu India.

However, when, in Iran, we walked through carefully tended Persian "paradise gardens," we felt we had found the inspiration for the *char baghs* of the Moghuls. Their beds of densely planted flowers—a fusion of pinks, reds, madders, maroons, deep blues and oranges—looked like living Persian carpets. Their water fountains disgorged spouts and rainbow mists; their water pools and channels reflected images of surrounding pleasure pavilions. Bees buzzed. Birds sang. The sights and scents reminded us of earlier visits to the Moghul gardens of Kashmir, with their marble pavilions, both black and white, and carpets of spring flowers—purple irises, red tulips and orange crown imperials—cascading down the terraced Shalimar Gardens to the waters of the Dal Lake beneath pink and white–blossomed fruit trees.

When we again reached India, we were eager not only to renew and broaden our appreciation of the architectural background to the Taj Mahal but also to gain a greater sense of how Shah Jahan and Mumtaz lived, from their luxurious existence as the favored son and daughter-in-law of the emperor, to their years in revolt and as fugitives, to the poignantly brief time that remained to them after Shah Jahan took the throne. In terms of architecture, we learned that what makes the Taj unique is not the presence or absence of a particular architectural feature. It is not the first garden tomb; not the first white marble mausoleum; not the first Moghul building to deploy the octagonal plan or to use *pietra dura*; and not the first to use elements from both Islamic and Hindu traditions. The secret of the Taj goes beyond this.

Burhanpur, the Moghul command center for their endless campaigns against the rulers of the Deccan and the scene of so many deaths including Mumtaz's own, is essential to understanding Shah Jahan's and Mumtaz's lives. As we drove south in the dusty heat of summer through a landscape of red, eroded hills and tablelands dotted with scrubby trees, we began to appreciate the jolting discomfort of travel, the eye-scorching glare of the sun Shah Jahan would have experienced as he scanned the horizon and hilltops for signs of enemies or of long-awaited messengers. The air was so dry we scarcely sweated, and our lips became parched as we passed tumbled watchtowers and the crumbling walls of strongpoints, evidence of the region's erstwhile strategic importance. Twelve miles north of Burhanpur, the dragon's teeth battlements of the formidable fortress of Asir, where Shah Jahan, Mumtaz and their children once sought refuge, rose up on a high escarpment, brooding and dominating the road below.

Burhanpur itself is now ringed with later redbrick walls. Narrow, twisting alleys, too small for a vehicle, led us to the fortress-palace appropriated by the Moghuls from earlier rulers and strengthened and beautified by them. The palace is smaller, more intimate than we had imagined. As familiar to Shah Jahan and Mumtaz as their palaces in Agra, much of it remains, such as the suite of marble *hammams* where Mumtaz once bathed in scented water warmed by perpetually burning oil. The domed ceilings still display painted flowers and intertwining leaves in reds, greens and blues, even if in places slightly flaked and fading. In the courtyard facing the *hammams*; the empty watercourses bear traces of once gushing, cooling fountains.

The ruins of Shah Jahan and Mumtaz Mahal's palace in Burhanpur, viewed from across the Tapti River

A pathway leads past guardhouses and latrines to a further courtyard, also once a formal garden with a large raised pool in its center. The high stone platform at one end was the imperial hall of public audience. The royal apartments lie beyond, traces of paintings still visible on the cracked plaster. The suite of rooms where Mumtaz is thought to have died is in a three-story building directly overlooking the broad Tapti River and open to any refreshing breezes from it. In the throes of childbirth Mumtaz would have heard the roaring and trumpeting of her husband's war elephants stabled in the nearby Hati Mahal, built into the riverbank. Shah Jahan's distress as his daughter Jahanara summoned him in the darkness to her dying mother's bedside became more real, and we imagined Mumtaz's body being borne out of the palace for temporary burial across the river.

We too crossed the Tapti. With the help of a local boy who guided us along rutted paths, past banana plantations and across fields plowed by oxen with blue-painted horns, we eventually found the large walled enclosure, today called the Ahukhana, or "Deer House," containing the sun-bleached pavilion where Mumtaz was briefly interred and where Shah Jahan poured out his "oceans of lustrous pearls of tears." It is much farther from the riverbank than we had thought but still visible from the palace. Despite the recent excavations, its lonely, dusty desolation seems to echo Shah Jahan's sorrows.

From Burhanpur we traveled northward to Agra, the setting for much of Mumtaz's happy but brief life as empress. In the Red Fort on the curve of the River Jumna, we saw the suite of marble pavilions that Shah Jahan commissioned the year he and Mumtaz rode into Agra in triumph to claim the throne. In Shah Jahan's private apartments, the Khas Mahal, the colors of the inlaid flowers are as vivid as when the gem cutters first sliced the semiprecious gems with their copper wire cutters to form the leaves and petals. The marble floors and pillars are cool to the touch. We tried to imagine the bare apartments lit by hundreds of oil lamps in the carved, cusped niches; strewn with rugs and brocade cushions; furnished with low divans, tables and rich hangings and the air scented with rosewater and the lingering heavy tang of spices and flowers.

Nearby, we saw where Jahangir's golden "chain of justice" had hung down, tempting the confident to summon imperial justice. We looked down from the crenellated red sandstone battlements of the fort toward the sandy banks of the Jumna on which the appellants clustered nervously and along which Shah Jahan's troops paraded as he stood in the surviving *jharokha* balconies. The banks were also where public executions were held and where elephants and other animals were made to fight for his entertainment. As Shah Jahan did in his years of imprisonment, we looked across to the Taj Mahal, a shadowy, milky presence in the mist.

We approached the Taj Mahal itself with mixed emotions. Though we had visited it many times over the years, finding it each time faultlessly and enduringly lovely, we were apprehensive. We remembered that Noël Coward refused to visit the Taj Mahal, even though staying around the corner, insisting, "I've seen it on biscuit boxes and I don't want to spoil the illusion." Perhaps having read about the Taj Mahal, thought about it, analyzed it so much would have diminished its impact. Salman

Rushdie had also been skeptical about visiting but exulted: "The building itself left my scepticism in shreds . . . insisting with absolute force on its sovereign authority, it simply obliterated the million counterfeits of it and glowingly filled, once and forever, the place in the mind previously occupied by its simulacra and this, finally, is why the Taj Mahal must be seen; to remind us that the world is real, that the sound is truer than the echo, the original more forceful than its image in a mirror. The beauty of beautiful things is still able, in these image-saturated times, to transcend imitations. And the Taj Mahal is beyond the power of words to say it, a lovely thing, perhaps the loveliest of things."

Rushdie was right. The Taj Mahal transcended any recollections, any scrutiny of plans, any detailed computation of symmetry, any overheated metaphors with which we had grappled. As we approached the gatehouse, the sudden appearance of the ethereal white mausoleum, framed mirage-like in the solid red sandstone arch, still made us pause to catch our breath. Then we moved through, and the vista opened to reveal the minarets and the rest of the complex in all its beauty.

Edward VII, who visited India when he was Prince of Wales in 1875, observed wearily that it had become commonplace for every writer who visited the Taj "to set out with the admission that it is indescribable and then to proceed to give some idea of it." Even if one agrees with Shakespeare that

> beauty itself doth of itself persuade
> the eyes of men without an orator,

and sympathizes with the view that beauty is so subjective, so intuitive, so much in the eye of the beholder, that what makes something beautiful is that someone thinks it is, it is indeed irresistible to pick out some of the elements which have made so many people from all over the world, all cultures, and both sexes, think the Taj Mahal is beautiful.

Most of us find symmetry and structure inherently appealing. When researchers showed people two pictures of the same person—one of the real face with the natural asymmetries common to us all and the other artificially composed of half of the face and its mirror image, thus producing greater symmetry—by far the majority preferred the symmetrical version. In appreciating music and other arts, structure seems required for beauty, although the former does not guarantee the latter. So it was for us with the Taj Mahal, whose symmetry and structural coherence we found deeply satisfying. We appreciated the way in which, as we walked toward the mausoleum, the shapes and architectural features built in an almost hierarchical ascent of ever-greater delicacy and definition.

Unlike other Islamic or Moghul buildings we had seen in India, the architecture of the Taj not only juxtaposed elements from Islamic and Hindu traditions but also synthesized and subtly modified them to produce a building that is much greater than the sum of its influences. We found the complex more fluid, more empathetic, more human than much Islamic architecture, simpler and more clearly structured than some Hindu buildings. We were struck by the combination of grand scale and attention to detail. The nineteenth-century bishop of Calcutta caught this feeling perfectly when he described the Taj Mahal as having been built by giants and finished by jewelers.

As we circled the mausoleum one hot afternoon, the curator pointed out that in addition to the jarring asymmetry of the placing of Shah Jahan's tomb, one other striking, if relatively small, lack of uniformity exists amid the careful hierarchy of shape and detail. On the chamfered northwest corner of the mausoleum one of the half-columns carved into the marble at the side of the dado differs entirely from the others that are uniformly the same all around the building. It is not faceted, nor does it have the same capital. To us and to him it seemed a deliberate fault introduced by the builders. They had perhaps done so to render the Taj imperfect since, in Islam, it is blasphemous to attempt to repeat the perfection of God's handiwork.*

At just the time that the Taj Mahal was being built, the Reverend Thomas Fuller, an essayist as well as cleric, wrote that "light (God's eldest daughter) is a principal beauty in building." We felt this observation was overwhelmingly true of both the interior and exterior of the Taj Mahal. The change of light within the building throws into greater relief the

---

* This is also the reason for the *abrash*, the deliberate discontinuity in the color or weave of the finest Persian carpets.

incised carving and, as it strengthens or softens as the day progresses, changes the mood. Outside, the sky remains the Taj's only backcloth as Shah Jahan planned. There is no competition or distraction from other buildings or even trees. The sunlight on the water of the pools and channels reflects the building; shadows increase and decrease the depth of the *iwans* (recesses) as the hours pass. The receptivity of the Makrana marble to the changing light and atmosphere produces shades of color and mood.

At sunrise we watched half the building blush softly pink. In the evening the sunset tinted the other half a peachy-orange. Just minutes later, as the dusk sky provided a mauve backdrop, the Taj faded into purple silhouette. The semiprecious stones sparkled in the setting sun. In moonlight they glittered and glimmered like fireflies as the Taj itself grew softly silvered, sometimes half dissolving into a melancholic, mysterious mist. Given the beauty of his impressions of the changing light on Rheims Cathedral, or on French haystacks so similar to those in fields around Agra, what would Monet have conjured from the interplay of light on the Taj Mahal? What nocturnes would Whistler have produced?

We found it impossible to keep simultaneously in focus all the ingredients that we thought contributed to the Taj Mahal's beauty. To concentrate clinically on one element, we discovered, quickly overemphasizes it and distorts its relationship with the others. In any case, there is something inherently elusive in the Taj Mahal's beauty. Francis Bacon wrote in 1625, "That is the best part of beauty that a picture cannot express." There is indeed an intangible dimension to one's perception of the Taj Mahal, perhaps encapsulated by Keats's assertion that beauty is truth and truth is beauty or perhaps related to the fact that the Taj itself transcends any reproduction, any secondhand enthusiasm. For Islamic visitors, the knowledge of the truth of the Koranic inscriptions, an appreciation that the complex was designed to represent a paradise on earth, can only add to their sense of beauty. For many, many others, ourselves included, the knowledge of the other central truth that the Taj Mahal is the expression of Shah Jahan's love for Mumtaz Mahal is fundamental. He was by no means an entirely admirable man, but the depth of his love and the scale of his loss as expressed in the Taj Mahal are overwhelming. The poet Sir Edwin Arnold wrote in 1886:

> *Not architecture, as all others are,*
> *But the proud passion of an Emperor's love*
> *Wrought into living stone which gleams and soars*
> *With body of beauty, shining soul and thought.*

Perceptions of this love color all responses to the monument, inducing in some a sensual feeling that the marble exhibits a fleshlike glow and that the dome represents a milky breast or in others the concept that the Taj Mahal is an enchanted castle in the air. Standing together beside the flower-inlaid cenotaphs of Shah Jahan and Mumtaz lying side by side, we understood that the Taj Mahal was, above all, the product of deep emotion. At the heart of all the grandeur and magnificence lie two human beings who loved each other.

The Taj Mahal viewed from the Mahtab Bagh

Acknowledgments

We could not have written this book without spending considerable time in India—a country which, despite the many times we have traveled there, still overwhelms our senses. In New Delhi Professor R. C. Agrawal, joint director general of the Archaeological Survey of India, gave generously to us of his own time and facilitated our visits to the Taj Mahal and other sites associated with the story of Shah Jahan and Mumtaz Mahal. In Agra we were very grateful for the expert advice of superintending archaeologist Dr. D. Dayalan and of his deputy, A. K. Tiwari, and to Dr. R. K. Dixit, who, in his atmospheric office perched in the southern gatehouse to the Taj, briefed us on recent excavations and future plans. He also led us extensively around the Taj complex and the excavations of the waterworks, helping us see things both figuratively and physically in a new light. Dr. K. K. Muhammed, superintending archaeologist of the Archaeological Survey of India in Bhopal, made possible our visit to the palace fortress of Burhanpur where Mumtaz Mahal died and the lonely site where she was temporarily laid to rest. We are also grateful to many others whom we met in India, especially Lucy Peck for her knowledge of the Moghul monuments of Delhi, Vibhuti Sachdev for insights into Hindu architectural principles and Dr. Giles Tillotson for advice on Moghul architecture.

The many Moghul chronicles were key to our understanding of this story. We must especially thank the staff of the Indian Institute of the Bodleian Library and those of the British Library, the London Library and the School of Oriental and African Studies for helping us access the sources of the period. We are equally indebted to many individuals. In the United States, Julia Bailey, the editor of *Muqarnas*, advised us on architectural sources. In the United Kingdom Philippa Vaughan guided us to material on the depiction of women in Moghul paintings.

Our research in India entailed traveling long distances to sometimes inaccessible places. Mehera Dalton and Tanya Dalton of Greaves Travel International (UK and USA) expertly organized our itinerary, and in New Delhi Mala Tandan of Greaves gave us invaluable support. We are also very grateful to the Imperial Hotel in New Delhi and to Prince Richard Holkar of the Ahilya Fort, Maheshwar, for their generous hospitality. Explore Limited gave us the chance in Uzbekistan to compare the tombs and palaces of the Moghuls' aesthetic ancestors and in Iran to trace the Persian influences discernible in the Taj Mahal.

The advice—and criticism—of friends were invaluable. In particular we are grateful to Robin and Justina Binks, Robert Binyon, Charlie Covell, Kim and Sharon Lewison and Neil Munro. We must also thank our family for their encouragement, especially Lily Bardi-Ullmann for her research in the New York Public Library and our parents, Leslie and Mary Preston and Vera Faith.

We have much appreciated the help and advice of our publishers. We are grateful to George Gibson of Walker & Company, New York, and his team, including Michele Lee Amundsen, Greg Villepique, Michael O'Connor and Peter Miller. At Doubleday in London we are grateful to Marianne Velmans, our editor Michele Hutchison and also Sheila Lee and Deborah Adams. In Delhi Vivek Ahuja of Random House India gave us hospitality and encouragement and fresh insights. Finally, we must thank our agents, Michael Carlisle of Inkwell Management in New York and Bill Hamilton and Sara Fisher of A. M. Heath in London, for their enthusiasm and support throughout.

Notes and Sources

The Moghuls were keen to record their actions and the details of their lives. The emperors Babur and Jahangir kept diaries. Akbar and Shah Jahan each employed court chroniclers to write the history of their reign from day to day and took care to scrutinize and to approve the results. Some courtiers kept diaries. Many of the imperial diaries and other memoirs have survived. Taken together with the accounts of European visitors to India, printed to satisfy public demand for accounts of the fabled "Great Moghul," these official chronicles and private memoirs provide a surprisingly multifaceted view of the imperial family and their doings, including the creation of the Taj Mahal. These sources are referenced in the notes, and full details are given in the bibliography.

For ease of reading, we modernized spellings, punctuation and capitalization where necessary in all sixteenth- and seventeenth-century accounts of India in English.

Since the following invaluable sources of Moghul documents appear so frequently, we abbreviated references to them as follows:

ED — *The History of India as Told by Its Own Historians* compiled and edited by H. M. Elliot and J. Dowson. This seven-volume work contains translations of long extracts from most of the major chronicles and histories of the Moghul period.

IT — *Taj Mahal—The Illumined Tomb. An Anthology of Seventeenth Century Mughal and European Documentary Sources.* Compiled and translated by W. E. Begley and Z. A. Desai.

Because translation between the Muslim and Western calendars and subsequent adjustment to the latter can cause confusion, we have included in these notes the key dates of Shah Jahan's and Mumtaz's birth, marriage and death according to the Muslim calendar.

Prologue

1 "When . . . oyster": Qazwini, *IT*, p. 15.
1 "His eyes . . . sadness": Ibid., p. 13.
3 "deserves . . . Egypt": F. Bernier, *Travels in the Mogul Empire*, p. 299.
3 "the eye . . . earth": Kalim, *IT*, p. 84.
3 "a tear . . . time": R. Tagore, quoted in the Internet source *Built Heritage of Agra and Fatehpur Sikri*.
3 "the ivory . . . unhappy": R. Kipling, *From Sea to Sea 1887*, quoted in D. Carroll, *The Taj Mahal*, p. 156.
3 "Descriptions . . . as hasn't": E. Lear, *Indian Journal*, 16 February 1874, p. 78.
3 "I held . . . the soul": E. Roosevelt, *India and the Awakening East*, p. 127.
3 "I cannot . . . over me": W. H. Sleeman, *Rambles and Recollections of an Indian Official*, vol. 1, p. 382.
3 "The Taj . . . all parts": T. Daniell, quoted in P. Pal et al., *Romance of the Taj Mahal*, p. 199.
5 "The building . . . stone": P. Mundy, *Travels in Europe and Asia*, vol. 2, p. 213.

1. "A Place of Few Charms"

All quotes in this chapter where not otherwise attributed are from Babur's memoirs, *The Baburnama*. We used the translations of Wheeler M. Thackston and Annette S. Beveridge. Both are excellent.

13 "the scourge of God": C. Marlowe, *Tamburlaine the Great*, pt. 2, 1.4641.
13 "were traversed . . . platforms": R. G. de Clavijo, *Embassy to the Court of Timur at Samarcand*, p. 131.
15–16 "calligraphy . . . work": Haidar, *Tarikh-i-Rashidi* (translated by E. Dennison Ross as *A History of the Moguls of Central Asia*), pp. 3–4.
16 "no wasteland . . . cut down": Quoted in *Footprint Guide to India*, p. 1294.
17 "candles without brilliance": Quoted in E. B. Moynihan, *Paradise as a Garden in Persia and Mughal India*, p. 72.

17 "a multitude . . . air": Quoted in B. Gascoigne, *The Great Moghuls*, p. 11.

17 "nothing . . . months": Ibid., p. 13.

18 "such a multitude"; "was . . . outside": R. G. de Clavijo, *Embassy to the Court of Timur at Samarcand*, p. 171.

20–21 Although Babur . . . "diminution of it in [Humayun]": All quotes in this paragraph are from Abul Fazl, *The Akbarnama*, vol. 1, p. 276.

21 "Do nought . . . deserve it": Ibid., p. 277.

21–22 The twenty-three-year-old . . . "feet and hands": All quotes in this paragraph are from A. Eraly, *The Mughal Throne*, p. 12.

22 "excessive": Ibid.

22–23 Humayun fled . . . August 1541: All quotes in these two paragraphs are from Gulbadan, *The Humayan-Nama*, pp. 144, 146 and 151.

24 "My very . . . cold": Ibid., p. 167.

24 "more . . . over": Abul Fazl, *The Akbarnama*, vol. 1, p. 439.

26 "brotherly . . . foe": Gulbadan, *The Humayan-Nama*, pp. 200–201.

26 "whatever . . . misconduct": Badauni, quoted in A. Eraly, *The Mughal Throne*, p. 111.

27 "his blessed . . . ear"; "I . . . call": Abul Fazl, *The Akbarnama*, vol. 1, p. 657.

2. Allah Akbar

Where no source is given for a quote in this chapter, and also in chapter 3, it comes from Abul Fazl's *The Akbarnama* for the relevant period of Akbar's life or from his *Ain-i-Akbari*, in which he set down the principles by which Akbar ruled his empire, together with a wealth of day-to-day detail about how he did so.

31 "did not . . . oppressors": Quoted in A. Eraly, *The Mughal Throne*, p. 139.

35 "in form . . . height": P. Mundy, *Travels in Europe and Asia*, vol. 2, p. 73.

37 "to venerate . . . dung"; Badauni, *Muntakhab al-Tawarikh*, ED, vol. 5, p. 529.

37 "following . . . fire"; "the parents . . . be heard": E. Terry's account, reproduced in *Early Travels in India*, ed. W. Foster, p. 323.

39 "with great reverence"; "on his head . . . respect": P. du Jarric, *Akbar and the Jesuits*, p. 19.

3. "Seizer of the World"

42 E. Koch's article "The Taj Mahal: Architecture, Symbolism and Urban Significance," *Muqarnas* 22 (2005): 128–49, discusses the use of red and white sandstone and the Hindu tradition.

43 "in order . . . together"; "Akbar . . . artisan": S. J. Monserrate, *Commentary*, pp. 200–201.

44 "[They] . . . populous": R. Fitch's account, reproduced in *Early Travels in India*, pp. 17–18.

46 "of a stature . . . foresight": S. J. Monserrate, *Commentary*, pp. 196–97.

46 "He was . . . nobles"; "often . . . dissimulation": P. du Jarric, *Akbar and the Jesuits*, pp. 205–6.

46–47 "illiterate . . . uneducated": Memoirs of Jahangir, ED, vol. 6, p. 290.

47 "well . . . foreigners": P. du Jarric, *Akbar and the Jesuits*, p. 9.

48 "in music . . . uncontrolled"; "the ladies . . . veils"; "could hardly . . . upon him"; "sternly . . . injustice": Ferishta, *History of Hindustan*, vol. 3, p. 21.

49 Shah Jahan (Khurram) was born on 30 Rabi II 1000 in the Muslim calendar.

49 Mumtaz Mahal (Arjumand Banu) was born on 19 Rajab 1001 in the Muslim calendar.

50 "true son": *Jahangirnama*, translated by W. M. Thackston, p. 30.

50 "I drank . . . me"; "twenty . . . spirits": Ibid., pp. 184–85 (quote adapted).

51 "was no friend of mine": Memoirs of Jahangir, ED, vol. 6, p. 3.

51 "if he would . . . kill him": *Tuzuk-i-Jahangiri* (Memoirs of Jahangir), translated by A. Rogers and edited by H. Beveridge, vol. 1, p. 25.

53 "So long . . . leave him": Quoted in M. Weatherly, *The Taj Mahal*, p. 25.

53 "Seizer of the World"; "the business . . . the world": *Tuzuk-i-Jahangiri* (Memoirs of Jahangir), translated by A. Rogers and edited by H. Beveridge, vol. 1, p. 3.

4. "Peerless Pearls and Heart-Pleasing Stuffs"

Where no source is given, quotes come from the memoirs of Jahangir (the translations in *IT*, ED [vol. 6], A. Rogers and W. M. Thackston).

56 "too much . . . blood": Sir T. Roe, *Embassy to India*, p. 104.

59 "who . . . him": W. Finch's account, reproduced in *Early Travels in India*, p. 186.

59 "all . . . Mahal": F. Bernier, *Travels in the Mogul Empire*, p. 293.

59–60 Khurram . . . "can find": The quotes in this paragraph come from W. Hawkins's account, reproduced in *Early Travels in India*, p. 118.

60 "whimsical . . . fair": F. Bernier, *Travels in the Mogul Empire*, p. 272.

60 "that bright . . . chastity"; "angelic character"; "pure lineage": Qazwini, one of Shah Jahan's official court historians, *IT*, p. 2.

61 "In the taking . . . fearless": Muhammad Hadi, *Tatimma-i Wakiat-i Jahangiri*, ED, vol. 6, p. 397.

62 "for a long . . . employment": Ibid., p. 398.

62 "Her appearance . . . harem": Mutamid Khan, *Ikbalnama-i Jahangiri*, ED, vol. 6, p. 406.

62 "the stars . . . arise": Muhammad Hadi, *Tatimma-i Wakiat-i Jahangiri*, ED, vol. 6, p. 398.

63 "and other . . . amazed at": Sir T. Roe, *Embassy to India*, pp. 378–79.

63 Shah Jahan (Khurram) and Mumtaz Mahal (Arjumand Banu) married on 9 Rabi I 1021 in the Muslim calendar.

63–65 The following year . . . "lasted a month": All quotes in these four paragraphs are from Shah Jahan's official court historians Qazwini and Lahori, *IT*.

65 "the people . . . coitus": R. Tannahill, *Sex in History*, p. 245.

65–66 "mine . . . royalty": Inayat Khan, *The Shah Jahan Nama*, edited by W. E. Begley and Z. A. Desai, p. 71.

66 Khurram's chroniclers . . . "fortune": Quotes in this paragraph are from Qazwini, *IT*, pp. 5–6.

67 Then . . . ran: The quotes in this paragraph come from P. Mundy, *Travels in Europe and Asia*, vol. 2, p. 216.

67 "win . . . world"; "remove . . . people": Asad Beg's account, given in ED, vol. 6, p. 173.

67 "this rope . . . accordingly": W. Hawkins's account, reproduced in *Early Travels in India*, p. 113.

68 "Right . . . commands": Ibid., p. 115.

68 "makes . . . consideration": P. della Valle, *Travels*, vol. 1, p. 30.

68 "his own invention": Sir T. Roe, *Embassy to India*, p. 270.

69 "rejected . . . vomit": Quoted in B. Gascoigne, *The Great Moghuls*, p. 115.

69 "much longer . . . broad": J. de Laet, *The Empire of the Great Mogol*, p. 37.

69 "his whole . . . for her": Inayat Khan, *The Shah Jahan Nama*, p. 71.

69 "lascivious . . . festivity": F. Pelsaert, *Jahangir's India* (translation of *Remonstrantie*), p. 64.

69 "Whatsover . . . shape"; "cut . . . abuse": T. Coryat's account, reproduced in *Early Travels in India*, pp. 278–79.

70 "chaste women"; "clever . . . writer": Abul Fazl, *Ain i Akbari*, vol 1, p. 44–45.

71 "condemned to the elephant": Sir T. Roe, *Embassy to India*, p. 191.

71 Richard Burton's observation is quoted in R. Tannahill, *Sex in History*, p. 249.

72 "great men . . . treasure": P. Mundy, *Travels in Europe and Asia*, vol. 2, 164.

72 "the greatest . . . world": N. Manucci, *Storia do Mogor*, vol. 2, p. 73.

72 "with no respect . . . person": Ibid., p. 328.

72 "the tongue . . . stories": Ibid., p. 74.

73 "hanging . . . feet"; "an eunuch . . . blind man": F. Bernier, *Travels in the Mogul Empire*, p. 267.

73 "in one month . . . survive": J.-B. Tavernier, *Travels in India*, vol. 1, p. 313.

73 "she erects . . . before": F. Pelsaert, *Jahangir's India*, p. 50.

74 "he never . . . abroad": Inayat Khan, *The Shah Jahan Nama*, p. 71.

5. The Warrior Prince

Where no source is given, quotes come from Jahangir's memoirs (the translations in *IT*, ED [vol. 6], A. Rogers and W. M. Thackston).

76 "when . . . resounds": N. Manucci, *Storia do Mogor*, vol. 2, p. 320.

78 "in a coat . . . firmament": Sir T. Roe, *Embassy to India*, p. 282.

78–79 The English ambassador . . . "Kandahar": All quotes in these five paragraphs are from ibid., pp. 119, 172, 177, 282, 283, 285 and 324 with the exception of "ambulans respublica," which is quoted in B. Gascoigne, *The Great Moghuls*, p. 154.

80 "in these . . . onsets": E. Terry's account, reproduced in *Early Travels in India*, p. 315.

80 "in wondrous triumph"; "having . . . bleeding"; "a scouring twenty weeks": Sir T. Roe, *Embassy to India*, pp. 385–86.

81 "due . . . expediency"; "content . . . only": Lahori, *IT*, p. 22.

81 "as the child . . . himself": Inayat Khan, *The Shah Jahan Nama*, p. 8.

84 "They . . . arms": J. de Laet, *The Empire of the Great Mogol*, p. 81.

86 "prevented . . . Bacchus": Sir T. Roe, *Embassy to India*, p. 325.

87 "thrust . . . by others": W. Hawkins's account, reproduced in *Early Travels in India*, p. 116.

87 "many fields . . . [drug taker]": P. Mundy, *Travels in Europe and Asia*, vol 2, p. 247.

87 "chafing . . . child": F. Pelsaert, *Jahangir's India*, p. 53.

87 "governs him . . . pleasure": Sir T. Roe, *Embassy to India*, p. 270.

87 "Easy . . . voluptuous": Ferishta, *History of Hindustan*, vol. 3, p. 32.

87 "her former . . . Queen": F. Pelsaert, *Jahangir's India*, p. 50.

88 "utterly . . . miseries": T. Coryat's account, reproduced in *Early Travels in India*, p. 277.

89 "the most . . . princes": *Intikhab-i Jahangir-Shahi*, ED, vol. 6, p. 450.

89 "feeble mind . . . character": Quoted in E. B. Findly, *Nur Jahan*, p. 49.

90 "a noble . . . favourite": Sir T. Roe, *Embassy to India*, p. 325.

6. Emperor in Waiting

Where no source is given, quotes come from the memoirs of Jahangir. We used the translations in ED (vol. 6), A. Rogers and W. M. Thackston.

93 "the author . . . plan"; "on . . . hunting"; "so . . . nothing": F. S. Manrique, *Travels*, p. 301.

93 "her husband . . . scream": P. Van Den Broeck, *A Contemporary Dutch Chronicle*, p. 54.

93 "Khusrau . . . non-existence": Inayat Khan, *The Shah Jahan Nama*, p. 10.

94 "laying . . . blood": Ferishta, *History of Hindustan*, p. 56.

94 "enquiring . . . some one": J. de Laet, *The Empire of the Great Mogol*, p. 199.

96 "shifted . . . world": Inayat Khan, *The Shah Jahan Nama*, p. 10.

97 "whose coin . . . time"; "the fire . . . years": Ibid., pp. 10–11.

100 "The King . . . age": E. Terry's account, reproduced in *Early Travels in India*, p. 329.

103 "was seized with illness": Muhammad Hadi, *Tatimma-i Wakiat-i Jahangiri*, ED, vol. 6, p. 396.

104 Under the circumstances . . . sacred: All quotes in these three paragraphs are from Muhammad Hadi, *Tatimma-i Wakiat-i Jahangiri*, ED, vol. 6, pp. 396–97.

7. Chosen One of the Palace

Where no source is given, quotes come from Jahangir's memoirs, continued by his personal scribe Mutamid Khan or from the latter's history of Jahangir's reign, the *Iqbal-nama-i-Jahangiri*. We used the translations in ED (vol. 6) and W. M. Thackston.

108 "They . . . cremation": N. Manucci, *Storia do Mogor*, vol. 2, p. 411.

112 "the young . . . Nur Mahal": Shah Jahan's official chronicler Lahori, translated in ED, vol. 7, p. 6

113 "there is . . . chance": P. Van Den Broeck, *A Contemporary Dutch Chronicle*, p. 90.

115 "Self-preservation . . . abhorred": Ferishta, *History of Hindustan*, p. 103.

115 "to carry . . . country"; "in a coffin . . . black": P. Mundy, *Travels in Europe and Asia*, vol. 2, p. 213.

115 "with all . . . went"; "the fictitious defunct": N. Manucci, *Storia do Mogor*, vol. 1, pp. 174–75.

115 "raised . . . army": J.-B. Tavernier, *Travels in India*, vol. 1, p. 271.

115 "scattering . . . right": Muhammad Hadi's appendix, *Jahangirnama* (Memoirs of Jahangir), translated and edited by W. M. Thackston, p. 460.

115–16 "the high . . . before": P. Pal et al., *Romance of the Taj Mahal*, p. 28.

116 "Her majesty . . . separation": Inayat Khan, *The Shah Jahan Nama*, p. 21.

117 "much . . . wife": Ferishta, *History of Hindustan*, p. 104.

118 "an auspicious star . . . sky"; "while everyone . . . world"; "the turbanned . . . dancers"; "owing . . . heaven"; "to the asylum . . . beyond": Inayat Khan, *The Shah Jahan Nama*, p. 23.

118 "As to the nature . . . insecure": J. de Laet, *The Empire of the Great Mogol*, p. 246.

8. The Peacock Throne

119 "during festivals . . . days": *Tuzuk-i-Jahangiri* (Memoirs of Jahangir), translated by A. Rogers and edited by H. Beveridge, vol. 1, p. 9.

120 "companion during travels"; "source . . . home": Kalim, *IT*, p. 34.

120 "sky touching": Lahori, *IT*, p.137.

121 "sensible . . . person": Ferishta, *History of Hindustan*, p. 105.

122 "spreading . . . head"; "presenting . . . trappings": *Tuzuk-i-Jahangiri* (Memoirs of Jahangir), translated by A. Rogers and edited by H. Beveridge, vol. 1, p. 26.

125 "the pompous . . . Shah Jahan": Ferishta, *History of Hindustan*, p. 103.

125 "square cisterns . . . middle": N. Manucci, *Storia do Mogor*, vol. 1, p. 198.

125 "the outside . . . of fine water": Lahori, *IT*, pp. 45–46.

126 "with elevated . . . thereabouts": J.-B. Tavernier, *Travels in India*, vol. 1, p. 304.

126 Festivals . . . Iraq: The information and quotes in this paragraph come from P. A. Andrews's article "The Generous Heart or The Mass of Clouds: The Court Tents of Shah Jahan," in *Muqarnas* 4:149–65.

127–130 The Augustinian friar . . . "avarice": The quotes in this paragraph are from F. S. Manrique, *Travels*, pp. 201, 202 and 204.

130 Good Mover . . . Ever Bold: N. Manucci, *Storia do Mogor*, vol. 2, pp. 338–39.

130 "each . . . down"; "The riders . . . trunks"; "formal . . . death": F. Bernier, *Travels in the Mogul Empire*, pp. 276–77.

131 "while . . . sky": Lahori's account appended to Inayat Khan, *The Shah Jahan Nama*, p. 567.

132 "The object . . . luminaries": Ibid.

132 "the harassed . . . population"; "freely . . . desires"; "furious . . . elephants": Ibid.

133 "like a wall": Quoted in M. A. Ansari, *The Social Life of the Mughal Emperors*, p. 97.

134 "broken-hearted . . . persons": Lahori's account, appended to Inayat Khan, *The Shah Jahan Nama*, p. 571.

134 "eloquent secretaries": Ibid., p. 570.

134 "sent . . . Mumtaz al-Zamani": Lahori, *IT*, p. 9.

134 "to adhere . . . wasted": Ibid., p.179.

134 "By the grace . . . God": S. A. I. Tirmizi, *Mughal Documents*, p. 32.

134 "so subject . . . wife": *Intikhab-i Jahangir-Shahi*, ED, vol. 6, p. 452.

134 "Nur . . . him": Ibid.

135 "No dust . . . to him": Kalim, *Padshahnama*, IT, p. 34.

135 "the fortunate . . . confidants": Lahori's account, appended to Inayat Khan, *The Shah Jahan Nama*, p. 571.

136 "when . . . good"; "unbelievably . . . taste": *Baburnama*, translated by W. M. Thackston, pp. 344–45.

136 "found . . . Agra": *Jahangirnama* (Memoirs of Jahangir), translated and edited by W. M. Thackston, p. 24.

137 "so artfully . . . middle": Quoted in M. Jaffrey, *A Taste of India*, p. 24.

138 "the molten snow": R. Nath, *The Private Life of the Mughals of India*, p. 70.

139 "Even . . . poor"; "owing . . . etiquette"; "beautiful songs . . . stirring melodies": Lahori's account, appended to Inayat Khan, *The Shah Jahan Nama*, p. 572.

140–41 "into a flat pad . . . rolled on": Quoted in H. Mukhia, *The Mughals of India*, p. 148.

141 "very rich . . . times": N. Manucci, *Storia do Mogor*, vol. 2, p. 317.

141 "[The ruler] . . . expense": J. Ovington's account, in *India in the Seventeenth Century*, ed. J. P. Guha, p. 83.

9. "Build for Me a Mausoleum"

143 A Moghul . . . behind: All quotes in these two paragraphs are from P. Mundy, *Travels in Europe and Asia*, vol. 2, pp. 193–94.

144 "If the treasury . . . too": Quoted in J. Gommans, *Mughal Warfare*, p. 105.

144–45 "Of the vast tracts . . . slaves"; "Thus . . . existence"; "as bearers . . . horsemen": F. Bernier, *Travels in the Mogul Empire*, p. 205.

145 "richer . . . rest". P. Mundy, *Travels in Europe and Asia*, vol. 2, p. 193.

145 "by far . . . trappings"; "field . . . attendance": F. Bernier, *Travels in the Mogul Empire*, p. 370.

145–46 "a certain . . . see": P. Mundy, *Travels in Europe and Asia*, vol. 2, p. 191.

146 Eunuchs . . . "gaze": All quotes in this paragraph are from F. Bernier, *Travels in the Mogul Empire*, pp. 372–73.

147 Given . . . "bronze": The quotes in this paragraph are from N. Manucci, *Storia do Mogor*, vol. 2, pp. 64–65.

148 "Though . . . prevalent": Quoted in J. Gommans, *Mughal Warfare*, p. 110.

149 "is . . . tents": F. Bernier, *Travels in the Mogul Empire*, p. 361.

149 "These brutes . . . miss": F. Pelsaert, *Jahangir's India*, p. 51.

150 "discord . . . enterprise": A. Eraly, *The Mughal Throne*, p. 317.

151 "The fortresses . . . determined": Ferishta, *History of Hindustan*, p. 127.

151 "desperate . . . feeding"; "a woeful spectacle"; "dying . . . great numbers": Letters from English merchants named Rastell and Bickford, quoted in P. Mundy, *Travels in Europe and Asia*, vol. 2, p. 341.

151 "to any . . . again": P. Mundy, *Travels in Europe and Asia*, vol. 2, p. 42.

151–52 Shah Jahan . . . "throne": The quotes in this paragraph come from Lahori, ED, vol. 7, pp. 24–25.

153 Mumtaz Mahal died on 17 Zil-Qada 1040 in the Muslim calendar.

153 "Today . . . separation"; "a beautiful . . . imagined": Disputed nineteenth-century Persian manuscript given in R. Nath, *The Taj Mahal and Its Incarnation*, pp. 5–6.

153 "build . . . earth": Another disputed nineteenth-century manuscript, ibid., p. 6.

153–54 Shah Jahan . . . "God": All quotes in this paragraph are from the account of Shah Jahan's chronicler Salih, *IT*, p. 25.

10. "Dust of Anguish"

155–56 Mumtaz's sudden . . . "seclusion": With the exception of "light . . . nightchamber" which is Lahori, *IT*, p. 22, all quotes in these two paragraphs are from Qazwini, *IT*, pp. 11–14.

156 "night illuminating . . . clothes": Lahori, *IT*, p. 20.

156 "white . . . dawn": Qazwini, *IT*, p. 12.

156 "running . . . mourning": Kalim, quoted in H. Mukhia, *The Mughals of India*, p. 149.

156 "all . . . music": Lahori, *IT*, p. 20.

156 "there . . . distress": Qazwini, *IT*, p. 13.

156 "from constant weeping . . . spectacles": Inayat Khan, *The Shah Jahan Nama*, p. 70.

156–57 "his auspicious beard . . . event": Qazwini, *IT*, p. 13.

157 "poured . . . tears": Salih, *IT*, p. 26.

157 "from that date . . . her": Inayat Khan, *The Shah Jahan Nama*, p. 74.

158 "The world . . . faces": Qudsi, *IT*, p. 46.

158 Although the Moghul chroniclers formally referred to the Taj as the *rauza-i-munavvara*, or "Illumined Tomb," Peter Mundy and other contemporary travelers wrote of the "Taje Mahal."

158–59 Some historians . . . "familiarity": All quotes in this paragraph are from Qazwini, *IT*, pp. 13–14.

159 "Mighty . . . power": Quoted in G. H. R. Tillotson, *Mughal India*, p. 20.

159 "Construction . . . fortune": Lahori, *IT*, p. 10.

159 "a memorial . . . ambition": Ibid., p. 43. See also E. Koch, "The Taj Mahal: Architecture, Symbolism, and Urban Significance," *Muqarnas* 22:128–49

164–65 "[The architect] . . . it": F. S. Manrique, *Travels*, p. 173.

167 "a mausoleum . . . earth": R. Nath, *The Taj Mahal and Its Incarnation*, p. 6.

167 "The royal . . . amendments": Lahori's account, appended to Inayat Khan, *The Shah Jahan Nama*, p. 570.

168 "distasteful . . . Majesty"; "the lamentable . . . Queen": Inayat Khan, *The Shah Jahan Nama*, p. 82.

168 "All . . . show": P. Mundy, *Travels in Europe and Asia*, vol. 2, p. 192.

168–69 "The comptrollers . . . assemblage"; "His majesty . . . crowds": Ibid., p. 84.

11. "The Builder Could Not Have Been of This Earth"

E. Koch's article "The Taj Mahal: Architecture, Symbolism and Urban Significance," *Muqarnas* 22: 128–49, provides much detailed and valuable information on the architectural theories behind the Taj Mahal and related matters.

171 "to evoke . . . paradise": Lahori, *IT*, p. 66.

173 "'Astibisti' . . . divisions": Quoted in R. A. Jairazbhoy, "The Taj Mahal in the Context of East and West," *Journal of the Warburg and Courtauld Institutes*, 24 (1961): 75. This article also contains other examples of the use of the octagonal design.

175 "of heavenly rank"; "shaped like a guava": Lahori, *IT*, p. 66.

175 "like ladders . . . heavens": Ibid., p. 67

175 "accepted . . . skies": Salih, *IT*, p. 79.

177 The author who suggested that the sight lines relate to Shah Jahan's height is R. Lane-Smith.

177 H. I. S. Kanwar discusses the significance of the fifty-eight foot diameter of the central chamber in "Harmonious Proportions of the Taj Mahal," *Islamic Culture* 49 (1975): 1–17.

177 A. J. Qaisar's *Building Construction in Mughal India* gives much useful information on Moghul building practices.

179 "made . . . prospect": P. Mundy, *Travels in Europe and Asia*, vol. 2, p. 213.

179–80 To bear . . . flower: All quotes in these three paragraphs come from Lahori, *IT*, pp. 65–66.

181 "We . . . order": Imperial order, quoted in *IT*, p. 163.

181 "The building . . . stones": P. Mundy, *Travels in Europe and Asia*, vol. 2, p. 213.

182 "Some . . . animals": F. S. Manrique, *Travels*, p. 172.

182 "Like . . . found": Kalim, *IT*, p. 84.

183 "the heaven-touching dome"; "glittering like the sun": Lahori, *IT*, p. 66.

184 "each line"; "as heart . . . Kashmir": Quoted in S. Stronge, *Painting for the Mughal Emperor*, p. 168.

186 "But . . . Paradise": Koranic inscription, *IT*, p. 195.

186 "the inscriptions . . . calligraphical writing [of others]": Salih, *IT*, p. 79.

188 "All . . . water": Ibid.

188 "everywhere . . . imaginable": F. Bernier, *Travels in the Mogul Empire*, p. 298.

189 "In . . . Jahan": J.-B. Tavernier, *Travels in India*, vol. 2, p. 101.

190 "They . . . flowers": Lines from the court poet Kalim, *Padshahnama*.

190 "look . . . topaz": Madame Blavatsky, quoted in P. Pal et al., *Romance of the Taj Mahal*, p. 130.

191 "wonder . . . magic making": Lahori, *IT*, p. 67.

12. "This Paradise-like Garden"

193 "Rose . . . diverse": J. Milton, *The English Poems*, p. 211.

194 The quote from the Koran comes from S. Crowe et al., *The Gardens of Mughul India*, p. 42.

196 "As . . . guidance": Abul Fazl, *The Akbarnama*, vol. 2., pp. 486 and 487.

197 "So long . . . rain": Kalim, *IT*, p. 85.

198 "the trees . . . herbs": Salih, *IT*, p. 80.

200 "full of flowers": F. Bernier, *Travels in the Mogul Empire*, p. 296.

201 "laborious . . . dung": *Baburnama*, translated by W. M. Thackston, p. 335.

203 "the black . . . speech": Salih, *IT*, p. 80.

13. The Illumined Tomb

204–5 Guests . . . "lamps": All quotes in these two paragraphs are from Kalim, *IT*, pp. 82–84.

205 "shining . . . perfections": J. Ovington's account, in *India in the Seventeenth Century*, p. 108.

205 "for . . . Paradise": Salih, *IT*, p. 77.

205 "highly polished . . . fasteners": Lahori, *IT*, p. 67.

205 "Shah . . . nights": *Tarikh-i Khafi Khan*, ED, vol. 7, p. 484.

206 "When . . . desert": Qudsi, *IT*, p. 86.

207 "Of all . . . preceptor": Quoted in P. Pal et al., *Romance of the Taj Mahal*, p. 48.

207 "great . . . rockets": P. Mundy, *Travels in Europe and Asia*, vol. 2, p. 202.

207 Shah Jahan . . . "burned": All quotes in this paragraph come from Inayat Khan, *The Shah Jahan Nama*, p. 309.

208 "the merchants . . . them": J.-B. Tavernier, *Travels in India*, vol. 1, pp. 46–47.

208–9 An anguished . . . celebrated: All quotes in these two paragraphs come from Inayat Khan, *The Shah Jahan Nama*, pp. 309–19.

210 "to so many . . . woman": The Latin text of J. de Laet, quoted in *IT*, p. 306.

210 "The Great . . . times": P. Mundy, *Travels in Europe and Asia*, vol. 2, pp. 202–3.

210–11 The stories . . . chew: All quotes in these two paragraphs are from F. Bernier, *Travels in the Mogul Empire*, pp. 11–13.

211 Not all Europeans . . . "service": All quotes in this paragraph come from N. Manucci, *Storia do Mogor*, vol. 1, pp. 208–11.

212 "she obtained . . . asked": Ibid., p. 212.

212 "is one . . . Hindustan": Lahori, ED, vol. 7, p. 50.

213 "great stronghold of infidelity": Ibid., p. 36.

213 "with cannon . . . war": Inayat Khan, *The Shah Jahan Nama*, p. 85.

213 "heretics": Ibid.

213–14 "Some . . . dear": N. Manucci, *Storia do Mogor*, vol. 1, p. 170.

214 "warriors of Islam": Inayat Khan, *The Shah Jahan Nama*, p. 87.

214 "The handsome . . . faith": F. Bernier, *Travels in the Mogul Empire*, p. 177.

214 "such . . . pieces": Lahori, *Badshah Nama*, ED, vol. 7, p. 43.

215 "under . . . companions"; "had determined . . . occupations": Ibid., p. 69.

215 "I knew . . . [of rivals]": Quoted in W. Hansen, *The Peacock Throne*, p. 128.

216 "due . . . sister": Inayat Khan, *The Shah Jahan Nama*, p. 319.

14. "The Sublime Throne"

217–18 Unlike . . . honor: All quotes in this paragraph are from F. S. Manrique, *Travels*, pp. 214–18.

218 "some . . . river": Inayat Khan, ED, vol. 7, p. 85.

219 "Nearly . . . felt": F. Bernier, *Travels in the Mogul Empire*, p. 267.

220 The gem-studded . . . "materials?": The quotes in this paragraph are from F. S. Manrique, *Travels*, pp. 197–98.

221 "the most . . . believer": Quoted in G. H. R. Tillotson, *Mughal India*, p. 22, and J. D. Hoag, *Islamic Architecture*, p. 10.

221–22 For a discussion of the costs of Shah Jahan's building projects and of the Taj Mahal, see S. Moosvi, "Expenditure on Buildings Under Shah Jahan—A Chapter of Imperial Financial History," *Proceedings of the Forty-Sixth Session of the Indian History Congress*, 1985, and R. Nath, *Art and Architecture of the Taj Mahal*, pp. 16–17.

222–23 The Venetian . . . "pleasure": The quotes in these two paragraphs come from N. Manucci, *Storia do Mogor*, vol. 1, pp. 187–88.

223 "with . . . follies"; "transgressed . . . decency": F. Bernier, *Travels in the Mogul Empire*, pp. 273–74.

223 "a good . . . shop": N. Manucci, *Storia do Mogor*, vol. 1, p. 189.

223–24 Preoccupied . . . "wine": Quotes in these two paragraphs are from F. Bernier, *Travels in the Mogul Empire*, pp. 6–7.

224 "reserved . . . dissimulation"; "contempt . . . elevation": Ibid., p. 10.

224 "undeserving . . . trust"; "Alas! . . . stars": Aurangzeb's letter to Jahanara written in the 1650s, in *Adab-i-Alamgiri*, translated by J. Scott p. 424.

224 "did not love him": N. Manucci, *Storia do Mogor*, vol. 1, p. 181.

225 "constant thought"; "was . . . himself"; "he trusted . . . arm": F. Bernier, *Travels in the Mogul Empire*, p. 10–11.

225 "the home . . . Timur": Lahori, ED, vol. 7, p. 70–71.

225 "Natural . . . climate": Ibid.

226 "from want of spirit": Inayat Khan, ED, vol. 7, p. 90.

226 "with such . . . reduced"; "the troops . . . recalled": Aurangzeb recalled his father's words in a letter to Shah Jahan, in *Adab-i-Alamgiri*, pp. 432 and 439.

226–28 In December . . . hand: All quotes in this paragraph are from W. M. Thackston's translation given in *The Moonlight Garden*, ed. E. B. Moynihan, p. 28.

228 "to seat . . . throne": Inayat Khan, ED, vol. 7, p. 105.

230 In early 1656 . . . his orders: The quotes in these two paragraphs come from A. Eraly, *The Mughal Throne*, p. 327.

15. "Sharper Than a Serpent's Tooth"

233 The chapter title comes from W. Shakespeare, *King Lear*, act 1, scene 4.

233 "a monarch . . . against him": Abul Fazl, quoted in A. Eraly, *The Mughal Throne*, p. 139.

234 Had . . . Murad: The quotes in this paragraph are from N. Manucci, *Storia do Mogor*, vol. 1, p. 230.

235 "the emperor . . . strangury": Inayat Khan, *The Shah Jahan Nama*, p. 543.

235 "was seized . . . constitution": F. Bernier, *Travels in the Mogul Empire*, pp. 24–25.

236 "turned . . . state"; "requesting . . . heir-apparent": Inayat Khan, *The Shah Jahan Nama*, p. 545.

236 "bigot and prayer-monger": Ibid., p. 220.

238 "The emperor . . . sinful"; "I shall not . . . design": W. Hansen, *The Peacock Throne*, pp. 235–36.

238 "with . . . meeting": Inayat Khan, *The Shah Jahan Nama*, p. 550.

238–42 Niccolao . . . murdered: All quotes in these eleven paragraphs are from N. Manucci, *Storia do Mogor*, vol. 1, pp. 255–57, 269, 276, 282, 295 and 352.

243 Dara . . . excuses: The quotes in this paragraph come from F. Bernier, *Travels in the Mogul Empire*, pp. 89–90.

244 "disgraceful procession": Ibid., p. 98.

244 "revived . . . empire"; "had not . . . Muslim": Aurangzeb's letter to Shah Jahan, in *Adab-i-Alamgiri*, pp. 358–59.

245 "not . . . blood": *Tarikh-i Khafi Khan*, ED, vol. 7, p. 267.

247 During . . . "occurred?": The quotes in this paragraph come from *Adab-i-Alamgiri*, pp. 358–59.

247 "the whole . . . others": F. Bernier, *Travels in the Mogul Empire*, p. 166.
247 "the Great Moghul . . . death": P. Mundy, quoted in *IT*, p. 309.
247 Shah Jahan died on 26 Rajab 1076 in the Muslim calendar.
248 "a grand . . . funeral": Salih, *IT*, p. 144.

16. Fall of the Peacock Throne

250 "bade . . . quick": N. Manucci, *Storia do Mogor*, vol. 3, p. 276.
251 "the boldest . . . turbulent": Ibid., vol. 2, p. 227.
251 "the inexperienced . . . Rajputs": The chronicler is Khafi Khan, translated in ED, vol. 7, p. 301.
251 "as he . . . instructed"; "that he . . . fire": Ibid., p. 304.
252 "to divert . . . drink": Quoted in W. Hansen, *The Peacock Throne*, p. 465.
253 "consulting . . . family": Quoted in A. Eraly, *The Mughal Throne*, p. 491.
254 "Never . . . 'barren' ": Quoted in W. Hansen, *The Peacock Throne*, p. 486.
255 "If you . . . India": Quoted in F. Watson, *India—A Concise History*, p. 120.
255 "repugnant . . . nation": Ibid, p.131.
256 "at an earlier . . . queen": Lord Curzon, *Speeches*, vol. 1, p. 223.
256 "it would . . . corner": Quoted in D. Carroll, *The Taj Mahal*, p. 133.
256 The question of Lord William Bentinck and the auctioning of the Taj Mahal is discussed in P. Spear, "Bentinck and the Taj," *Journal of the Royal Asiatic Society* (October 1949): 180–87.
257–58 Curzon . . . remains: The quotes in these two paragraphs come from Lord Curzon, *Speeches*, vol. 4, p. 347, except "My name . . . person" and "makes . . . plebeian," which come from the *Oxford Book of Political Anecdotes*.
259 "Must we . . . mausoleum?": B. Gautam, *Japan Times*, 11 October 2004.

17. "His Own Tomb on the Other Side of the River"

262 The theory that the Taj was a symbolic representation of the throne of God is contained in W. E. Begley's article "The Myth of the Taj Mahal and a New Theory of Its Symbolic Meaning," *Art Bulletin*, 61, no. 1 (March 1979): 7–37. E. Koch in her article "The Taj Mahal: Architecture, Symbolism and Urban Significance," *Muqarnas* 22 (2005): 128–49, is among those advancing the proposition that the placement of the Taj Mahal derives from the practice in Agra riverside gardens.
263 The recent excavations in the Mahtab Bagh are the subject of *The Moonlight Garden* edited by E. B. Moynihan.
263 "one . . . garden": *Jahangirnama*, translated in S. Crowe et al., *The Gardens of Mughul India*, p. 192.
267 "Shah Jahan . . . plan": J.-B. Tavernier, *Travels in India*, vol.1, p. 91.

267–70 Among those who consider that it was Shah Jahan's intention to be interred in the Mahtab Bagh is Professor R. C. Agrawal, current joint director general of the Archaeological Survey of India.

270–72 The underground chambers are discussed by H. I. S. Kanwar in "Subterranean Chambers of the Taj Mahal," *Islamic Quarterly* 48 (July 1974): 159–75.

272–74 The theory that the Taj Mahal was a Hindu temple is advanced in V. S. Godbole's *Taj Mahal and the Great British Conspiracy* and P. N. Oak's *Taj Mahal The True Story—The Tale of a Temple Vandalised*. G. H. R. Tillotson in *Oriental Art*, autumn 1986, pp. 266–69, discusses politics and the Taj Mahal.

272 "The Hindu . . . Mahal": A. Huxley, *Jesting Pilate*, p. 50.

273 "laying the foundations"; "the water table": Lahori, *IT*, p. 65.

273 "The building is begun": P. Mundy, *Travels in Europe and Asia*, vol. 2, p. 213.

274 "a wonder of the world": F. Bernier, *Travels in the Mogul Empire*, p. 299.

Epilogue

280 "I've seen . . . illusion": N. Coward, quoted by J. Heilpern in the *Observer*, 14 December 1969.

281 "The building . . . things": S. Rushdie, *National Geographic Traveler*, October 1999.

281 "to set out . . . of it": Quoted in P. Pal et al., *Romance of the Taj Mahal*, p. 206.

281 "beauty . . . orator": W. Shakespeare, *The Rape of Lucretia*, line 29.

282 "light . . . building": T. Fuller, *The Holy State and the Profane State*, chapter 7, "Of Building."

283 "That is . . . express": F. Bacon, essay no 43, *Of Beauty*.

284 "Not architecture . . . thought": E. Arnold, quoted in the Internet source *Built Heritage of Agra and Fatehpur Sikri*.

Bibliography

Original Sources (Including Translations)

Moghul and Indian Sources

Abul Fazl. *The Ain-i-Akbari*. Translated by H. Blochmann and H. S. Jarrett. 3 vols. Calcutta: Asiatic Society of Bengal, 1873–94.

————. *The Akbarnama*. Translated by H. Beveridge. 3 vols. Calcutta: Asiatic Society, 1907–39.

Adab-i-Alamgiri (Aurangzeb's letters). Extracts translated by J. Scott, contained in *Tales, Anecdotes and Letters*. London: Cadell and Davies, 1800.

Baburnama. Translated by A. S. Beveridge. 2 vols. London: Luzac, 1921.

Baburnama. Translated by W. M. Thackston. New York: Modern Library, 2002.

Ferishta. *History of Hindustan*. Translated by A. Dow. 3 vols. London: J. Walker, 1812.

Gulbadan. *The Humayan-Nama*. Translated by A. S. Beveridge. London: Royal Asiatic Society, 1902.

Haidar. *Tarikh-i-Rashidi*. Translated by E. D. Ross as *A History of the Moghuls of Central Asia*. London: Sampson Low, 1895.

The History of India as Told by Its Own Historians. Compiled and edited by H. M. Elliot and J. Dowson. 7 vols. London: Trubner, 1867–77.

Inayat Khan. *The Shah Jahan Nama*. Edited by W. E. Begley and Z. A. Desai. Delhi: Oxford University Press, 1990.

Jahangirnama. Translated by W. M. Thackston. Oxford: Oxford University Press, 1999.

Taj Mahal—The Illumined Tomb. An Anthology of Seventeenth Century Mughal and European Documentary Sources. Compiled and translated by W. E. Begley and Z. A. Desai. Cambridge, MA: Aga Khan Programme for Islamic Architecture, 1989.

Tirmizi, S. A. I. *Mughal Documents*. Delhi: Manohar Books, 1995.

The Tuzuk-i-Jahangiri (Memoirs of Jahangir). Edited by H. Beveridge. Translated by A. Rogers. London: Royal Asiatic Society, 1909.

Accounts of European Travelers to the Moghul Empire

INDIVIDUAL ACCOUNTS

Bernier, F. *Travels in the Mogul Empire*. Delhi: Low Price Publications, 1999.

Broecke, P. van den. *A Contemporary Dutch Chronicle of Mughal India*. Calcutta: Susil Gupta (India), 1957.

De Clavijo, R. G. *Embassy to the Court of Timur at Samarcand, A. D. 1403–6.* Translated by C. R. Markham. London: Hakluyt Society, 1899.

Floris, P. *Voyage of Peter Floris to the East Indies*. London: Hakluyt Society, 1934.

Jourdain, J. *The Journal of John Jourdain*. Edited by W. Foster. London: Hakluyt Society, 1905.

Manrique, F. S. *Travels of F. S. Manrique*. London: Hakluyt Society, 1927.

Manucci, N. *Storia do Mogor*. Vols. 1 to 4. Delhi: Low Price Publications, 1996.

Monserrate, S. J. *The Commentary of Father S. J. Monserrate on his Journey to the Court of Akbar*. Translated by J. Hoyland. Oxford: Oxford University Press, 1922.

Mundy, P. *The Travels of Peter Mundy in Europe and Asia*. Vols. 1 to 5. London: Hakluyt Society, 1914.

Pelsaert, F. *Remonstrantie.*Translated by W. H. Moreland as *Jahangir's India*. Cambridge: W. Heffer, 1925.

Roe, Sir. T. *The Embassy of Sir Thomas Roe to India*. Edited by W. Foster. New Delhi: Munshiram Manoharlal, 1990.

Tavernier, J.-B. *Travels in India*. Vols. 1 and 2. New Delhi: Munshiram Manoharlal, 1995.

Vallee, P. della. *The Travels of Pietro della Vallee*. Edited by E. Grey (from a translation of 1664 by G. Havers). 2 vols. London: Hakluyt Society, 1892.

COMPILATIONS

Early Travels in India—1583–1619. (Contains the accounts of Ralph Fitch, John Mildenhall, William Hawkins, William Finch, Nicholas Withington, Thomas Coryat and Edward Terry.) Edited by W. Foster. New Delhi: Munshiram Manoharlal, 1985.

India in the Seventeenth Century. (Contains the accounts of John Ovington, Jean de Thevenot and Giovanni Careri). Edited by J. P. Gupta. New Delhi: Associated Publishing, 1984.

Laet, J. de. *The Empire of the Great Mogol*. Translated by J. S. Hoyland. Bombay: D. B. Taraporevala Sons, 1928.

Other Sources

Books

Ansari, M. A. *The Social Life of the Mughal Emperors (1526–1707)*. Allahabad and New Delhi: Shanti Prakashan, 1974.

Asher, C. E. *Architecture of Moghal India*. Cambridge: Cambridge University Press, 1992.

Berinstin, V. *Mughal India—Splendours of the Peacock Throne*. London: Thames and Hudson, 1998.

Blair, S., and J. Bloom. *The Art and Architecture of Islam, 1250–1800*. London: Pelican, 1994.

Byron, R. *The Road to Oxiana*. London: Pimlico, 2004.

Canby, S., ed. *Humayun's Garden Party*. Mumbai, India: Marg, 1995.

Carroll, D. *The Taj Mahal*. New York: Newsweek, 1978.

Chakrabarti, V. *Indian Architectural Theory*. London: Curzon, 1999.

Craven, R. C. *Indian Art*. London: Thames and Hudson, 1976.

Crowe, S., S. Haywood, S. Jellicoe and G. Patterson, *The Gardens of Mughul India*. London: Thames and Hudson, 1972.

Curzon of Kedleston, Lord. *Speeches*. Vol. 1 1898–1900 and vol. 3 1902–1904. Calcutta: Office of the Superintendent of Government Printing, 1900 and 1904.

Dutemple, L. A. *The Taj Mahal*. Minneapolis, MN: Lerner, 2003.

Eraly, A. *The Mughal Throne*. London: Phoenix, 2004.

Findly, E. B. *Nur Jahan, Empress of India*. New York: Oxford University Press, 1993.

Footprint Guide to India. Bath: Footprint Handbooks, 2005.

Gascoigne, B. *The Great Moghuls*. London: Jonathan Cape, 1971.

Godbole, V. S. *Taj Mahal and the Great British Conspiracy*. Thane, India: Itihas Patrike Prakashan, 1996.

Gommans, J. *Mughal Warfare*. London: Routledge, 2002.

Hambly, G. *Cities of Mughal India*. London: Elek Books, 1968.

Hansen, W. *The Peacock Throne*. New York: Holt, Rinehart and Winston, 1972.

Hoag, J. D. *Islamic Architecture*. London: Faber and Faber, 1987.

Huxley, A. *Jesting Pilate*. London: Triad Paladin, 1985.

Jaffrey, M. *A Taste of India*. London: Pavilion Books, 1985.

Jarric, P. du. *Akbar and the Jesuits*. London: Routledge, 1926.

King, R. *Brunelleschi's Dome*. New York: Walker, 2000.

Koch, E. *Mughal Architecture*. New Delhi: Oxford University Press, 2002.

Krishnan, U., and M. Kumar. *Indian Jewellery*. Bombay: India Bookhouse, 2001.

Lall, J. *The Taj Mahal and Mughal Agra*. New Delhi: Roli Books, 2005.

———. *The Taj Mahal and the Saga of the Great Mughals*. Delhi: Lustre Press, 1994.

Lall, K. S. *The Mughal Harem*. New Delhi: Aditya Prakashan, 1988.

Lall, M. *Shah Jahan*. Delhi: Vikas, 1986.

Lane-Smith, R. *The Taj Mahal of Agra*. Delhi: Stonehenge, 1999.

Lear, E. *Indian Journal*. Edited by R. Murphy. London: Jarrolds, 1953.

Milton, J. *The English Poems*. Ware: Wordsworth Editions, 2004.

Mitford, N. *The Sun King*. London: Hamish Hamilton, 1966.

Moynihan, E. B., ed. *The Moonlight Garden—New Discoveries at the Taj Mahal*. Washington D.C.: Smithsonian Institution, 2000.

———. *Paradise as a Garden in Persia and Mughal India*. London: Scolar Press, 1980.

Mukhia, H. *The Mughals of India*. Oxford: Blackwell, 2004.

Nath, R. *Art and Architecture of the Taj Mahal*. Agra: Historical Research Documentation Programme, 1996.

———. *The Private Life of the Mughals of India*. Jaipur: Historical Research Documentation Programme, 1994.

———. *The Taj Mahal and Its Incarnation*. Jaipur: Historical Research Documentation Programme, 1985.

Oak, P. N. *Taj Mahal The True Story—The Tale of a Temple Vandalised*. Houston, Texas: A. Ghosh, 1969.

Okada, A., M. C. Joshi and J. L. Nou. *The Taj Mahal*. New York: Abbeville Press, 1993.

Pal, P., J. Leoshko, J. M. Dye and S. Markel. *Romance of the Taj Mahal*. Los Angeles and London: Los Angeles County Museum of Art and Thames and Hudson, 1989.

Peck, L. *Delhi, A Thousand Years of Building*. New Delhi: Roli Books. 2005.

Prawdin, M. *The Builders of the Mogul Empire*. London: Allen and Unwin, 1963.

Qaisar, A. J. *Building Construction in Mughal India*. Delhi, Oxford University Press, 1988.

Richards, J. D. *The Mughal Empire*. Cambridge: Cambridge University Press, 1993.

Roosevelt, E. *India and the Awakening East*. London: Hutchison, 1954.

Savory, R. M., ed. *Islamic Civilisation*. Cambridge: Cambridge University Press, 1976.

Sleeman, W. H. *Rambles and Recollections of an Indian Official*. Vols 1 and 2. New Delhi: Asian Educational Series, 1995.

Stronge, S. *Painting for the Mughal Emperor—The Art of the Book, 1560–1660.*
    London: V and A Publications, 2002.
Tannahill, R. *Sex in History.* London: Hamish Hamilton, 1980.
Tillotson, G. H. R. *Mughal India.* London: Viking, 1990.
Victoria and Albert Museum. *The Indian Heritage.* London: Victoria and Al-
    bert Museum, 1982.
Watson, F. *India—A Concise History.* London: Thames and Hudson, 2002.
Weatherly, M. *The Taj Mahal.* Farmington Hills, MI: Lucent Books, 2003.
Ziad, Z. *The Magnificent Mughals.* Karachi: Oxford University Press, 2002

Journals and Magazines

The Art Bulletin
The Indian Historical Quarterly
Islamic Culture
Islamic Quarterly
The Journal of Imperial and Commonwealth History
The Journal of Indian History
The Journal of the Pakistan Historical Society
The Journal of the Royal Asiatic Society
The Journal of the Warburg and Courtauld Institutes
Muqarnas
National Geographic Traveler
Oriental Art
South Asian Studies

Newspapers

The Observer
The Japan Times
The Times (London)
The Sydney Morning Herald

Other

Built Heritage of Agra and Fatehpur Sikri Web site.
Indian History Congress. *Proceedings of the Forty-Sixth Session.* Guru
Nanak Dev University, Amritsar, 1985.

Index

A Note on the Authors

Diana and Michael Preston are graduates of Oxford University where Diana read modern history and Michael read old and medieval English. When not traveling they live in London, England. Diana is the author of *A First Rate Tragedy*, *The Boxer Rebellion*, *Lusitania: An Epic Tragedy* and *Before the Fallout: From Marie Curie to Hiroshima*, which won the 2006 Los Angeles Times Book Prize for Science and Technology. She and Michael coauthored *A Pirate of Exquisite Mind*, a biography of the great seventeenth-century adventurer William Dampier.